Sean

This is the follow-on from the article [look]
a couple of years
a good read for our work.

Ben

Govern Like Us

Govern Like Us

U.S. Expectations of Poor Countries

M. A. THOMAS

Columbia University Press
New York

Columbia University Press
Publishers Since 1893
New York   Chichester, West Sussex
cup.columbia.edu
Copyright © 2015 Columbia University Press
All rights reserved
Library of Congress Cataloging-in-Publication Data

Thomas, Melissa Annette.
Govern like us : U.S. expectations of poor countries / M.A. Thomas.
pages cm
Includes bibliographical references and index.
ISBN 978-0-231-17120-5 (cloth : alk. paper) — ISBN 978-0-231-53911-1 (electronic)
1. Developing countries—Politics and government. 2. Public administration—
Developing countries. 3. Poverty—Political aspects—Developing countries.
4. Political culture—Developing countries. 5. Developing countries—
Foreign relations—Western countries. 6. Western countries—
Foreign relations—Developing countries. I. Title.

JF60.T48 2015
320.9172'4—dc23

2014025326

Columbia University Press books are printed on permanent
and durable acid-free paper.
This book is printed on paper with recycled content.
Printed in the United States of America
c 10 9 8 7 6 5 4 3 2 1

COVER PHOTO: © Jan Banning/www.janbanning.com
COVER DESIGN: Milenda Nan Ok Lee

References to websites (URLs) were accurate at the time of writing. Neither the author nor
Columbia University Press is responsible for URLs that may have expired or changed since the
manuscript was prepared.

Contents

Acknowledgments

Writing this book was a challenge. I have benefited from seven years of field research, but I have been unable to call on any of that work explicitly for this book. The interviews I conducted and the reports I wrote were confidential and for other purposes. Academia would have liked me to attempt to conduct some of these interviews over again so that I could quote people, but it was simply not possible for reasons of both cost and access. Instead, I was obliged to support and illustrate my argument where I could by drawing on the existing secondary literature.

Much of it is already there, if fragmented across the disciplines and buried in technical jargon. Many parts of this puzzle have been considered and explored by political scientists, economists, sociologists, lawyers, and aid practitioners. Part of the reason why our foreign policy has lagged beyond the insights from the academic and practitioner worlds is because those insights are not always easily available to the general audience. As a lawyer and a political economist, I understand terms like "ethnolinguistic fractionalization," "neopatrimonialism," "purchasing power parity," "constitutive theory of statehood," and "tax effort," but I saw no reason to burden the reader with them. I've tried to keep it straightforward, albeit sometimes at the expense of nuance.

I owe enormous thanks to many people and can only thank a few of them here. Thanks to Francis Fukuyama, who hired me at SAIS and was kind enough to read and comment on the manuscript; to SAIS, which gave me a home while I was writing it; to the Max M. Fisher Excellence in Teaching Award that helped me write the first paper that crystallized this line of thought in 2008, and to *Policy Review* that eventually published it; to the foundation that provided grant support and the program officer whose demand for regular updates helped keep me to the task; to mentors and colleagues Robert Bates, Deborah Brautigam, Thomas Carothers, Gerald

VIII

ACKNOWLEDGMENTS

Hyman, Seth Kaplan, and Richard Messick for their unflagging encouragement, comments on the manuscript, and advice on dealing with the publishing world; to research assistants Nate Hanson, Rachel Ort, and Megan Vaughn-Albert; to SAIS students that devoured and mercilessly shredded parts of the manuscript like a school of intellectual piranhas; to the colleagues, friends, and family who encouraged me and patiently bore my unavailability as I worked on the book; to the people who opened their homes, lives, and hearts to me over the years as I learned about governance in poor countries.

Govern Like Us

1. Blind Spot

The United States has been embroiled in Afghanistan in the longest running war in its history, so long that I now teach graduate students who barely remember the attack on New York and Washington, D.C. on September 11, 2001. The objective of the United States and its Coalition partners in Afghanistan was not simply to rout the Taliban government and its al Qaeda allies—this was accomplished quickly and effectively in 2001. Instead, it has been to change the way Afghanistan is governed on the theory that a stable, prosperous, and well-governed country would provide no future foothold for terrorism. To do this, they sought to create a government that governed according to the American, and more broadly, Western governance ideal: a constitutional democracy operating under the rule of law that protects human rights and delivers public goods and services to its citizens, such as security, economic opportunity, health, education, and infrastructure.

These objectives dovetailed with those of people in the development community who seek generally to improve the welfare of the poor. In fact, many in the development community had been quick to argue after the attack that poverty causes terrorism and that development is the solution. In March 2002, the United Nations secretary general spoke at a meeting of fifty countries, saying that "no-one in this world can feel comfortable, or safe, while so many are suffering and deprived," and urged wealthy countries to double foreign aid.[1] President George W. Bush promised that the United States would "challenge the poverty and hopelessness and lack of education and failed governments that too often allow conditions that terrorists can seize and try to turn to their advantage."[2]

To establish a democratic government in Afghanistan, in 2001 the United Nations organized a conference in Bonn, Germany, to put together a provisional government for Afghanistan, which Hamid Karzai was chosen to lead. In 2002, President Karzai and the international community adapted an Afghan institution called the *loya jirga* as a representative assembly to ratify the Bonn Agreement until a constitution was drafted and elections were held. A second such meeting in 2003 approved the newly drafted constitution, which provided for a strong president at the head of a centralized government. Presidential elections were held in 2004, and parliamentary elections in 2005.

At the same time, the international community went to work to strengthen the rule of law, ensure human rights (including equal rights for women), build the Afghan army and police, and strengthen the capacity of the Afghan government to deliver public services such as security, justice, health, and education and improve Afghan livelihoods. Aiddata 3.0, a database of international aid projects, lists more than 8,800 development projects in Afghanistan from 2001 to 2011, funded by everyone from the Asian Development Bank to the World Bank. All told, the government of Afghanistan would receive about $36.5 billion from foreign aid donors between 2001 and 2010.[3]

The military was also engaged in activities that had traditionally been undertaken in the name of development, but were now done with the aim of stabilization. The Commander's Emergency Response Program gave U.S. battalion commanders "walking around money" to use in an attempt to purchase goodwill or information or to reward cooperative communities. These projects included building or renovating schools, roads, dams, canals, and bridges and providing equipment or agricultural supplies.[4]

The cost of this effort in money and lives has been substantial. As of March 2011 the Congressional Research Service (CRS) estimated that the United States alone had spent $444 billion for Afghanistan (including expenditures of the Department of Defense, State Department/United States Agency for International Development, and the Department of Veterans Administration), approximately 35 percent of the total of $1.283 trillion spent for the Global War on Terror.[5] More than 2,000 U.S. soldiers and 88 Coalition soldiers had been killed in Operation Enduring Freedom and another 19,000 wounded.[6] As of 2011, more than 800 contractors were also killed, a consequence of the U.S. government's increased outsourcing of functions that were previously carried out by the military and U.S. government employees.[7] It is not clear how the focus on state building affected civilian casualties from conflict, but no discussion of the cost of war could overlook them. Although there was no regular reporting on Afghan civilian casualties before 2007, the CRS notes, "Up to 11,864 civilians were killed in Afghanistan from 2007, when the United Nations began reporting statistics, to the end of 2011."[8]

It is often the case that the international community sets such ambitious goals that important improvements are overshadowed and overlooked. A look through World Bank statistics shows some gains for Afghan citizens in terms of quality of life and access to services. From 2001 to 2010, infant mortality declined by more than 20 percent; life expectancy at birth rose from 46 years to 48 years; and the percentage of rural Afghans with access to improved water sources rose from 22 percent to 42 percent, while the percentage of urban Afghans with access to improved sanitation rose from 48 percent to 60 percent. The percentage of girls in school has climbed. More than half the population has cell phones. As of this writing, despite Taliban attacks, the 2014 presidential elections have been held, considered by most observers to be successful, and bring the promise of a democratic transition to a new government.

But the broader objective of establishing a sustainable strong central government in Afghanistan that is legitimate, democratically elected, free of corruption, and capable of ensuring security and economic growth, protecting human rights, and delivering public goods and services has not been met. As Professor Thomas Barfield describes in his excellent history of Afghanistan, trouble was brewing already in 2004.[9] The Karzai government had failed to deliver security or economic development and was seen as corrupt and abusive. The government was unable to deliver reliable electricity or water in the capital. The Taliban was allowed to regroup. Beginning in 2005 and accelerating after 2007, there was an increase in assassinations, suicide bombings, and armed attacks led by resurgent Taliban and al Qaeda forces. In 2009, President Karzai won reelection through a combination of massive electoral fraud and generous gifts of money and government positions to accused drug traffickers and war criminals.

In 2013, Freedom House ranked Afghanistan as "Not Free," scoring Afghanistan's civil liberties and political rights as six out of seven, where seven is the lowest score possible.[10] The State Department flagged a number of issues in its 2012 Human Rights report, including widespread violence; attacks on civilians; the use of torture; arbitrary arrests; corruption; violence and discrimination against women and girls; restrictions on freedom of the press, of assembly, of religion, and freedom of movement; and widespread disregard for the rule of law.[11] In 2012, Transparency International's

Corruption Perceptions Index listed Afghanistan as perceived to be one of the most corrupt countries in the world, tied for last place with North Korea and Somalia.[12]

Narcotrafficking remains central to Afghanistan's economy. Despite eradication efforts, Afghanistan remains the world's top opium producer, responsible for 90 percent of the world's supply of heroin—an industry worth about $61 billion that funds both drug traffickers and insurgents.[13] Foreign currency and gold are leaving Afghanistan for Dubai, with cash in suitcases and shrink wrapped on pallets. The *New York Times* reported that an estimated $4.5 billion in cash flowed out of Afghanistan in 2011 alone and that in October 2012 a single courier boarded an airplane with 60 pounds of gold worth almost $1.5 million.[14] Despite concerns that the dollars may be diverted foreign aid funds or money laundered from drug trafficking, in December 2012 the Special Inspector for Afghanistan Reconstruction reported that the Afghan government was still not using the bulk currency counters installed in the airport to count cash outflows and record bill serial numbers.[15]

General John Allen, former commander of the International Security Assistance Force and U.S. Forces Afghanistan, testified to Congress in the form of a letter to the next Afghan president:

> The great challenge to Afghanistan's future isn't the Taliban, or the Pakistani safe havens, or even an incipiently hostile Pakistan. The existential threat to the long term viability of modern Afghanistan is corruption. Indeed, across your great country, the ideological insurgency, the criminal patronage networks, and the drug enterprise have formed an unholy alliance, which relies for its success on the criminal capture of your government functions at all levels. For too long, we've focused our attention on the Taliban as the existential threat to Afghanistan. They are an annoyance compared to the scope and magnitude of corruption with which you must contend.[16]

What Went Wrong?

What went wrong with the effort to build the new government of Afghanistan? One critique is essentially a critique of technique: that the U.S. and international effort was too little, too late. The United States remained focused on the war in Iraq until the end of the Iraq surge in 2007. Only as violence grew in Afghanistan in 2007 and 2008 did the United States sharply increase both the number of troops (in 2008) and its spending (in fiscal year 2010).[17] Anthony Cordesman, who holds the Burke Chair in Strategy at the Center for Strategic & International Studies, wrote: "The present state of the war is now very serious, but this should not be ascribed to the difficulties in nation building and [counterinsurgency], or cultural issues. It took half a decade of gross underreaction and under-resourcing, and a US focus on Iraq that led the US to ignore key developments and trends in Afghanistan to create the current situation."[18]

Another argument blames the Afghans, and in particular the elites. Steven Metz, chairman of the Regional Strategy Department of the Strategic Studies Institute at the Army War College, explained:

> The American conceptualization of counterinsurgency assumed that partner regimes shared the Western notion of what a state should be: an entity that reflected the beliefs of all the people of a country and dispersed goods and services based on formal procedures such as the rule of law and democratic elections. The reality is that in many parts of the world, the state is a mechanism by which the group that controls it extracts as many resources as possible, whether money, concessions, government jobs, natural resources or pure power. When a parasitic political system is threatened by insurgency, those who control it will only make the minimum concessions necessary to hold on to power. The last thing they want to do is fundamentally alter a system that deeply rewards them. Yet that is what American counterinsurgency thinking expects them to do.[19]

A congressional staff report similarly cautions:

> Our stabilization strategy . . . presumes that the international community and the Afghan Government have shared objectives when it comes to promoting longer term development, good governance, and the rule of law. These assumptions may not be correct.[20]

This argument—the lack of "political will" for change at the top—is one that is frequently raised in international development when projects to reform governments fail.

But it is unlikely that the governance reform effort in Afghanistan can succeed even with the best efforts of sincere and public-spirited Afghan elites. The idea of building a strong central government in Afghanistan that operates under the rule of law and delivers public goods and services to all citizens was flawed from the start. While there are many challenges to that project—including elite opposition, a lack of history of centralization, a lack of popular demand for a strong central government in some quarters, geographic barriers, ethnic and cultural tensions—there is one indisputable necessary prerequisite that is missing: sufficient government revenue. The government of Afghanistan does not have enough domestic revenue to govern this way. With annual domestic revenue per capita of about $73 per person in 2014, according to one estimate in current exchange rates,[21] there is a real limit to what the government of Afghanistan can do.

It should have been obvious that Afghanistan cannot sustain the kind of government the United States had in mind, and indeed a number of people raised this concern. From 2006 to 2010, the United States and other donors funded 90 percent of Afghanistan's total public expenditures, with the Afghan government paying the remainder from its own domestic revenues.[22] The U.S. Government Accountability Office (GAO) repeatedly raised the alarm that the government and military that the international community built in Afghanistan are too expensive for the Afghans to operate and maintain. Its September 2011 report is worth quoting at length because a summary would miss what appears to be politely expressed frustration:

The United States has allocated over $72 billion to secure, stabilize, and rebuild Afghanistan since 2002, and the President requested over $18 billion for these purposes for fiscal year 2012. GAO has on numerous occasions raised doubts about the Government of the Islamic Republic of Afghanistan's (GIRoA) ability to fund its public expenditures—funds spent to provide public services to the Afghan population, such as security, infrastructure projects, and government salaries. In 2005, we reported that Afghanistan had limited resources and recommended the Secretaries of State and Defense develop plans for funding the Afghan national security forces (ANSF). In 2007 and 2008, we reported that it was essential to develop future funding requirements for the ANSF and a strategy for transitioning these responsibilities to GIRoA. In 2008, Congress also mandated that the Department of Defense provide a long-term plan for sustaining the ANSF, including future funding requirements. The Department of Defense, however, has yet to provide the Congress an estimate of the cost to sustain the Afghanistan National Security Forces. In 2011, we again recommended that the U.S. and international partners develop estimates of the future funding needed to grow the Afghan National Army. We have also raised concerns about Afghanistan's inability to fund planned government expenditures without foreign assistance and raised questions about the sustainability of U.S.-funded efforts to build and enhance Afghanistan's road, agriculture, and water infrastructures.[23]

Foreign funding for Afghanistan will not last forever. Congress has approved only half the amount for Afghanistan requested by the Obama administration in 2014.[24] At the same time, donor-funded efforts to develop new revenue sources for Afghanistan are yielding little. The growing budget shortfall threatens to leave civil servants unpaid and to close public programs.

The government of Afghanistan cannot afford to provide the basket of goods and services that those in rich liberal democracies equate with government. It is not even clear that it can maintain control of its territory without outside help. As Professor Barfield argued, no government in Afghanistan was ever able to maintain centralized control without external financing and supplies of arms, first from the British, then from the Soviet Union, and finally from the West.[25] Instead, Afghan rulers had varying degrees of control of different parts of Afghan territory in what he calls "the Swiss cheese model" of statehood.[26] Rulers sought direct control of populated and economically valuable regional centers and ignored or claimed nominal rulership of marginal territory between and beyond them.

But in this, Afghanistan is not different from any other poor government. With fewer resources and less capacity, poor governments govern less—much less. They have less territorial control and deliver fewer and lower quality public goods and services to fewer people. They have fewer and less well-equipped and staffed hospitals and schools. They have fewer paved roads. They enforce laws unevenly and sporadically and most, like Afghanistan, are unable to provide basic security.

The problems of poor governments are often framed exclusively as problems of ability and capacity to deliver goods and services given their low revenue, lack of equipment and infrastructure, and shortage of well-trained staff. But if poor governments simply governed less—if they were just weaker versions of rich liberal democracies—then the solution would be simple. We could "fix" poor governments by giving them money. And indeed, as in Afghanistan, much of our foreign aid seems to be premised on this idea. Poor governments would happily accept the money and use it to provide more public goods and services, building hospitals and schools, distributing food, strengthening the rule of law, and improving government accountability through democratic elections. *But poor governments don't just govern less than rich liberal democracies. Because they are poor, they govern differently.* They face different challenges; they have different constraints; they have fewer options; and therefore they govern using different strategies.

One of the central problems of a government is to govern, which can only happen if people comply with government mandates or, at the very least, don't challenge the government's authority to govern. There are many reasons why people might choose to comply with government mandates, and many strategies that governments and leaders can employ to persuade people to follow. People might follow leaders because they are charismatic or because they see them as effective advocates for values that are important to them. They might follow leaders because rules that people respect confer authority upon those leaders, whether these rules come from tradition (monarchies), religion (theocracies), or a political bargain (constitutional republics). People might follow leaders through naked self-interest, because they are receiving or anticipate receiving a personal benefit, because they fear punishment if they do not, or because they seek protection against an outside threat. People might follow leaders because doing so gives them a sense of belonging and group identity. People might support a leader or a government for any combination of these reasons. Accordingly, leaders may claim descent from gods, kings, or freedom fighters; carefully maintain their public image as courageous, intelligent, honest, pious, or generous people; govern according to well-accepted laws; provide public goods and services; appeal to ethnic identity or religious ideology; provide special benefits to some followers and punish some challengers and opponents; or work to create a sense of patriotism or national identity through a common struggle, establishment of a national language, religion, or school curriculum, or the fear of a common enemy.

The sociologist Max Weber posed the question: "If the state is to exist, the dominated must obey the authority claimed by the powers that be. When and why do men obey?"[27] He developed a typology of the bases of the legitimate authority of governments, identifying three main types of legitimate authority: legitimacy that derives from the personal charisma of a ruler; legitimacy that derives from tradition (for example, monarchies); and legitimacy that derives from the government's adherence to a set of widely accepted laws and rules that determine who should govern and how.[28] This way of looking at governance was enormously innovative, and has been influential in political science, sociology, and regional studies. Weber was very clear that his three types were idealized abstractions not found in reality.[29] Nevertheless, a lot of academic ink has been spilled attempting to characterize various governments according to their basis of legitimate authority using Weber's typology.

In reality, governments hold power to govern by means seen as both legitimate and illegitimate, and they do not have a single means of holding power. The question of how a government holds power to govern is not an either/or problem. Governments hold power based on a dynamic mix of means and strategies; the mix is fluid and differs with each constituency. Insurgents who contest governments to win popular support also use different strategies—for example, these may offer public services, unite their followers with ideology, or punish citizens who disobey.

Not all strategies are equally available to all governments at all times. In North Korea, Kim Jong-Il claimed divine authority. The state-sponsored account of Kim's birth on Mount Paektu contends that there were "flashes of light and thunder, the iceberg in the pond of Mount Paektu emitted a mysterious sound as it broke, and bright double rainbows rose up."[30] Claiming magical or divine authority would not be as effective a strategy in the United States. Perhaps a milder version can be seen in the attempts of U.S. politicians to cloak themselves in the mantle of well-regarded people who went before them, including Ronald Reagan, John F. Kennedy, and Martin Luther King, Jr.

Rich liberal democracies have come to see only one type of governance as legitimate: the provision of public goods and services impersonally to all citizens by a democratically elected government that governs according to law, an idea referred to in this book as the "Western governance ideal" or sometimes "good governance."[31] The modern basket of government goods and services in rich liberal democracies includes national defense; justice; public safety; infrastructure such as roads and hospitals; health services and education; regulation; and social safety nets such as pensions and unemployment compensation and may include public utilities that provide electricity, gas, water, sanitation, telephone, and garbage collection services. But this type of government is expensive. It did not exist before the twentieth century, where it came into being in a handful of rich countries as political participation and claims on government services were widened to the entire adult population at the same time that government took on a broader role in ensuring individual well-being.

Poor governments do supply some public goods and services, but these are of low quality and concentrated in the capital, where population density is the highest and there are economies of scale. Most people still live in rural areas and see little of them. Because poor governments cannot offer even a modest basket of public goods and services impersonally to the entire population, they must rely more heavily on older, cheaper strategies of governance such as patronage, clientelism, repression, ideology (religious, Marxist, idiosyncratic), tradition, cult of personality, the creation of a common enemy, and neglect (benign and otherwise). The costs of governing different constituencies or parts of the country may also be highly variable and require the use of different strategies. For example, poor governments routinely ignore hinterlands far from the capital because they are unable to establish presence there or because doing so is not cost effective. What Barfield calls "the Swiss cheese model" is not a cultural or historical peculiarity of Afghanistan—it is a good description of how all poor governments govern and how, historically, all governments have governed.

We might analogize to the diet of rich and poor people. People who are very poor eat fewer calories than those who are rich. But poor people do not just eat less than rich people do; they eat differently. Rich people and poor people may both eat meat and rice, but over the course of a year, meat is more often on the table of a rich person. Some luxury foods that the rich buy the poor simply cannot afford, while the poor may eat foods that the rich wouldn't touch because they are not as healthy or nutritious, not as appealing to taste or smell, or simply because they are stigmatized because they are strongly associated with poverty.

There is no single governance strategy used by all poor governments (although patronage is very common). Instead, poor governments' strategic options for governance are constrained by poverty, and so their mix of strategies is different than that of rich liberal democracies, and very different than the expensive governance ideal. We consider some of the strategies of governance on which poor governments rely to be undesirable, suboptimal, or even abhorrent.

Just as some people are so poor that, no matter what they eat, they do not eat enough calories to stay healthy or even to stay alive, some governments are so poor that they can't govern their territories no matter what strategies they use. While they have the right and the responsibility to govern their territories under international law, they do not have the ability. Their power evaporates rapidly outside of the capital, and other power brokers govern there. Their statehood is a legal fiction introduced by the international community in order to end colonialism, and the task of establishing the government's control of the allotted territory still remains before it. If their territories were defined by the places in which government is effective, their actual borders would be smaller and fuzzier than those marked on the map. We will take a look at how that came about in chapter 3.

I use the term "poor government" to mean governments that do not have enough domestic revenue to hold elections and offer a basic package of public goods and services to all citizens (such as health services, education, roads, security, justice, or a social safety net), cannot afford to enforce their own laws with any regularity, and may not be able to control their own territories. But naming that group of countries is difficult. Ideally, to identify them we would define (and agree on) a basic package of public services and cost out the rule of law, democracy, and public service delivery. We would need to cost these out for every country, because the cost would vary, affected by a variety of factors such as population and population density, geography, and troublesome and poor neighbors. We could then compare this cost to the government's domestic revenue and, if the revenue were inadequate, put the government on our list of poor governments.

Unfortunately, the costing exercise has not been done. There is no consensus on a "basic package" of government services, and in any event, the information to conduct this exercise is not available. Among the many things that poor governments cannot provide well is official statistics. Poor governments do not have good information on the size of their populations or the size of their economies—or even their own revenue. In fact, as a general rule, the quality of information deteriorates the poorer the country. One need only look at "Bureaucratics," the photo essay of the world's bureaucrats in their offices by the photographer Jan Banning, to understand why, with photos of bureaucrats surrounded by heaps of moldering papers or, worse, with nothing at all.[32] In chapter 4, we'll take a look at some of the available information on government revenue per capita, but suffice it to say that there are governments that appear to have less than $300 per person per year to spend for everything that a government does.

That there exist governments that are too poor to provide public goods and services to all their citizens, or pay for national elections, or enforce their own laws, or assure basic security in their own territories is not a subject of debate. Certainly the governments of the poorest of the world's countries fall into this group. We might think of Afghanistan, the Democratic Republic of Congo, or Yemen. The poorest countries are classified by the World Bank as "low-income economies" (see box 1.1). Some of the world's lower-middle-income countries may also have poor governments. Although they have greater national wealth, their governments may not raise revenue effectively, or the cost of governing may be high because of challenging geography, large territories, large populations, or bad neighbors.

As we talk about richer governments, however, it is not always easy to tell the difference between a government that *cannot* govern according to the governance ideal and a government that *chooses not* to govern according to the governance ideal; between governments that do not have enough revenue, and governments that divert so much of the revenue into private pockets that there is not enough left over; or between governments that have chosen to spend their revenue very unequally, privileging one group or region at the expense of another, and governments that lack the resources to provide services to all citizens. Both scholars and development practitioners usually blame elites who would lose their wealth or status and who block governance reforms.[33]

Box 1.1 World Bank Low-Income Economies
(GNI per capita of $1,035 or less), as of June 2014

Afghanistan, Bangladesh, Benin, Burkina Faso, Burundi, Cambodia, Central African Republic, Chad, Comoros, Democratic People's Republic of Congo, Democratic Republic of Korea (North Korea), Eritrea, Ethiopia, The Gambia, Guinea, Guinea-Bisau, Haiti, Kenya, Kyrgyz Republic, Liberia, Madagascar, Malawi, Mali, Mozambique, Myanmar, Nepal, Niger, Rwanda, Sierra Leone, Somalia, Tajikistan, Tanzania, Togo, Uganda, Zimbabawe

That poor countries govern less is widely known and well documented, although people from rich liberal democracies still tend to overestimate by far what poor governments can do and make extravagant demands on them. Over the years I and many others have pointed out periodically that we expect too much of poor governments and press them to take on more than they can afford or manage, particularly when we want them to extend the services of a welfare state.[34]

That they govern differently is less widely understood but is also no secret. Academics have generated specialized vocabulary to describe how they govern: authoritarianism, patrimonialism, neopatrimonialism, clientelism, prebendalism, kleptocracy, limited access orders, extractive institutions, predatory states, weak states, fragile states, and failed states. Governments and organizations working in the field of international development produce mountains of "grey literature"—field reports, assessments, evaluations, and surveys that assess corruption levels, bemoan the lack of enforcement of law, discuss informal governance practices, or confess the failure of ambitious projects to change the way poor countries govern. There is now a light industry in the creation of "governance indicators" that seek to measure how well governments govern (with the governance ideal as the yardstick), and the poorest governments usually fare poorly on such measures. Finally, the uneven territorial control of the governments of poor countries has attracted the attention of the military and security specialists who are concerned about "ungoverned spaces" (by the government, in any event) that might be exploited by terrorists or criminals.

Revenue is not the only prerequisite for the governance ideal. The governance problems of the poorest governments are not solved simply by giving them money (and here we can again turn to Afghanistan as an example). However, the reason this book focuses on the need for adequate government revenue out of all the possible missing prerequisites for the establishment of the governance ideal is that while one can debate whether there is sufficient political will for reform among elites, good leadership, national identity, or other unobservable qualities, revenue is observable and there are governments that do not have enough. Without adequate revenue, the poorest governments could not govern according to the governance ideal even if they were led by brilliant and selfless leaders. When we focus on revenue, it becomes clear that the ideal is not universally available—and this means that simply insisting that all governments govern according to it is not an effective foreign policy.

And Then There's Us

There is a disconnect between the academic literature and our foreign policy. The academic literature explores various strategies of governance and considers the costs, benefits, and possibilities of different types of governance. By contrast, our foreign policy tends to insist on the governance ideal as the single legitimate and acceptable form. What is more, there is a tendency to consider the governance ideal as the default system, as if it can be achieved simply and quickly by providing the necessary resources, transferring our formal institutions and laws, or pressuring or replacing elites.

To say that Afghanistan can't afford the kind of government the United States was building for it only answers half the question of what went wrong. If everyone already knows that poor governments can't deliver the same goods and services as rich ones, why do we (and by "we" I mean "we Americans," although much of what I say will be relevant to others) keep demanding that they do? If poor governments govern differently of necessity, why haven't we already developed policies and strategies that seek to meet them where they are? And why do we keep imagining that "fixing" the way poor governments govern is something we can do easily, painlessly, and relatively quickly when it has never worked that way, not even once? There are two parties in every dysfunctional relationship. It can't always be the other person's fault.

One problem is cultural naïveté. Citizens of rich liberal democracies have difficulty grasping the enormity of the gap between the resources and wealth of their home governments and those of the poor. They assume institutions, capacities, resources, and services that do not exist, such as reliable electricity, a functioning postal system, an educated civil service, or a literate citizenry. At the same time, they do not imagine the challenges that some poor governments confront that are not problems at home, such as the need to consolidate territorial control or to manage ethnic or religious tensions. This is essentially a problem of class, on an international scale. We are often not even setting our expectations of poor governments based on the operations of our own, richer, government. We are comparing them to a simple idealized notion of governance, which my colleague Thomas Carothers calls the "Schoolhouse Rock" version of government, referring to educational cartoons that were shown on U.S. television between 1973 and 1999.

Another cultural problem is legalism and formalism. Rule of law is a very important Western political value. Domestic law plays an important role in coordinating behavior in the United States and other rich liberal democracies, and in particular in guiding the actions of government. International law plays a role in coordinating the actions of states under the international state system. We assume that governments govern their territories, that laws are enforced and describe and constrain how the government works, that government power is wielded by government actors in government offices, that authority is vested in the persons in government who hold the appropriate title or in the ministry with the appropriate name, and that the organizational chart of government describes a functioning command structure. Adding to our confusion is the fact that, because of a history of both voluntary and involuntary transfer, many poor governments have constitutions, laws, organizations, and ministries that look the same as those of Western democracies.

Behind the formal legal picture of every government is a very different one in practice. But in the poorest countries, the gap between law and practice is particularly wide. The government may have only nominal authority and control, government power could be wielded by private parties, the organizational chart could be fictional, laws may be both unknown and unenforced, the entire situation could vary substantially from one part of the country to the next, and there may be little or no effective government in parts of the country. Prisoners of our own legal fictions, we have difficulty setting aside the formal rules to ask who really makes decisions and how, when, and why those decisions are implemented.

Because these are cultural beliefs about what governments do, should do, and how they work, we tend to make the same mistakes over and over again. Academics and practitioners point repeatedly to these erroneous assumptions in dealing with poor governments, but they have had little impact on our foreign policy. Their insights are scattered among academic disciplines, in different areas of practitioner expertise, and buried in impenetrable jargon. Lawyers working on rule of law and anticorruption programs, economists working on public finance, political scientists thinking about patronage and power, health specialists working to promote public health, and security specialists seeking to battle counterinsurgencies do not read or reference each other's work. This is why some lawyers and economists think that passing more severe criminal laws will reduce corruption in poor countries, some health specialists think that poor governments should offer free universal public health, and some aid and security specialists think that poor governments can counteract insurgencies by governing based on the legitimacy acquired from the provision of universal public goods and services.

But our failure to adapt runs much deeper. It is not just that we have mistaken assumptions about what government is in poor countries; we have very deeply held moral convictions about what government—all governments—should be. Unsurprisingly, our discussion of government in poor countries is heavily freighted with normative judgments and moral language. We do not talk about effective governance, but about "good" governance. The solicitation of side payments by government actors is called "corrupt," a word that in English also means "depraved" or "wicked." We believe that our governance values are universal, applying equally to all people in all places at all times. The United States in particular believes that it has a moral mission to champion democracy, rule of law, and good governance, and politicians routinely appeal to this conviction when they justify their international actions to the domestic public. In this context, even a diplomat or a governance specialist who suggests some form of accommodation with the realities of governance of poor governments faces the very difficult task of convincing a home audience. One does not compromise with or accommodate evil.

This is our blind spot—the inability to recognize that our singular notion of governance is not available to everyone and from there to adapt accordingly. The necessarily different governance of poor governments creates a dilemma that we can't and don't want to confront. It is an American dilemma because of the unique role of our governance values in binding us as a nation, and because of our position as a superpower, but it is also more generally a Western dilemma, because the United States is not alone in its conception of the governance ideal. It is not just that we want too much from poor governments, it is that we want things that are mutually incompatible. We want to preserve the existing state system that gives poor governments responsibility for their territory (so that we don't have to take responsibility for it); we want them to govern their territory using their own domestic revenues (so that we don't have to pay for it); and we want them to do it using a model of governance that we see as a moral imperative, but that they can't afford. We do not want to compromise any of these, which is why our foreign policy churns incoherently.

I would not want to leave the impression that I believe that all U.S. engagement in poor countries has been altruistically concerned with improving the quality of governance. We have often taken actions to protect our own interests at the expense of these more high-minded goals. But just as all of our foreign policy is not idealistic missionary work, neither is it all *realpolitik*. Sometimes, where we convince ourselves that extending the governance ideal will be in our own direct interest—as where we convince ourselves that it will stabilize Afghanistan and neutralize a terrorist threat—it is both. A belief in the value of the governance ideal is a core part of our national identity. The missionary impulse to extend the governance ideal is sufficiently important to tie up a good bit of our discussion and energies. Politicians appeal to these values because these appeals work.

About This Book

As a lawyer and a political economist, I worked as a governance specialist for foreign aid donors such as the World Bank and the U.S. Agency for International Development in some of the poorest countries in the world. I conducted qualitative and quantitative studies of governance, negotiated governance reforms, monitored the implementation of reforms, provided technical assistance on governance issues to recipient governments, and ran donor-financed governance reform projects. My work for donors gave me rare access to government actors and an intimate window into some governments that are otherwise closed. In the course of that work I conducted hundreds of confidential interviews about governance, corruption, and rule of law with politicians, civil servants, business people, civil society leaders, religious leaders, and citizens.

As time passed, I became increasingly frustrated with the shortcomings of our governance dialogue, which largely ignored the actual operations of government and focused instead on formal rules and organizations, ignoring the fiscal constraints of poor governments. More deeply, that dialogue assumed that aid donors and recipient governments can and do share the same objectives when it comes to governance and have the same priorities. When people working on the ground came to a new understanding through experience, their insights were quickly lost as they rotated out. Major policy decisions were dictated not by people with field experience, but by people in rich liberal democracies who had never set foot in poor countries and never had their assumptions about governance challenged. Our dialogue becomes a sham when our aid-dependent government counterparts pretend to agree with our governance values and goals and we pretend to believe them, or as our people on the ground do what they think best and repackage it for domestic sensibilities.

I found some of my government counterparts very difficult to work with. Some embezzled; some lied; some allocated themselves or their relatives government contracts; some were thugs; some, it was whispered, had had people murdered. In late-night discussions, local staff and I argued about whether the donors were simply naïve (a level of naïveté that local staff usually found hard to imagine) or complicit as they continued to funnel money into the hands of government officials who charmed donors and deftly used donor buzzwords like "livelihoods" or "gender mainstreaming," but were locally famous for extravagant spending that far outstripped their meager official salaries.

I say this because I have felt and understand the anger toward those government elites whose greed seems to know no bounds and who seem so indifferent to the responsibilities of government office or the welfare of the people of their country. I understand why Westerners labeled some of the first independence governments in Africa "kleptocracies"—rule by thieves—and why, in francophone Africa, the people say of this or that elite, "il exagère" (he goes too far).[35] I am not excusing those elites and I am no relativist. Like most of my colleagues who work in governance, I am also a true believer in our governance ideal. However, I came to understand that that ideal costs more money than poor governments have. I believe this to be true even though some of the principal people who make this argument are its least attractive advocates—the very same elites who use their government power to amass personal fortunes, who benefit from the status quo, whom we routinely accuse of selfishly blocking change.

An understanding that the rich and the poor do not have the same options is not moral relativism. Just because poor governments cannot govern like rich liberal democracies does not mean that some cannot govern more justly, more accountably, more fairly, more effectively, or more in the public interest. But if we would change the way they govern, we need to have a realistic idea of their possibilities, understand the tradeoffs, and develop moral standards that do not carelessly criminalize being poor by measuring poor governments against a standard they cannot afford to meet. We must destigmatize the governance of the poor, allowing a more open dialogue, and be open to supporting shifts from more disfavored strategies of governance to less disfavored strategies, instead of insisting on the adoption of the governance ideal.

The discussion of how to adapt to the realities of how poor governments do and must govern is difficult for us to have. Acknowledging that our governance ideals cannot be implemented by everyone necessitates moral compromises in engaging poor governments that make us intensely uncomfortable, risks eroding standards we have erected at home, and reopens the wounds of recently won (or ongoing) domestic policy conflicts. There is a tendency to refocus the discussion immediately and talk instead about how poor countries can become richer. After all, if poor countries became richer, then poor governments would get more revenue. They would have more options, and we would be more justified in making demands on them and wouldn't have to make any tough decisions. There are some great success stories of very poor countries that rapidly became both wealthy and (by our standards) better governed. But this is not a book about why countries are poor or about how poor countries can become rich. This book is an appeal for an honest conversation about handling the indefinite interim. The world of foreign policy has yet to wrestle with the question of how best to engage governments that govern differently because they must.

I wrote this book to help start that conversation. This is an analysis shaped by my experience in the field and informed by both the academic and practitioner literature. This is not an academic book. It does not test a hypothesis, start with a review of the academic literature, or introduce country case studies; it eschews technical jargon; and it does the violence to detail and nuance that is necessary to make a very broad argument in a single volume. Yet much of what is in this book is well accepted in the academic and practitioner literature, and readers will find citations to some of that literature in the notes. Because I was barred from using my own field research, which had been conducted for another purpose, stories from the press and in the policy and academic literature are used to illustrate how poor governments govern, how people navigate their interactions with them, and how we have often failed to come to terms with them.

This book is organized as follows. Chapter 2, "The Governance Ideal," explains the Western governance agenda and how the emergence of our current conception of governance in a handful of countries in the mid-twentieth century was concomitant with and dependent on increased government revenue. Chapter 3, "Paper Empires, Paper Countries," explains how nineteenth-century colonialism and twentieth-century decolonization resulted in the formation of a number of poor countries whose governments were in no position to govern according to that ideal.

Chapters 4, 5, and 6 provide a broad description of the operation of poor country governments to explain how and why they differ from the Western governance ideal. Chapter 4, "Poor Countries, Poor Governments," explains just how poor the governments of the poorest countries are and what this means in terms of both what their governments can provide and how they are financed. Given that they cannot provide public goods and services to all under the rule of law, chapter 5, "Governing Cheaply," focuses on the strategies that poor governments use to govern, with particular attention to patronage and monetization of government positions. Chapter 6, "The Rule of Law," explains why rule of law is weak and what this means on the ground for those negotiating their interactions with the government.

The final chapters turn the discussion back to us. Chapter 7, "Governance as It Is," provides examples of the difficulties of well-intentioned Westerners (and some poor country elites) in grappling with the more limited possibilities of poor governments. Finally, chapter 8, "A Different Conversation," describes our difficult choices in dealing with poor governments—so difficult that we have largely declined to make them.

2. The Governance Ideal

The attempt to restructure the government of Afghanistan is arguably one of the more ambitious efforts of the governance agenda, a Western effort to change the way other countries are governed. Over the last twenty years, both the development and the security communities have focused with increasing intensity on changing the way poor governments govern. The development community sees government as playing an essential role in fostering economic growth, contributing to individual well-being, and lifting the poor out of poverty. The security community sees government as necessary to address problems that threaten to expand beyond national borders, such as conflict, terrorism, drugs and arms trafficking, and pandemic diseases. The government that is seen as necessary to accomplish these goals is a constitutional democracy with universal adult franchise, operating under the rule of law, managing government resources, using government authority effectively for the public good, respecting and guaranteeing human rights, facilitating economic activity, helping to ensure economic growth, and providing public goods and services impersonally to citizens, such as personal security, justice, health and education services, and infrastructure.

There is debate among and within rich liberal democracies about how to implement this vision and substantial variation among rich liberal democracies, particularly about which human rights to protect, how to protect them, which public goods and services to deliver, and how to deliver them. However, the governance ideal itself is an unchallenged common core, and all of this debate happens within its framework. There are no mainstream voices arguing that government should rule to benefit the governing rather than the governed, that democracy should be eliminated, or that government need not provide any public goods and services or should provide them only to friends of people in power.

This governance ideal is a moral vision of government. We consider such a government to be "good." Americans have a strong investment in the governance ideal, which is central to American national identity and entwined with American religiosity.

Even though we now think of this governance ideal as timeless and universal, our ideas of good government have changed over time, often emerging from violent political struggles. As we changed our expectations of government, the basis of government legitimacy changed, and we marginalized, abandoned, and even criminalized older strategies of governance, such as patronage, repression, or the claim of a right to rule based on tradition or divine right.

The current governance ideal emerged in the twentieth century. While some of our governance ideals have ancient roots, such as democracy and the rule of law, others are not even a century old, such as an egalitarian ideal that allows all adults to participate equally in the political process and guarantees equality under the law and the expectation that government will provide a wide variety of public goods and services. This change in the functions and ideas of government was enabled by increased wealth and government revenue. But if our moral vision of government requires wealth, how are we to judge governments that are too poor to provide this type of government?

The Governance Agenda

Aid agencies, militaries, international organizations, and nongovernmental organizations (NGOs) are all engaged in promoting the governance agenda. The agenda is pursued in a number of ways: through aid projects that seek to change the way poor governments govern, advocacy efforts, declarations and covenants of international organizations, and military efforts to counter insurgents by strengthening government legitimacy. A host of overlapping constituencies work to advance one or more components of the governance ideal.

The United Nations Millennium Declaration states that democratic governance and equality are "fundamental values" that are "essential to international relations in the twenty first century."[1] As the website of the United States Agency for International Development (USAID) puts it, "democratic governance and human rights are critical components of sustainable development and lasting peace."[2] In 2009, the United States alone spent about $2.3 billion for foreign aid to promote rule of law, human rights, democracy, and good governance abroad, including funding small NGOs in other countries to campaign in their own countries.[3] NGOs such as Amnesty International, the Carter Center, Freedom House, and the Lawyers' Committee for Human Rights campaign and work for human rights overseas. The U.S. Congress requires the State Department to produce an annual report on human rights for every country in the world, and some countries have been singled out for sanctions based on human rights concerns. The rights discussed include the right to security of person; freedom from torture; freedom of speech, association, and religion; freedom from discrimination; and the rights of democratic political participation.

Barred by its charter from interfering in politics, the World Bank has nevertheless been active in attempting to reform the governance of its members in those areas it deems to be technical rather than political. In 1994, the Bank defined "good governance" as:

> epitomized by predictable, open, and enlightened policymaking (that is, transparent processes); a bureaucracy imbued with a professional ethos; an executive arm of government accountable for its actions; and a strong civil society participating in public affairs; and all behaving under the rule of law.[4]

Through lending and technical services, the Bank has been engaged in supporting almost all aspects of public sector reform among its member countries, except those dealing with democratic processes and human rights. This includes strengthening public financial management, improving civil service performance, strengthening justice systems, and increasing the effectiveness of government agencies providing public services. From 2009 to 2012, the World Bank lent more for public administration, law, and justice than for any other sector, including health or education.[5] Many other international organizations and foreign aid donors are also engaged in programs designed to strengthen the public sectors of poorer countries. The public financial management component is particularly important to foreign aid donors because they seek reassurance that aid funds transferred to poorer governments will be used responsibly and effectively.

The Millennium Declaration commits the United Nations to work to strengthen the rule of law.[6] Advocates for the rule of law seek to strengthen the enforcement of laws in poor countries and the extent to which the government itself abides by and is constrained by law. Because human rights are often enshrined in law and corruption is criminalized, this concern overlaps both the human rights and anticorruption agendas. NGOs such as Transparency International and Global Integrity conduct research and advocate for measures to control corruption worldwide. In 2003, the United Nations adopted the "United Nations Convention Against Corruption," which requires signatory governments to criminalize a broad range of acts under domestic law.[7]

Foreign aid donors and international organizations also support projects in poor countries designed to promote economic growth by a variety of means, including changes to laws or government economic policy, or loans to governments to permit them to construct needed infrastructure. Governments, NGOs, and international organizations focus on improving the welfare of the poor abroad by working on issues such as food security, education, health, personal security, and social safety nets. They often deliver services directly; in other cases, they work to strengthen the ability of governments to provide services. Access to education, health services, and housing are also framed as part of a bundle of social and economic human rights and are part of the human rights discussion.

Finally, the U.S. military and its partners have also focused on the issue of governance. Because an insurgency is a violent political struggle for control of government, counterinsurgency (COIN) focuses on delegitimizing insurgents and strengthening the legitimacy of government. The U.S. Counterinsurgency Manual counsels: "Success in COIN can be difficult to define, but improved governance will usually bring about marginalization of the insurgents to the point at which they are destroyed, co-opted or reduced to irrelevance in numbers and capability. . . . The intent of a COIN campaign is to build popular support for a government while marginalizing the insurgents; it is therefore fundamentally an *armed political competition* with the insurgents."[8] Many COIN specialists see strengthening the legitimacy of a government as equivalent to widening political participation and improving government accountability, strengthening the rule of law, reducing corruption, and improving the government's ability to guarantee security, protect human rights, and deliver services—in other words, equivalent to advancing the broad governance agenda.[9] As the Joint Chiefs of Staff reported, "Building an effective Afghan government is an integral part of the 'clear, hold, and build' COIN strategy because it is the Afghan government that is ultimately responsible for protecting the population, delivering public services, and enabling economic growth."[10]

These different actors focus on different aspects of the governance ideal. The World Bank, for example, because of its Articles of Agreement, does not address democracy and human rights, while the United Nations focuses strongly on human rights and the Coalition in Afghanistan includes a focus on support to the Afghan military. The actors may also disagree on what governments should do or how policies should be implemented. But this debate takes place within the common frame of reference of the governance ideal, a shared vision of a constitutional democracy under the rule of law, protecting human rights, and providing public goods and services impersonally to all citizens.

A Governance Revolution

Given the fervor with which we promote these governance values, and our assumption that they are timeless and universal, it would be easy to imagine that we ourselves always had such a government and always subscribed to these values, but our ideas of governance have evolved over time. Changing ideas about the legitimate role of government led in turn to demands for changes in the way governments govern that sometimes led to violent conflict.

CHANGING IDEAS. The Enlightenment was an intellectual revolution in Western Europe during the seventeenth and eighteenth centuries, as the modern nation-state was forming.[11] Urbanization gave rise to new public places where people could meet and argue about ideas in salons, clubs, Masonic lodges, and coffee houses. National identities began to trump local identities, as people were united by increased mobility, the creation of national languages, and national laws. There was an explosion of printed material, now addressed to the new national "public."

A literate urban elite challenged the absolutism of the monarchy and the authority of the church, revived and diffused ancient Greek and Roman political ideas, embraced science and rationality, questioned the foundations of the political and social order, and argued for equality, including women's rights, the abolition of slavery, and freedom of speech and thought. The idea that kings were divinely ordained, answerable only to God, was gradually overturned in favor of republican ideals in which the people are sovereign and delegate power to the government to be used for their own benefit. With this came an idea of a citizen's duty not to the king, but to the nation and the public. Thinkers emphasized the idea of the natural rights of the individual, the birthright of every person, which could be secured or violated by governments, but not granted or taken away by them. Older ways in which governments claimed and held power—such as appeals to monarchical tradition or divine authority to rule—no longer sufficed; they were rejected and cast aside.

This fundamental shift in Western beliefs about the nature of government was not accomplished through drawing room debate. Britain plunged into a civil war between an increasingly assertive Parliament and the king. The war ended in 1649 when King Charles I was tried for his "wicked design totally to subvert the ancient and fundamental laws and liberties of this nation, and, in their place, to introduce an arbitrary and tyrannical government."[12] He demanded to know by what lawful authority he had been brought to trial. "I am your king . . . I shall not betray my trust; I have a trust committed to me by God, by old and lawful descent; I will not betray it to answer a new and unlawful authority."[13] He threatened them with divine vengeance. Since the House of Commons had resolved "that the people, under God, are the original of all just power," the court claimed "the authority of the Commons of England assembled in Parliament," found him guilty, and executed him.[14]

In the United States, a revolution was launched in 1776. The ideas of the Framers of the Constitution were informed by the Greek philosophers and the European Enlightenment thinkers about the purpose of government, the power of the people, and human freedoms and liberties. The themes of the natural rights of man, the sovereignty of the people, and the subordination of the government to the people echo in the Declaration of Independence:

> We hold these Truths to be self-evident, that all Men are created equal, that they are endowed by their Creator with certain unalienable Rights, that among these are Life, Liberty, and the Pursuit of Happiness—That to secure these Rights, Governments are instituted among Men, deriving their just Powers from the Consent of the Governed, that whenever

any Form of Government becomes destructive of these Ends, it is the Right of the People to alter or to abolish it, and to institute new Government, laying its Foundation on such Principles, and organizing its Powers in such Form, as to them shall seem most likely to effect their Safety and Happiness.

The French Revolution began about a decade later. The first three articles of the Declaration of the Rights of Man and the Citizen, one of the fundamental documents of the revolution, reiterate these beliefs:

1. Men are born free and remain free and equal in rights. Social distinctions can be based only on public utility.

2. The aim of every political association is the preservation of the natural and imprescriptible rights of man. These rights are liberty, property, security, and resistance to oppression.

3. The source of all sovereignty resides essentially in the nation; no body, no individual can exercise authority that does not proceed from it in plain terms.[15]

CHANGING ADMINISTRATION. The new ideas about the relationship between the government and the governed and about the function and purpose of government required changes in the structure of government administration. In feudal Europe, government depended on a fluid hierarchy of personal relationships. Kings held power by maintaining personal relationships with powerful nobles. In return for their loyalty and political support, the king granted them rights to income from lands, monopolies, or government positions that could be used for personal profit. They in turn held power by maintaining similar relationships with their supporters. As central government strengthened, it became less dependent on these relationships to extend control over territory, but government positions still functioned primarily as personal rewards for some time thereafter. When pressed for cash, governments sold government positions outright.[16] "Venality," as it was called, was a frequent desperate financing mechanism of prerevolutionary France.[17]

Men sought government positions as a road to wealth. Government offices were treated by office holders as a form of personal financial investment. Those who purchased their offices did so with the expectation that they would recoup the cost and make a profit through use of that office.

Officials pocketed fees, sold and traded decision-making authority, and handled procurement to their own advantage.

In Britain, until at least 1780, government offices, with their salaries and perquisites, were widely and openly thought of as private property. In the eighteenth and early nineteenth centuries,

> rewards did not accord with effort or duty; promotion did not occur according to merit or seniority even in a nominal sense; the highest and most lucrative places had the fewest duties, and, often, the least *raison d'être*. Indeed, the most lucrative and impressive offices frequently had no duties at all, and their holders no objective qualifications for having them. Succession to responsible office was often determined by hereditary succession to that office or by open sale.[18]

However, the idea of government power as a public trust meant that the use of government authority or resources for any purpose other than public benefit was increasingly unacceptable, even as governments began to find that they could no longer bear the inefficiencies of the old system. A British newspaper in 1820 described, in tones of outrage, the emoluments of Lord Liverpool, whom historians view as a government reformer:

> He is first set down as First Lord of the Treasury, at £6000 a year! . . . After discharging all the business of the treasury, as first lord, and pocketing the £6000 a year I find him with enough time on his hands *to be a commissioner of affairs in India*, with room enough in his pocket for £1500 more every year! I have scarcely recovered my astonishment at this, when I am also informed that he has also time to discharge the duty of *a Warden of the Cinque Ports* which consists, I am told, of putting £4,100 a year more in his bottomless purse! But even this is not all—he has leisure enough, by working over hours, I suppose, to be *Clerk of the Rolls in Ireland*, for which he pockets £3500 a year more! . . . They whisper, that he neither keeps the Rolls of Ireland, nor attends to the affairs of India, nor knows anything about the Cinque Ports; and that a deputy does all his work at the Treasury for a few hundred a year which is also paid by the *country!*[19]

A line was drawn between public and private offices and roles.[20] Government salaries were tied to the performance of government duties, the sale of offices was abolished, and a new elite social class of professional government administrators was created.

The professionalization of government began early in Prussia; the basic model of Prussian government was established by the 1830s. Robert Neild has argued that the reason for Prussia's early reform was the need to improve the efficiency of both revenue collection and expenditure in order to pay a standing army and ensure its military readiness.[21] France followed shortly thereafter, as Napoleon modernized after the French Revolution. Britain reformed later, drawing on administrative experiments in British India. The buying and selling of government offices and the promising of a seat in Parliament were outlawed in 1809; competitive examinations for candidates to the senior civil service were introduced in 1870; and the purchase and sale of military commissions was finally abolished in 1871.[22]

Perhaps because it faced no serious external military threat, reform came much later in the United States. Federal government in the United States suffered from President Andrew Jackson's introduction of the spoils system, in which an incoming administration reallocated government jobs as patronage to its political supporters. Civil servants got their jobs through local politicians and lost them if their patron lost influence or if they ceased to provide useful political support, such as campaigning for him or paying an assessment into his campaign fund of 2 to 7 percent of their salary.[23] Federal government offices did not begin to be staffed on the basis of merit until the passage of the Pendleton Act in 1883, and implementation occurred over the following decades.

Standards in state and city government were lower. In the words of a British observer, focusing only on federal civil service reform in the United States is "as if one were looking at a painting by Pieter Bruegel and had focused on an upper corner where priests are guiding virtuous people away from a village binge and had not lowered one's eyes to the scenes of lust and debauchery in the rest of the canvas."[24] Political machines dominated major cities until well into the twentieth century. The most famous of these was Tammany Hall, a political organization that ruled New York City for almost a hundred years. Tammany's "bosses" used access to government for self-enrichment; the most successful became multimillionaires by awarding government contracts to themselves, selling government influence, and collecting kickbacks and protection money from the "vice" industries, such as gambling and prostitution, that they were nominally responsible for shutting down.[25]

By the end of the nineteenth century, however, moral standards were changing and such practices were increasingly loudly condemned. George Washington Plunkitt, a Tammany leader made famous through the publication of his interviews with a journalist in 1905, was regarded by his interviewer as refreshingly frank and unconventional because he "dared to say publicly what others of his class whisper among themselves," while Plunkitt himself carefully drew a distinction between making money from "honest graft" (awarding government contracts to himself and using inside knowledge of government infrastructure projects to buy land and sell it to the government at an inflated price) and "dishonest graft" (embezzlement and protection rackets).[26]

Patronage politics still exists in rich liberal democracies, but the sale of government offices and the pocketing of fees for government decision-making were criminalized and vilified. These older strategies of governance and technologies of government administration were labeled "corruption," a word that has inextricable moral overtones. The Merriam-Webster dictionary defines "corruption" as: "impairment of integrity, virtue, or moral principle: depravity b : decay, decomposition c : inducement to wrong by improper or unlawful means (as bribery) d : a departure from the original or from what is pure or correct."[27]

Modern mores can be seen in the public reaction to the attempt by Rod Blagojevich, then-governor of Illinois, to sell President Obama's vacated Senate seat. ("I've got this thing and it's [expletive] golden, and uh, uh, I'm just not giving it up for [expletive] nothing," he famously said.)[28] Perhaps he was simply born too late. Blagojevich's behavior invited national scorn. Salon.com published "Glengarry Rod Blagojevich," portraying a conversation with Blagojevich as written by playwright David Mamet.[29] Blagojevich was also lampooned by "Saturday Night Live" and by *The Onion*. He was the subject of a musical satire by Chicago's "Second City" and dozens of editorial cartoons. In one cartoon, mobster Al Capone scolds Blagojevich as he signs over his soul to Satan. In another, he is likened to a Tammany Hall boss. It is not that the older administrative practices have entirely vanished in rich liberal democracies, but they are no longer acceptable.

WIDER AND DEEPER. The Enlightenment "public" did not include everyone, despite calls for greater inclusion. Political participation was limited to a minority. For decades chattel slavery continued. Pseudoscientific theories

Figure 2.1. John Darkow, "Al Capone Scolds Rod Blagojevich." (Courtesy of Cagle Cartoons)

of racial inferiority lent their weight to both colonialism and the Holocaust; pseudoscientific theories of female inferiority justified the exclusion of women. In the United States, the franchise was initially limited to white men with property. Even a hundred years ago, women and American Indians did not have the legal right to vote, while African American men were excluded in practice.

Over the course of the twentieth century, egalitarianism became better established as a value, and political participation and access to government services were expanded to all adult citizens. These changes also involved conflict. They required an end to the nobility and to discrimination on the basis of religion. In the United States, the Civil War—which still stands as the war with the most U.S. casualties—was fought about the right to own slaves. Suffragettes marched for women's right to vote, and the Civil Rights movement ended the acceptability of racial "separate but equal" policies. These battles for equal rights are recent, scars are fresh, and they are not yet over. It was only in 2013, for example, that qualified women were given the equal right to enter combat positions in the military, and while American

Indians got the right to vote in the Voting Rights Act of 1965, enforcement continues to be an issue.[30]

Even as the pool of political participants grew, the twentieth century saw an explosive growth in government functions throughout the industrialized world. After the Great Depression, the government stepped in to attempt to revive the economy and provide a social safety net. Social insurance functions such as caring for the poor and the sick that had previously been provided by family or religious groups (to the extent that they were provided at all) became part of the function of government. In the United States, a few of the new government activities of the twentieth century include the Social Security Act of 1965 (including the creation of Medicare and Medicaid); unemployment compensation; federal aid to public education and federal financial aid for students; and a host of new regulatory activities including protections against discrimination; labor laws such as those providing for workplace safety and restricting child labor; environmental laws and regulations including the Clear Air, Water Quality and Clean Water Restoration Acts, and the Endangered Species Act; and market-supporting laws and regulations such as antitrust, securities, and consumer protection laws. In other Western countries, the social safety net was expanded earlier and even further, including such benefits as free higher education and national public health. The establishment of equal treatment under the law as an important value and the increase in the number of services that government was to provide reinforced the need for professional government staff.

Older functions of government grew in extent, complexity, and quality. Nearly all childbirth in the United States took place at home in 1900, and nearly all of it occurred in hospitals by 1945.[31] Medical technology advanced, and hospitals offered new treatment options, including renal dialysis and open-heart surgery. Staff-patient ratios dropped in hospitals, and student-teacher ratios dropped in schools where today computers are increasingly seen as necessary learning aids.

People came to see the government as having the responsibility to ensure the well-being of citizens in a broad spectrum of areas. The "welfare state" was born. The idea that the government could intervene usefully in the national economy for good has given way to the idea that it is largely responsible for the state of the national economy and has an obligation to ensure national economic growth. What we now debate is just what basket of public goods and services government should provide. (As comedian Jon Stewart put it, "They're really only 'entitlements' when they're something other people want. When it's something you want, they're a hallmark of a civilized society, the foundation of a great people."[32]) Today, most Republicans and Democrats who argue about the optimal size of government and its redistributive and social insurance functions do not contemplate turning the clock back to the early 1900s before the routinization of federal income tax, before Social Security, Medicaid and Medicare, federal student loans, or unemployment benefits, much less to the 1800s before free universal primary education.

The role of government in enforcing rights also expanded, as did the list of human rights to be enforced. The Universal Declaration of Human Rights, drafted shortly after World War II with strong participation from socialist countries, specifies a right to "food, clothing, housing and medical care and necessary social services, and the right to security in the event of unemployment, sickness, disability, widowhood, old age or other lack of livelihood in circumstances beyond [the individual's] control."[33] Regarding education, it states:

> Everyone has the right to education. Education shall be free, at least in the elementary and fundamental stages. Elementary education shall be compulsory. Technical and professional education shall be made generally available and higher education shall be equally accessible to all on the basis of merit.[34]

While the drafting committee was deliberately ambiguous about the corresponding duty of governments to supply these goods,[35] these articles have been used to support an argument of government duty where such a duty has not simply been assumed.

New rights are emerging all the time, with corresponding obligations for governments. Almost seventy countries have adopted legislation granting a right of access to government information,[36] a right that implies the duty and ability of the government to keep, organize, and retrieve records and to photocopy them on demand. The very wealth of rich countries is used as an argument for the development of new rights. In the United States, Jesse Jackson has argued that government-provided health care "of the highest quality" is a human right on the grounds that "we can afford health care for all our citizens."[37] President Obama, defending legislation to extend health insurance, stated, "In the wealthiest nation on Earth, no one should go broke just because they get sick. In the United States, health care is not a privilege for the fortunate few, it is a right."[38] The Poverty and Race Research Action Council argued for a "right to housing" because "America has the resources to guarantee" it.[39]

Our demands and expectations of government and the standards by which we evaluate it have changed with the idea that government should derive its power from the people and use that power for their benefit, and with democratization, with egalitarianism and equality under the law, and with an expanded idea of government responsibilities for individual and national welfare. This in turn has implications for how governments should be staffed, how government workers should be remunerated, and how they should use the authority and resources at their disposal.

In rich liberal democracies, the political debates about the principles of the Enlightenment are largely over. We are no longer discussing whether we should be ruled by a king, or whether the government should be accountable to the people, or whether classes of people should be excluded from political participation or government services—instead we are largely arguing about implementation. What were daring arguments during the Enlightenment are for us today nonnegotiable articles of faith. The conflict that followed the Enlightenment left us with absolute moral convictions about human rights, the proper nature of government, and the proper use of government power. If we feel passionately about these notions of governance perhaps it is because a price was paid in blood to replace the older strategies of government, which were rejected and condemned. We represent the winning side. We are the inheritors of the victors of the political struggles of the Enlightenment.

Like a fire that starts as a thin red line on the edge of the paper, then quickly begins to consume, these ideas that began in Western Europe are spreading, violently remaking the world. The West has used its political power and dominance in the international community to project these ideas outward, and they are not limited to Western Europe and its settler countries. When I call this ideal "Western," it is a tribute paid to its origins, not a description of its followers. Many people around the world aspire to this governance ideal. Within the common frame is great diversity in ideas about implementation and the role of government—from maximalist socialism to minimalist libertarianism—but there is a shared understanding that the legitimacy of government is based on rule of law, democratic accountability, and the provision of public goods and services in support of the general welfare.

Not Open to Compromise

The United States is not the only proponent of the governance agenda, but as the world's only superpower and an economic powerhouse its voice on the international stage is loud, whether acting alone, in coalition, or as a member of international organizations such as the World Bank, the International Monetary Fund, the United Nations, or the Organisation for Economic Co-operation and Development. Although its governance values do not always trump its self-interest, they are nonetheless real, influence American foreign policy, and politicians and civil society organizations appeal to them to mobilize American public opinion.

In broad lines these values are similar to those espoused in other rich liberal democracies like those of Western Europe, but American governance values are culturally distinct both in their content and their cultural role.[40] Shared political values are the foundation of American national identity. The United States remains more religious than Western Europe, and its governance values are intertwined with American religiosity. As a consequence, the universality of these values is largely beyond question, open compromise on these values can be domestically costly, and they give rise to a missionary impulse to remake governance abroad either because of a moral obligation to assist or on the basis of expected benefits to the United States, such as peace, prosperity, reduction of terrorism, or the creation of friendly and accommodating partners.

Both President George W. Bush (who coined the term "Axis of Evil" to refer to Iran, Iraq, and North Korea) and President Obama each pledged to support the export of democratic governance and the assurance of human rights.[41] President George W. Bush said in his second inaugural address:

> We are led, by events and common sense, to one conclusion: The survival of liberty in our land increasingly depends on the success of liberty in other lands. The best hope for peace in our world is the expansion of freedom in all the world.
>
> America's vital interests and our deepest beliefs are now one. From the day of our Founding, we have proclaimed that every man and woman on this earth has rights, and dignity, and matchless value, because they bear the image of the Maker of Heaven and earth. Across the generations we have proclaimed the imperative of self-government, because no one is fit to be a master, and no one deserves to be a slave. Advancing these ideals

is the mission that created our Nation. It is the honorable achievement of our fathers. Now it is the urgent requirement of our nation's security, and the calling of our time.

So it is the policy of the United States to seek and support the growth of democratic movements and institutions in every nation and culture, with the ultimate goal of ending tyranny in our world.[42]

Or as President Obama put it with fewer religious references in his address on the Arab Spring:

We support a set of universal rights. Those rights include free speech; the freedom of peaceful assembly; freedom of religion; equality for men and women under the rule of law; and the right to choose your own leaders—whether you live in Baghdad or Damascus; Sanaa or Tehran. And finally, we support political and economic reform in the Middle East and North Africa that can meet the legitimate aspirations of ordinary people throughout the region. Our support for these principles is not a secondary interest—today I am making it clear that it is a top priority that must be translated into concrete actions, and supported by all of the diplomatic, economic and strategic tools at our disposal.[43]

While in Britain the national constitutional order was gradually articulated in a series of documents, in the United States it was the drafting and ratification of the constitutional documents that defined and founded the nation. This gives the U.S. Constitution a unique cultural place. In his presidential oath, an incoming president swears to "preserve, protect and defend" not the country, not the people, but the Constitution of the United States.[44]

The way in which Americans handle the Constitution has no parallel unless it can be likened to the handling of a medieval relic. In the winter of 1952 original copies of the United States Constitution and the Declaration of Independence were transferred from the Library of Congress to a specially built rotunda in the National Archives built to house the "Charters of Freedom."

At 11 a.m., December 13, 1952, Brigadier General Stoyte O. Ross, commanding general of the Air Force Headquarters Command, formally received the documents at the Library of Congress. Twelve members of the Armed Forces Special Police carried the 6 pieces of parchment in their helium-filled glass cases, enclosed in wooden crates, down the Library steps through a line of 88 servicewomen. An armored Marine Corps personnel carrier awaited the documents. Once they had been placed on mattresses inside the vehicle, they were accompanied by a color guard, ceremonial troops, the Army Band, the Air Force Drum and Bugle Corps, two light tanks, four servicemen carrying submachine guns, and a motorcycle escort in a parade down Pennsylvania and Constitution Avenues to the Archives Building. Both sides of the parade route were lined by Army, Navy, Coast Guard, Marine, and Air Force personnel. At 11:35 a.m. General Ross and the 12 special policemen arrived at the National Archives Building, carried the crates up the steps, and formally delivered them into the custody of Archivist of the United States Wayne Grover.[45]

Figure 2.2. Transfer of the Declaration of Independence and the Constitution to the National Archives, National Archives and Records Administration, 64-NA-1–434. (Courtesy of the National Archives)

President Truman spoke at the ceremony in language replete with religious imagery:

> The Constitution and the Declaration of Independence can live only as long as they are enshrined in our hearts and minds. If they are not so enshrined, they would be no better than mummies in their glass cases and they could, in time, become idols whose worship would be a grim mockery of the true faith. Only as these documents are reflected in the thoughts and acts of Americans, can they remain symbols of power that can move the world. That power, is our faith in human liberty.[46]

In their hermetically sealed cases, the pages were placed in the rotunda on special platforms for public viewing. At night the platforms descended twenty feet, lowering the pages into a bomb-proof vault.[47] (I was unable to confirm whether this is still the case, as the National Archives declined to comment on its security arrangements.)

In 1995 it was discovered that the glass was deteriorating and a project was launched to create new encasements. The new encasements consist of a gold-plated titanium frame, in which the documents rest on specially made pure cellulose paper "on top of an anodized aluminum support platform that is machined to conform precisely to the irregular shape of the document."[48] The base was cut from a block of solid aluminum alloy, with windows made of sapphire. When a page of the Constitution was unveiled in its new encasement in 2000, the Archivist of the United States remarked that "without the sacred document that contains this page, we might be living in a country dominated by tyrants or a foreign power."[49]

Now, on any given day, a quiet stream of visitors files past to gaze upon the Constitution in its display in the rotunda. British author G. K. Chesterton observed that America is founded on a creed; that it is "a nation with the soul of a church."[50] It is probably more than a coincidence that our most revered civil rights leader was also a pastor.

These strong feelings set the tone of our dialogue abroad and constrain the choices of our policymakers and our people on the ground engaging poor governments. While we are patient when we think about economic growth and understand that it takes time, because our governance ideal is equated with the universal good, and contrasted with evil and tyranny, we have little patience for incrementalism when it comes to governance.

Figure 2.3. Visitors to the Rotunda for the Charters of Freedom. (Courtesy of the National Archives)

The Cost of Governance

Many interconnected factors contributed to these changes to government, the basis of government legitimacy, and technologies of government administration in the West. Two recent prominent books focus on the self-interest of elites in blocking change and the circumstances under which change can happen.[51] Francis Fukuyama has pointed to the critical role of the Christian religion and the church in the rise of the rule of law.[52] Others have considered the role of the emerging middle class and the bargains it was able to strike with government in return for the payment of taxes.[53] However, one prerequisite for this type of government is adequate government revenue.

Increased centralization of government allowed nationwide taxation, which reduced reliance on older systems of revenue raising such as feudal dues or sale of monopolies.[54] Arguably, the reimagining of government as a servant of the people and stronger popular control of the budget increased people's willingness to pay taxes. As governments were increasingly bound by law, their promises became more reliable and they were better able to borrow. As the country became wealthier, governments raised more in taxes. When governments then spent their increased revenue wisely for the public benefit, they increased their capacity, legitimacy, and credibility, and helped foster national economic growth and innovation (or at least did not hinder it), leading to higher revenues in a virtuous circle.[55]

The evolution of the Western governance ideal was enabled by increased government revenue. Government revenue was needed so that central governments could control their territories directly instead of relying on a fragile and fluid network of personal relationships with local power brokers. Alternate sources of government revenue were needed to end the practice of selling government positions. Revenue was also needed to replace a system in which government positions were financial benefits in and of themselves, giving the holder a right to hunt his own pay, with a system in which government jobs came with fixed salaries. Yet more revenue was needed to ensure that those salaries were sufficient to allow rules prohibiting civil servants from engaging in any other kind of remunerated work in order to minimize conflicts of interest.

Finally, substantial government revenue was needed to create a system of government in which government provides a broad number of public goods and services impersonally to the entire adult population, including those we now think of as human rights, such as universal free primary education. Both extending the type and complexity of government services and delivering them to more people required more revenue. The Western governance ideal is expensive. The welfare state as it emerged in Western Europe is so expensive that it is not clear that even those wealthy countries can sustain it.

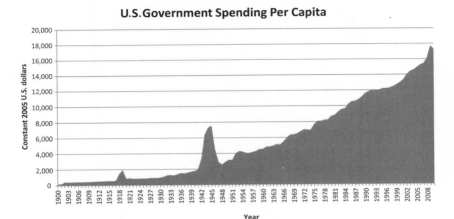

Figure 2.4. U.S. Government Spending Per Capita in Constant 2005 Dollars. (Courtesy of Christopher Chantrill, usgovernmentspending.com)

Revenue per capita in rich liberal democracies increased precipitously. The quality of financial recordkeeping in seventeenth- and eighteenth-century Europe leaves a great deal to be desired, but one scholar attempted to trace the rise in government revenue per capita that accompanied Western European centralization, as evidenced by the birth of national taxation, and the subsequent establishment of popular control of government spending during the nineteenth century.[56] He estimates that French revenue per capita doubled from the 1780s to 1815, doubled again by the end of the 1860s, and doubled again by the start of World War I. Increased public sector spending prompted economist Adolph Wagner to propose Wagner's Law in 1893—that there is a long-run tendency for the public sector to grow in relationship to the size of the economy in industrialized countries. In 1902 in the United States total government spending at all levels was about $438 per person per year in 2011 dollars; in 2013, it was $13,782.[57]

To a colleague who huffed that "it is not all about money"—that's right, it isn't. The historic coevolution of changing ideas and institutions, centralization, increased state capacity, better fiscal and administrative technologies, and economic growth is a soupy mess from which scholars attempt to tease out causal relationships. It may not be replicable elsewhere. But without adequate government revenue it is certainly not possible. While richer governments may not have good governance, poor governments cannot afford good governance—or in some cases any governance at all. Poor governments are too poor to provide either quantity or quality in public goods and services. While in poor countries many if not most people live in rural areas, delivery of public goods and services is concentrated in the few urban centers. Poor governments are too poor to provide rule of law, particularly when this task is complicated by the lack of a national consensus on appropriate legal rules and norms and the lack of a widely spoken national language. Because they cannot provide public goods and services to most people under the rule of law, they cannot govern by relying on the legitimacy that comes from providing them. They must use other means to hold power, relying more heavily on older, cheaper strategies of governance, such as appeals to tradition or religion, or patronage and repression. They also rely more heavily on older, cheaper technologies of government administration, such as sale of public offices or allowing government actors to monetize their positions and "pay themselves." They do this despite the fact that they have borrowed, received, or had thrust upon them constitutions, formal government structures, and laws modeled on those of much richer Western countries that criminalize these practices, creating an extra-wide gap between law and practice.

To say that poor governments cannot afford to govern according to the Western governance ideal is not to deny the value or the rightness of those ideals. It is not an argument for cultural relativism. People would have every reason to prefer, for example, a country with a well-functioning and impartial court system when deciding where to do business, or a country that is stable, peaceful, and respectful of human rights when deciding where to travel or live. But it does mean that we should have different expectations of poor governments. We should not expect poor governments to govern like rich liberal democracies and consequently to have the same objectives, priorities, processes, or approaches to problem solving. It means that if we assume that their formal institutions and rules play the same role as similar institutions and rules are supposed to play in rich liberal democracies we will be utterly misled. It also means that our system of governance is not transferable to poor countries, and it is not clear that our current expertise in governance is very relevant to them. Finally it means that we cannot erect the Western governance ideal as the *moral* standard by which to judge all governments unless we simply wish to condemn the poor for not being rich.

The problem is even more serious than that. Not only do poor govern-ments govern out of necessity with heavier reliance on disfavored strategies and administrative methods, some governments are so poor that they can't govern their territories no matter what strategies they use. The problem of territorial consolidation and the difficulty of establishing any kind of central government remains one of their biggest challenges. In the process of the formation of the international state system, these governments were given the right and responsibility to govern their territories, but they do not have the ability. They will not have it in the short or medium term, and some may never have it. To understand how this came about, we need to first take a brief look at how they came to be considered states, and we will do so in the next chapter.

3. Paper Empires, Paper Countries

To attempt a history of colonialism and decolonization in a single chapter is a thankless but necessary task. The governance problems of many of today's poor countries are rooted in the way they came into being during the formation of the modern state system. The modern state system was formed through the process of "second wave" colonialism that occurred in the late nineteenth and the early twentieth centuries and the subsequent process of decolonization that followed in the mid-twentieth century. During second wave colonialism, the colonial powers claimed large territories and held most of them with a minimum of investment and, in some cases, for as little as sixty years before decolonization. Most of today's poor countries were yesterday's poor dependencies, colonized during the second wave, and most had never been previously governed as states.

Colonization and decolonization were haphazard processes of state formation that were not concerned with the creation of economically viable states. For today's poor countries, for most of the period, it was not the ambition of colonizers to build independent states or to govern colonial subjects by winning popular legitimacy. The economies of the poorer dependencies were built to service the needs of the colonizing power, and some did not generate enough tax revenue to pay for their own administration. Colonial powers controlled these dependencies not by winning popular support through the provision of public goods and services, but by a combination of patronage and indirect rule, repression, and neglect—just as poor governments govern today.

Decolonization was unexpected, rapid, and accomplished by expressly waiving the requirement of an effective territorial government. The result was the international recognition of a number of states that have never governed their entire territories. Accordingly, decolonization left these governments with an unprecedented task: instead of establishing a state, whose power and control would determine its boundaries, the new governments were tasked with building a state capable of controlling territory out to pre-determined boundaries. While it was assumed that the newly recognized governments would eventually govern their territories with domestically generated revenue, today's poor countries still do not.

The Second Wave: Legal Claims

The modern state system, in which the entire world was divided into states with defined territories and permanent populations, is a creation of the nineteenth and early twentieth centuries. Beginning in the nineteenth century, more powerful states began laying claims to territory, both territory that was claimed by weaker states whose rights they did not recognize and territory that was not claimed by any state, but was occupied by people living in other forms of political and social organization. Western Europe was very active in this expansion, but it was not alone. Imperial Russia, Japan, and the United States also claimed territory.

Most of today's poor countries are products of the nineteenth-century European colonization of Africa and Asia (see table 3.1); some had more than one European colonizer. Historians sometimes refer to this as the "second wave" of European colonization to distinguish it from an earlier period of European expansion that started in the fifteenth century with the colonization of the Americas.[1] By the time the second wave occurred, North and Latin American colonies had already obtained their independence. European settlement played a far smaller role in second wave colonialism than it had in first wave colonialism.[2] There were, by the nineteenth century, more comfortable and less dangerous destinations for would-be European émigrés in Australia and the Americas.

Second wave colonialism was not the beginning of Western engagement in these territories. European control had been gradually extended through private agents, sometimes acting under the color of their government flag and sometimes acting on their own impetus. Some regions in Africa had already been devastated by centuries of the transatlantic slave trade, in which private traders traded European manufactured goods in Africa in return for slaves, who were traded in the Americas for export crops like sugar that were then carried back to Europe. But the second wave of colonization was a turning point because it was the extension

TABLE 3.1 Low-Income Economies and Their Most Recent Former Colonizers

Region	Colonial Power							Not Colonized
	France	Britain	Belgium	Portugal	Italy	Imperial Russia	Other	
Africa (27)	Benin Burkina Faso Central African Republic Chad Comoros Guinea Madagascar Mali Niger Togo*	Gambia, The Kenya Malawi Sierra Leone Somalia Tanzania Uganda Zimbabwe	Burundi* Congo, Democratic Republic of Rwanda*	Guinea-Bissau Mozambique	Eritrea Somalia		Liberia (private company)	Ethiopia
South Asia (3)		Bangladesh						Afghanistan Nepal
Central Asia (1)						Tajikistan		
Southeast Asia (2)	Cambodia	Myanmar						
East Asia (1)							Korea, Democratic People's Republic of (Japan)	
Caribbean (1)	Haiti							

*indicates a country that was in whole or part a former German colony whose administration was assumed by one of the Allies after World War I.

by European governments of legal claims over territories. These claims were extended under an international legal system that at the time was restricted to Christian or "civilized" nations. These claims would determine the boundaries of states in the modern international system and of today's poor countries in particular.

A number of factors contributed to second wave European colonialism. Certainly economic motivations were important. Industrialized Europe required supplies of tropical goods, such as rubber, to feed its factories and to maintain employment; it also required markets for its manufactured goods. European competition for markets was intense. By claiming colonies, European countries could establish preferential trading arrangements, if not outright monopolies. However, that great voice of British colonialism, Dame Marjery Perham, identified five different reasons for the British Empire: economic, security, emigration, power and prestige, and philanthropy, and "they were neither all simultaneous nor neatly consecutive";[3] nor, it should be added, were they mutually exclusive.

Scholars of Africa refer to this expansion as "the Scramble for Africa." As European powers began to collide with each other in Africa, they competed to expand and lock in their exclusive claims. One author marks the beginning of the Scramble for Africa as the year 1879, when Stanley and de Brazza were sent by the French and the Belgians to conclude treaties in an area of the Congo Basin that Portugal and Britain had considered to be theirs.[4] France annexed Port Novo and Little Popo in 1883, and in response Britain declared a protectorate over the Oil Rivers and Cameroon in 1884. In 1887 King Leopold II of Belgium wrote to one of his ambassadors, "I don't want to miss the chance of getting us a slice of this magnificent African cake."[5] Responding to an argument that Britain should have seized the Congo River for itself, Earl Granville asked Britain's House of Lords, "But are we really to take possession of every navigable river all over the world and every avenue of commerce for fear somebody else should take possession of it?"[6]

The competition over Africa threatened European relations. In 1884 to 1885 a conference was held in Berlin that set the ground rules for European claims, trade, and activities in Africa in order to minimize inter-European conflict.[7] Under the agreed upon rules, a colonial power had to notify other signatory powers when it took possession of a territory or established a protectorate. It had an obligation to establish authority in the coastal regions it occupied sufficient to protect existing European rights, including freedom of trade and transit. Nothing was said about claims to the interior regions. "The Berlin Congo Conference thus set a precedent in allowing a European power to preclude others from contesting a piece of territory that was merely under its sphere of influence."[8] Herbst called it "boundary creation on the cheap."[9] Alternately, where colonial powers encountered a larger polity, a protectorate could be claimed, which in theory allowed a local ruler to maintain control of domestic affairs, but in practice allowed the European power to intervene at will without assuming the administrative costs of managing a colony.[10] Within fifteen years, the carving up of Africa was all but complete, with the exception of Morocco, Liberia, and Abyssinia (Ethiopia). The 1901 International Year Book concluded: "All Africa, practically, seems destined to be governed by Europe."[11]

Colonial powers scrambled for control of Africa, but unlike scholars of Africa, their vision was global, not regional. They were simultaneously scrambling for territory in Asia and the Pacific. For example, the French established a protectorate over Cambodia in 1863, annexed Tahiti in 1880, and extended protectorates over Annam (Vietnam) in 1883 and Madagascar in 1885.[12] Some colonial powers were not engaged in Africa at all.[13] Imperial Russia expanded into and claimed Central Asia. Japan laid claim to Korea. The United States expanded westward across the North American continent, annexed Hawaii, and claimed Samoa, Cuba, the Philippines, Puerto Rico, and Guam. Some territories were claimed for noneconomic reasons, such as the desire to build a buffer around a more valuable territory, but in the haste to beat out competitors, European powers claimed some territories that they had not even explored, and badly overestimated their economic value.[14] In the end, almost every square mile of the earth had been swept into the international system of states—at least on paper—in what Jackson has called "an international enclosure movement."[15]

Nineteenth-century legal scholars justified colonialism by arguing that "international law applied only to the sovereign states that composed the civilized 'Family of Nations.'"[16] They wrestled throughout the century with definitions of sovereignty and statehood, and with identifying "family" members, but the conclusion was that non-European peoples did not live in states, and were not part of the family. As one scholar explained, "The public law, with slight exceptions, has always been, and still is, limited to the civilized and Christian people of Europe or to those of European origin."[17] Accordingly, non-Europeans had no rights under international law; nor did European nations owe them any duties. Although European powers had been signing treaties with non-European rulers since the fifteenth century, jurists held that such treaties could create binding obligations for the non-Europeans who signed them, but not for European governments.[18] While countries subject to the General Act that emerged from the Berlin Conference pledged to "watch over the preservation of the native tribes, and to care for the improvement of the conditions of their moral and material well-being, and to help in suppressing slavery, and especially the slave trade," as well as to allow freedom of religion, the obligation was between European countries as a result of their mutual pledge, rather than an obligation from a European government to the "native tribes."[19]

Colonization had two faces: a legal face, in which Europeans defined their territorial claims *as against each other*, and a face of power, which defined relationships between Europeans and the non-Europeans whose territory they claimed. The word "colonize" therefore refers to two different things: the international legal act of declaring a territory to be a colony, and the de facto process of asserting control over a territory and its people. Declaring a colony was a legal act aimed at a European audience; it was not a reflection of the degree of the colonial power's effective control on the ground. While European powers made efforts to limit European claims to territories that European powers actually occupied, no clear standard for effective occupation was ever set.[20] Even after 1945, much of Africa was only nominally under colonial control; people were often faced with serious violence and crime, institutional violence by traditional rulers, ethnic disputes, and religious conflicts.[21]

The establishment of legal claims of right was much easier than the establishment of actual control, and so there were two empires—the juridical empire, a legal fiction represented by European maps with boundaries and colored-in dependencies that described European claims to territory, and the real one, in which European control was often fragile, territorially limited, and repeatedly challenged.[22] An older European map of Africa attempted to represent the political realities of territorial control. See figure 3.1. It was a map of power. But by 1910, political maps of the world no longer represented power and control; they represented European legal claims as against each other. See figure 3.2. A European world map from 1910 shows the extent of colonial claims and ambitions. The world is neatly colored in—pink for the British Empire, blue for the French, orange for Germany and its dependencies, grass green for Portugal and its dependencies, a muddy purple for the Netherlands and its dependencies, lime

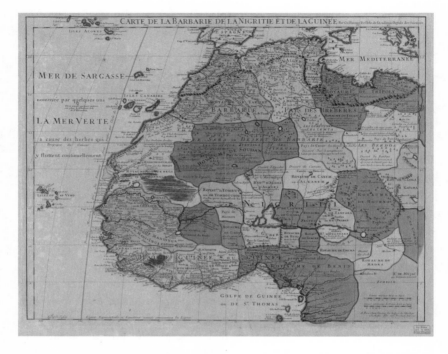

Figure 3.1. Guillaume Delisle, North West Africa, 1707. (Courtesy of Wikimedia Commons)

green for the United States and its dependencies, dark grey for the Russian Empire. By World War I, except for parts of Antarctica, all the world's territory had been claimed by at least one state.

Economy

If the colonial powers did not look ahead to statehood when claiming and conquering territory during second wave colonialism, neither did they do so in building the local economy. Colonial territories were made to serve the economy of the metropole. These patterns of economic development persist in many of today's poor countries.

The declared economic purpose of dependencies was to provide the metropole with unprocessed tropical goods and to serve as markets for its manufactured products. To this end, the colonies were developed narrowly as exporters of tropical goods that could not be produced at home, including

Figure 3.2. "The World: Colonial Possessions and Commercial Highways 1910." From Sir Adolphus William Ward, G. W. Prothero, Sir Stanley Mordaunt Leathes, and E. A. Benians, eds., "The Cambridge Modern History Atlas" (London: Cambridge University Press, 1912). (Courtesy of the University of Texas Libraries, The University of Texas at Austin)

needed inputs for manufacturing. For example, dependencies in the British Empire produced rubber, palm oil, cocoa, gold, manganese, cotton, cattle, sisal, tea, tobacco, sugar, bananas, and copra.[23] Dependencies did not print their own currency, and so from their exports gained the currency necessary to purchase imports such as textiles, trade spirits, firearms, tobacco, salt, sugar, opium, flour, matches, clothing, jewelry, furniture, work tools, paper products, industrial machinery, fishing, cooking, and farming utensils, glassware, metal goods, industrial equipment, radios, and bicycles.[24]

Through preferential trade agreements and colonial economic policy the colonial powers encouraged dependencies to specialize in raw materials and agricultural products that were needed by the metropole, and typically each dependency was concentrated in the production of one or two of these. Of seventeen British colonies through 1964, fourteen of them depended on just three export commodities for at least 70 percent of their export earnings, and for six of them, the percentage was higher than 90 percent.[25] By putting the entire economy's eggs in one basket, as it were, this narrow export base left the dependencies very vulnerable to swings in world prices for their primary exports, as well as to changes in international shipping costs and availability. This economic structure, which continues to this day for many poor countries, particularly those in Africa, creates unpredictable boom-and-bust cycles that affect both their economies and their tax yields. Moreover, because each empire wanted to assure itself of an independent supply of these goods, dependencies as a whole were encouraged to supply similar goods. Later, when no longer shielded by preferential trade agreements, these dependencies would find themselves in fierce competition.

The development of exports in the dependencies was not only the result of market incentives or special trade agreements. Plantations and mines needed workers, but colonial subjects were primarily subsistence farmers—people who raised their own food and traded the surplus. They were neither seeking wage labor nor available for it in the numbers that colonists required, nor were they conveniently located near colonial capitals, plantations, and mines. One way to generate labor was through taxation. Taxes on colonial subjects were often imposed not primarily to raise revenue, but to compel peasants to hire themselves out to raise the tax money as wage laborers, to enter cash crop production, or to work in forced labor as tax defaulters.[26] In 1936, the government treasurer of Uganda wrote that "in Uganda taxation is the principal incentive to labour and production."[27]

Infrastructure was built to facilitate the trade between metropole and dependency. In the late 1800s and early 1900s, the colonial powers organized the construction of railroads and roads to facilitate the transportation of goods and troops.[28] The purpose of these transportation links was to facilitate the movement of goods to the port and troops to the interior when needed. "The Germans in Togo actually named their railway lines after the products they served: Coconut line, cocoa line, cotton line, iron line and palm-oil line (öl-bahn)."[29] The hub-and-spoke structure of roads and railways connecting the capital to the interior served the economic relationship of colony and colonial power and persists today.[30] Because of the desire to monopolize railroad revenue, colonial powers did not link their railroads to those of other powers. In West Africa, where French and British territorial claims alternated, this created a series of disconnected railroad lines pushing from the interior to the ports.[31]

According to the *Economist*, in much of Africa little has changed in intercontinental transportation infrastructure since independence:

> The continent has only a few broken-down railways. It has nothing resembling a transcontinental motorway. Even the British colonial dream of a road connecting Cape Town with Cairo failed. Today, getting a container to the heart of Africa—from Douala in Cameroon to Bangassou in the Central African Republic, say—still means a wait of up to three weeks at the port on arrival; roadblocks, bribes, pot-holes and mud-drifts on the road along the way; malarial fevers, prostitutes and monkey-meat stews in the lorry cabin; hyenas and soldiers on the road at night. The costs of fuel and repairs make even the few arterial routes (beyond southern Africa) uneconomic. A study by America's trade department found that it cost more to ship a ton of wheat from Mombasa in Kenya to Kampala in Uganda than it did to ship it from Chicago to Mombasa.[32]

Chicago is some 8,200 miles from the port at Mombasa as the crow flies, while Kampala is just over 500 miles away.[33]

The colonial powers did not promote industrialization in the dependencies or promote a domestic economy. Neither Britain nor France wanted to create industries in the dependencies that would compete with industries at home. Even the more socially liberal political parties did not imagine support for indigenous industrialization.[34] As Jules Méline, former French prime minister, wrote in 1906:

> Within a sound colonial system, colonial production must be limited to supplying the mother country with raw material or with non-competitive products. If colonial production should step out of this field and offer competition ruinous to our own production then it would become a dangerous opponent.[35]

Similar concerns were advanced in Britain.[36] In 1934, Neville Chamberlain, chancellor of the exchequer stated:

> While it was improbable that West Africa would set up factories to compete with those at home, there was a real and serious danger of such factories being established in Malaya and possibly other parts of the Colonial Empire, and we might well be faced with very serious

developments of a problem of industrial competition of which we had already had some experience in the case of India.[37]

Not only was local industrialization not supported, financed, or encouraged, it was actively discouraged to prevent competition with Europeans. More generally, local trade and cash cropping were discriminated against and disadvantaged as against European business interests.[38] In some places, such as Guinea, Democratic Republic of Congo, and Cameroon, existing local commercial networks were actively stamped out.[39]

By the 1920s, facing postwar unemployment, there were advocates in both France and Britain who argued for the further development of the colonies to stimulate the home economy, although most stopped short of recommending industrialization. In Britain, Winston Churchill and Leo Amery argued that development of the colonies would benefit Britain by reducing unemployment.[40] In France, Albert Sarraut proposed the creation of "poles of development" to facilitate exporting, stopping short of recommending industrialization; this call was later echoed by Giscard D'Estaing in 1932.[41] In the mid-1930s, Paul Bernard called for industrialization in Indochina. However, the governments were hard to convince. A plan to industrialize Indochina was finally ratified in 1948 but never implemented because it was superseded by independence.[42] In Britain, serious investment in colonial development did not begin until after World War II, and this investment was made in social services rather than industrialization.[43]

In short, the economy built under colonial policies was not the economy that would serve an independent country well. The domestic revenue base depended on taxes on trade and was inadequate to provide more than minimal public goods and services concentrated in the capital. There was little industrialization, or it was actively suppressed. The export-based economy focused narrowly on just a few primary products, leaving the economy vulnerable to swings in world prices. While some infrastructure was built, it was in the service of moving products to the port where such existed and moving troops to the interior. Other public works, such as sewerage, electrification, hospitals, and schools, were heavily concentrated in the colonial capital city. Rural areas, where the vast majority of the countries' populations lived, had been largely neglected; once free to do so, people would leave the countryside to come to the city seeking jobs and access to these services, overwhelming the city infrastructure and surrounding the capital with a ring of slums.

Governance

Colonial powers did not govern colonial subjects by winning popular support through the delivery of a modern basket of universal public goods and services under the rule of law or by being accountable to them through democratic elections with a universal franchise. They did provide some public goods and services, notably roads, rail lines, courts, and schools. However, they relied heavily on cheaper strategies of governance, a combination of neglect, patronage and indirect rule, and repression.

To begin with, the governance ideal wasn't yet how they governed their own citizens. Purchase of military commissions was abolished in Britain in 1871. Britain did not grant equal voting rights to women until 1928. Neither France nor Italy granted the right to vote to women until 1945. At the turn of the century, Europe did not have universal primary education; child labor was still legal.[44] The British National Health Service was not established until 1948.

Dependencies were acquired to benefit the metropole, not the other way around. The purpose of the administration was to protect the rights of colonial citizens, generate revenue and labor for colonial enterprises, and exclude competing colonial powers. The questions of when and whether dependencies would become independent, of the extent of the obligation to colonial subjects, and the extent to which the interests of colonial subjects would be represented to the government were discussed. In the meantime, a sharp line was drawn between citizen and subject. Subjects were governed and treated differently than citizens. While some colonial administrations also saw themselves as having a trusteeship or guardianship with regard to colonial subjects, their very slender lines of accountability ran upward to their own governments, far away.

Even had they wanted to, colonial administrations could not have provided that type of government because they could not afford it. By 1946 Great Britain claimed the largest empire the world had ever seen, with a quarter of the world's land area and more than a quarter of its population.[45] France claimed dependencies that were nineteen times its own size in area and almost twice its size in population.[46] Portugal claimed dependencies more than twenty-two times its own area and with a population greater than its own.[47] The Netherlands claimed dependencies of sixty-one times its own size in land area and almost eight times its own population.[48]

Yet the resources they had available to govern their newly claimed territories were very limited.

Some businesses made important profits in the dependencies, and business interests were typically supportive of the extension of empire. European domestic public opinion was another matter. Empire had to be actively marketed to the public by the small constituencies in favor of expansion. The public enjoyed the sense of status that came with having an empire, but was never entirely convinced of its material benefits and was reluctant to pay for it or die for it. Before the 1890s, French public opinion toward colonialism wavered between hostility and indifference, becoming more enthusiastic only when sparked by indignation over British and German overseas expansion at the expense of French interests—they were "colonialists only in a moment of national crisis."[49] Belgians hesitated to assume King Leopold's private domain in the Congo as a colony because of fear of expenditures.[50] In Germany, enthusiasm for colonies was limited to a small group of patriots interested in empire for prestige and a few merchants hoping for investment opportunities and government contracts.[51] The Portuguese public understood Africa to be a "far and dangerous place inhabited by Negroes and exiles."[52]

Colonial powers accordingly adopted the general principle that colonies should pay for themselves, which meant that colonial administration should be self-financing.[53] Even though this policy was never entirely implemented—there were transfers from the metropoles to build colonial infrastructure, pay down debts, and even to pay routine administrative expenses—it meant that the colonial enterprise was run as cheaply as possible: "a gimcrack effort run by two men and a dog."[54]

Efforts to estimate the ratio of European colonial administrators to colonial populations are hampered by the quality of statistics (and in particular, population statistics for the dependencies), but in 1936 there were just 316 Belgian colonial administrators in the Congo; in 1926 in French Equatorial Africa, there were 112 French administrators. In 1939, there were 3,073 British Colonial Service posts in British East Africa, which had an estimated population of almost thirteen million people. A quarter to a third of those posts were vacant at any one time because of death, illness, and administrative leave.[55] A district commissioner, typically a young unmarried man, "might have a district the size of a large or medium English county, and its population might number anywhere from twenty thousand to nearly half a million, though in this case he would have one or two assistants and perhaps a sub-district."[56]

The poorer dependencies did not produce enough revenue to pay for the cost of their colonial administrations. Instead they were subsidized by the colonial power directly or with revenues derived from richer dependencies. Laos, for example, was annexed as a possible route to China and to create a defensive buffer for Vietnam, and it never provided enough revenue to cover the cost of its own administration.[57]

The British Somali Protectorate was acquired for its Red Sea port at Berbera.[58] The revenues raised never paid for its meager colonial administration, as it was "without any exploitable resources or viable commercial activities."[59] Sayyid Muhammad, the leader of Somali resistance in the interior, protested to the British, "I have no forts, no houses, I have no cultivated fields, silver or gold for you to take. If the country was cultivated or contained houses or property, it would be worth your while to fight, but the country is all jungle and that is of no use to you."[60]

Attempts to levy taxes resulted in rebellion. Instead, the Protectorate depended on colonial grants-in-aid. In the face of armed resistance, the British abandoned the interior and discussed abandoning the Protectorate altogether. They tried to trade the interior with Italy in return for one of its territories, but Italy wasn't interested. They then unsuccessfully attempted to donate the interior to Ethiopia and Italy. The Protectorate became self-supporting for the first time in 1938 as a result of increased economic activity that resulted from the Italian invasion of Ethiopia.

Other dependencies were able to support the cost of minimal administration. After conquering Chad for France, a French commander reflected

'that it truly was not worth having killed so many and having suffered so much to conquer such a forsaken country.' The military territory of Chad played home to only 20 Europeans at the turn of the twentieth century. . . . Forced labour and various taxes imposed on the population produced revenues equal to half the cost of administration. A single French businessman, who traded in ivory and rubber, represented French commerce.[61]

Yet in Chad the administration ultimately managed to log a fiscal surplus, through a combination of extortion and creative accounting.[62]

A contemporaneous scholar discussing France's 1900 law that put forth the principle of colonial support remarked that many colonies were still far from self-supporting.[63] Germany was in worse shape. With the exception of Togo, colonies were paying less than two-fifths of their ordinary running expenses, due in part to the construction of public works in China.[64]

São Tomé and Principe were uninhabited islands off the coast of Africa that the Portuguese claimed, and on which they established profitable cocoa operations. However, the profitability of the cocoa operations depended entirely on slave labor. Once slavery was abolished, cocoa farming became less profitable, and few of the islands' inhabitants had any further desire to work in the cocoa fields. One scholar has gone so far as to call São Tomé a country that is economically "unviable."[65]

Poor dependencies certainly did not generate enough revenue to pay for the cost of providing universal public goods and services. As Lord Hailey wrote in 1938, "If African administrations are to be able to attain higher standards in expenditure or social improvements, the African population must pay the price which is necessary to earn them."[66] Social investment in the dependencies was not begun with any seriousness until after World War I, reflecting changing norms at home that emphasized growing egalitarianism, a greater social role for government, and a growing international challenge to the legitimacy of colonialism. It was also at the precise moment when colonial powers, ravaged by war and the Great Depression, had the least to give, and in some cases, paradoxically, increasing intrusion in social affairs by colonial powers was resented by local elites and fed nationalist movements. Decolonization followed soon after.

Much of the claimed territory was simply neglected, the colonial claim of interest only to exclude other European powers. In some cases, colonizers had not even explored the territories they claimed. In 1930, two Australian prospectors crossed the mountains of the Central Highlands of New Guinea—administered by Australia after having been claimed by Britain and Germany—and found more than a million people living there, almost half the population of New Guinea.[67] This moment, remarkably, was caught on film.[68] This last major episode of European first contact overlapped the Golden Age of Hollywood.

The British system of "indirect rule" relied, where possible, on coopting local rulers using both the carrot and the stick. As one of the architects of British colonial policy, Lord Lugard, stated, "The object to be aimed at in the administration of the country is to rule through its own executive government."[69] In practice, however, sometimes a British political officer interfered "more than he should,"[70] and the British were willing to appoint intermediaries if there was no suitable executive government, as they did in Igbo in Nigeria and in Papua New Guinea.[71] The French appointed all their intermediate *chefs des cantons*, who in theory could be dismissed at will.[72] Stretched so thin, all colonial powers relied on local intermediaries both as auxiliaries and for actual territorial governance, tax collection, and conscription of labor. In exchange, they were backed by the colonial authority and its military might.[73] This method of control was dictated by "convenience for conquest, ease of administration, economy."[74]

The treatment of the local population by the auxiliaries and intermediaries of the colonial regime was usually not the concern of the colonial administration unless problems threatened to spill over to the European community or posed a direct threat to colonial rule.[75] As a consequence, much of colonial administration as it affected the local population is undocumented, and intermediaries were free to use their authority to their own advantage, provided that the needs of colonial administrations were met.[76] One French colonial administrator complained that he was surrounded by a "circle of iron," a "wall of deceptions and lies built by the local interpreter and the local chief," who had used his name and authority to levy fines, imprison rivals, and confiscate property.[77]

In many cases, colonial powers also relied on repression to keep the population quiescent.[78] Orders from the metropole might dictate abuse of colonial subjects, as where it required or incentivized colonial administrators to produce a quantity of native labor or taxes or conduct a punitive raid, and there was little to stop a colonial administrator from going even further, abusing his authority through plunder, rape, torture, and murder, which tended to rise to official attention only when the victims were white. A persistent German parliamentarian raised a number of such incidents publicly after the administration had failed to react.[79] They included cases such as the administrator who tortured African criminals to death; the station master in Togo who maintained a large harem of young African girls obtained through coercion; or the case of the official whose sleep was disturbed by a crying baby and killed mother and baby alike before going back to sleep.

Some colonial powers controlled populations by terror, through plunder, torture, and punitive raids. Such raids might involve burning a village whose terrified inhabitants had fled so that they were left without food or slaughtering all the inhabitants before putting the village to the torch. In 1927, the colonial government representative was murdered in the Solomon Islands while collecting taxes. The punitive expedition in response involved an Australian gunboat and a "breathless army" of Australian planters and volunteers who engaged in random slaughter of the Kwaio, raped the women, and destroyed and desecrated their shrines and sacred objects.[80] Recounting his life as a Papuan resident magistrate, Monckton recalled that he was asked what the response of the administration should be to a series of murders. He answered that the administration should demand that the community turn over the men responsible. "'If you don't get them, what then?' he was asked. 'Shoot and loot,' I answered laconically."[81] A rebellious leader captured by the Portuguese was reportedly "tied up, mutilated, his eyes plucked out, and buried alive," while his pregnant wife was "shot in the belly."[82] In the Congo Free State, villagers that failed to meet their rubber quota were killed, and to ensure that ammunition was not wasted, proof of a kill was required in the form of a hand or a head from the corpse.[83]

Repression also included organized military actions to respond to organized resistance. In South West Africa, the Bondelswarts rebelled in 1922 and were bombed by South Africa, which was administering the territory under a League of Nations mandate; in 1931 the Pende revolted; there was rebellion in Mozambique from 1917 until 1921; in Sudan, Mahdist uprisings occurred until 1922; and uprisings also occurred in 1930 in Vietnam, and in Guinea-Bissau and Somaliland as late as 1936.[84] Conquest could even mean the genocide of an ethnic group. When the Herero and Hottentots in South West Africa revolted in 1905 in a reaction to forced labor, taxes, and whippings, the German commander ordered all Herero males shot and the women and children driven into the Kalahari desert. The Herero population was reduced from 100,000 to 20,000.[85]

Repression was a relatively cheap strategy that allowed the colonial powers to dominate large territories with small numbers because of their superior technology, organization, and wealth. While during the first wave of colonization Europeans did not necessarily hold these advantages, by the time of the second wave they were far ahead technologically, much better organized, and commanded vastly superior military force, which they were able to wield successfully against many smaller, less well-organized, and less well-armed polities.[86] The colonial powers had professionally organized armies and superior weaponry, including the Maxim gun (an early machine gun) at the beginning of the period and aircraft and aerial bombardment

by the end of it.[87] Their opponents were typically unarmed, armed with traditional weapons such as bows or spears, or armed with elderly muskets
designed for the Africa trade that were so badly made that they were likely
to explode when fired.[88] While the colonial powers were each a single polity, capable of organizing action on a national scale, their opponents were
thousands of much smaller polities, some no larger than a village, divided
by language, culture, and in some cases, traditional enmities.

Where force was required, the colonial powers were also able to make
extensive use of locally recruited or conscripted men or mercenaries, who
were cheaper (as they were paid less and outfitted more poorly than European troops), were thought to be better acclimatized to the local environment, and whose deaths would not cause domestic political problems in the
metropole.[89] They transported labor and soldiers from one dependency to
another. Indian troops were used by the British in the conquest of Nyasaland
(Malawi); in 1859 the French took Saigon using Senegalese troops.[90] The
Portuguese drew on Senegalese irregulars to conquer Guinea; the mercenaries killed men, women, the elderly, and children, sacked and burned their
villages, and destroyed their fields.[91] Punitive raids might be accompanied
by local enemies of the peoples targeted. Private companies, where granted
territorial concessions, maintained private police forces.[92] Such colonial
policies both strengthened the definition of ethnic identities and increased
ethnic tensions that would become ethnic violence after independence.[93]

Africans lost almost every pitched battle that they fought against European forces. The few exceptions included a battle between the Portuguese
and Felupe/Djola warriors in 1878 and the battle of Emperor Menelik of
Ethiopia against the Italian army in 1896.[94]

Often, however, force was not applied. As one scholar writes:

For most of the colonial period British administration in colonial
Africa "rested on a minimum of force." Even in the years of conquest
and "pacification" colonial military and police forces were numerically
small; their disciplined fire-power, machine guns and artillery usually
ensured victory over numerically larger African opponents.[95]

It was certainly the case that some local leaders allied with the colonial
powers voluntarily, particularly if they thought they would gain an advantage in the new status quo or escape a threat from another more powerful
group. But the fact that military force did not often need to be applied

did not mean that colonial rule did not rest upon force. Demonstrations of the overwhelming military, material, organizational, and technological superiority of the colonial powers were often sufficient to discourage direct resistance. As one scholar noted, "Even if to the imperial power they were 'little wars,' to the colonial peoples they were 'big wars,' upon which all their energies were concentrated, and which they lost."[96]

•Decolonization and Independence

The futures that the colonial powers had envisioned for their different dependencies were varied, plural, and changed over time.[97] Britain imagined independence as a hazy ultimate outcome for some that was generations or centuries away; for other territories, judged less able to operate independently, she imagined permanent dependence. France wandered between policies of assimilation and of association; a conference in Brazzaville in 1944 concluded that "the attainment of self-government even in the most distant future must be excluded."[98] Germany had two dominant colonial ideologies.[99] While one imagined using colonies as suppliers of tropical goods and purchasers of German manufactures, the other imagined using colonies for German expansion, a process that would, according to the geographer Ratzel, involve the destruction and displacement of "inferior" peoples, just as more successful species displaced less successful ones.[100] In neither case did the Germans imagine eventual self-government for their colonies. A parliamentary speech in 1908 that suggested that Africans, like Europeans, were humans with souls and divine destinies brought murmurs and loud laughter.[101] Italian colonial minister Allessandro Lessona spoke of an "Ethiopia without Ethiopians."[102]

However, second wave colonialism came to a rapid end, unforeseen by colonial powers that, weakened by war, were unable to cling to their colonies in the face of rising nationalist movements and changing global norms. Just as colonial powers had not intended to create viable states, anticolonialists did not seek to create viable states either. The need to end colonialism meant that concerns about the viability of the new states were swept aside. Independence governments were recognized as having sovereignty over their territories regardless of whether they actually governed them or were capable of governing them. Statehood in fact was divorced from statehood under law.

World War I was an important turning point. Both the Axis and the Allies attempted to use propaganda to destabilize each other's dependencies.[103] At the same time, the war was proclaimed to be a war for freedom and democracy against aggression and annexation, and for a new and more just world order—rhetoric that raised powerful questions about the status of colonized peoples. Colonial powers had also recruited troops in their dependencies, which required political concessions in some cases, such as Great Britain's promise of eventual self-government to India and its promise to the Middle East of independent Arab states, or France's declaration that four communes in Senegal would be fully integrated and assimilated. The war also demystified Europeans to colonial subjects, who fought with them and against them or who observed their wartime losses. Colonial subjects who returned as veterans were bitterly disappointed in their expectations of benefits or opportunities. All of these accelerated the growth of nationalist movements.

The war also gave rise to the League of Nations, the predecessor of the United Nations. While accepting colonialism, it asserted an international norm of colonization in the interest of the colonized peoples, rather than for the benefit of the colonizer, and recognized eventual self-government for some dependencies.

> To those colonies and territories which as a consequence of the late war have ceased to be under the sovereignty of the States which formerly governed them and which are inhabited by peoples not yet able to stand by themselves under the strenuous conditions of the modern world, there should be applied the principle that the well-being and development of such peoples form a sacred trust of civilisation and that securities for the performance of this trust should be embodied in this Covenant. The best method of giving practical effect to this principle is that the tutelage of such peoples should be entrusted to advanced nations who by reason of their resources, their experience or their geographical position can best undertake this responsibility, and who are willing to accept it, and that this tutelage should be exercised by them as Mandatories on behalf of the League.[104]

The European powers then faced the Great Depression in the interwar years, which motivated them to think about industrialization of their dependencies. Before they could act on these discussions, however, World

War II ravaged Europe completely and left Western Europe a recipient of foreign aid from the United States for reconstruction. The old ways of maintaining control of dependencies—for example, the punitive raid—were no longer either feasible or internationally acceptable, and the small but growing population of elites in the dependencies rejected the notion of tutelage described by the League of Nations.

Americans tended to see the issue of colonialism as a problem of denial of political liberties and analogized to their own colonial experience.[105] They insisted that the Atlantic Charter, a joint statement of British prime minister Churchill and U.S. president Roosevelt, include a provision specifying that the parties "respect the right of all peoples to choose the form of government under which they will live; and they wish to see sovereign rights and self government restored to those who have been forcibly deprived of them."[106] A year later, Roosevelt attempted to persuade Churchill to extend the language to apply to all colonial territories, while Churchill insisted that it applied only to those countries that had been conquered by the Nazis.[107]

The British were suspicious that Americans sought to replace British influence with their own and to benefit from the dismantling of the system of imperial trade preferences.[108] However, Roosevelt's argument was echoed by church groups, labor unions, and professional organizations on purely moral grounds.[109] An "Open letter to the people of England," published by the editors of the American magazine *Life* in 1942, stated:

> One thing we are sure we are *not* fighting for is to hold the British Empire together. We don't like to put the matter so bluntly, but we don't want you to have any illusions. If your strategists are planning a war to hold the British Empire together they will sooner or later find themselves strategizing all alone. . . . In the light of what you are doing in India, how do you expect us to talk about "principles" and look our soldiers in the eye?[110]

At the same time, rising nationalist movements in the dependencies networked effectively with international supporters and challenged the legitimacy of continued colonial domination, by appeals to public opinion and in some cases through strikes and rebellion.[111] After 1945, elites were no longer seeking reform of the colonial system, but seeking its abolition, and as quickly as possible.[112]

By the time of the San Francisco Conference that launched the United Nations, Russia, China, the Philippines, and other voices were already calling for complete and immediate independence of all the dependencies.[113] Iraq pressed for the abandonment of language about peoples unable to govern themselves. In 1946, a Committee on Information from Non-Self-Governing Territories was formed to force colonial powers to set timetables for independence.[114] (This committee still exists, and notes that some two million people "remain to be decolonized."[115] Among the oppressed peoples listed as awaiting decolonization are the inhabitants of Pitcairn Island, an island of two square miles with a fifty-person population composed of persons "descended from the mutineers of HMAV Bounty and their Tahitian companions."[116])

The British position was that not all dependencies were equally ready for independence, and that self-government in some cases might be more meaningfully achieved in other ways. The parting words of Lord Cranborne were, "We are all in favour of freedom, but freedom for many of those territories means assistance and guidance and protection."[117] Some Americans were sympathetic to the idea that not every dependency was ready for independence. Nelson Rockefeller observed with respect to some dependencies, "If they achieved independence, the assistance which they needed from the larger states to advance their economic and social status, would collapse."[118]

Arguments against independence were based on the idea that the dependencies could not govern themselves effectively. This argument was made on various grounds. The first was that the colonial peoples lacked the capacity for self-government because they were deficient in reason, judgment, or moral character. This was an old argument for colonization that harkened back to Aristotle's argument that some peoples are natural slaves, better off under the control of masters.[119] By World War II, this argument was losing both legitimacy and currency, but could still occasionally be heard. In Britain, Herbert Morrison, the socialist home secretary, said, "It would be sheer nonsense—ignorant, dangerous nonsense—to talk about grants of full government to many of the dependent territories for some time to come. In these instances it would be like giving a child of ten a latchkey, a bank account and a shotgun."[120]

A second argument was that all or some of the dependencies were not yet ready, in that they lacked political, economic, or social institutions necessary for effective self-government. The 1933 Montevideo Convention on the Rights and Duties of States sets out four requirements for statehood: a permanent population, a defined territory, a government, and the capacity to enter into relations with other states. It was certainly difficult to see how those dependencies that had illiterate populations and no more than a handful of university graduates, lacked a tax base, had no formal institutions of or experience with national self-government would govern themselves. Some had the added complication of existing ethnic tensions.

Many anticolonialists who believed strongly in the right of dependent people to self-government accepted that some period of transition or preparation would be necessary.[121] This was already recognized by the Covenant of the League of Nations, which separated dependencies into classes based on their readiness for independence. However, colonial powers and their critics tended to disagree on the extent of the period necessary for such preparation. The colonial powers also felt that critics, without experience as colonial powers, underestimated the complexities involved, while the critics could reasonably question whether colonial powers could be entrusted with preparing their dependencies for independence because of their conflicts of interest.

A third argument, made regarding some of the dependencies, was that they would never be capable of effective self-government because they were too small and too isolated. A number of dependencies are mentioned by different authors in this regard. Article 22 of the Covenant of the League of Nations had separated out South West Africa and the South Pacific Islands as best administered by another power. Robinson mentions Malta, the Gambia, and the Seychelles.[122] Perham sniffed that "the Gambia, two riverbanks cut off by another accident of history, is about as ready to stand alone as, shall we say, a Samoan island"—a dig at the United States for railing against colonialism while holding American Samoa.[123]

The question of whether a dependency would be a viable state was raised during decolonization, but was directed primarily at small isolated islands.[124] It had been occasionally raised with respect to other countries. Considering the future of small landlocked Basutoland (modern Lesotho), one observer posited that the only possible economic activity would be "pony-trekking."[125] Today, remittances—money sent home by citizens working abroad—account for almost a quarter of Lesotho's gross national product.[126] (It also has pony trekking.)

There were also practical concerns about granting independence too hastily to a dependency unable to govern itself effectively. One key concern was that it would result in a power vacuum that would soon be filled by another external power. In the era of the Cold War, Western policymakers and scholars were most concerned about a Soviet takeover.[127] Another concern raised was that in the absence of effective domestic accountability, such dependencies would soon be governed by despots (an ironic concern given the authoritarian nature of colonial rule). In dependencies with ethnic tensions, there was fear of the possibility of civil war or the abuse of one ethnic group by another. Britain was particularly concerned about the likely treatment of non-Europeans by European settlers in southern Africa—a concern that was not unfounded.[128] For dependencies that were not economically independent, and would not be in the near future, the grant of political independence could mean abandonment of support for their populations by larger states or domestic pressure to adopt public policies that could not be implemented, such as universal primary education.[129]

Anticolonialists brushed aside all arguments of lack of readiness and viability. There could no longer be an indefinite "tutelage" of "backward" people that would last until they had been deemed by their colonizers to have "graduated."[130] Anticolonial arguments centered not on empirical arguments about the ability of dependencies to mount effective self-government, or on legal requirements of sovereignty, but rather on the claim that all people had a natural right to determine their own governance arrangements as part of a core belief of democratic theory—what one contemporary declared in 1945 "the fundamental democratic principle of self-determination."[131] Objections of lack of effective government were swept aside, first informally, and then explicitly in the 1960 United Nations Declaration on the Granting of Independence to Colonial Countries and Peoples, which stated: "Inadequacy of political, economic, social or educational preparedness should never serve as a pretext for delaying independence."[132] Just as colonial powers had established claims recognized under international law to territories they did not control, decolonization awarded the same claims to independence governments that did not control the territory either. Former colonies, protectorates, and other dependencies, as well as a few territories that were not former colonies, were recognized as states under this legal fiction.

Indian independence in 1947 was the beginning of a cascade in which dependent territories sought and obtained their independence under a newly articulated right of self-determination. Remarkably, in most cases independence was granted peacefully. As each dependency became independent, it set a precedent and raised the expectations of colonial subjects in the remaining dependencies, encouraging them in their own quest for independence. According to Perham,

> Ex-British Somaliland gained independence, in spite of the poverty and inexperience of her semi-nomad population, because the United Nations had named a date for her neighbor, Italian Somaliland. . . . The promised emancipation of such unready peoples proved a strong argument in the hands of those other Africans who could rightly claim to be more ready.[133]

The pace accelerated and the number of recognized countries in the world grew rapidly. The new countries joined the United Nations, where each country had an equal vote, and added their voices to the call for the end of colonialism. In 1960, the United Nations issued a "Declaration on the Granting of Independence to Colonial Countries and Peoples,"[134] which called for immediate steps to transfer all powers to the peoples of non-self-governing territories without any conditions or reservations. Founded by 51 country members, as of 2011, the United Nations listed 193 country members.[135]

A Backward Task

The processes of colonization and decolonization created some countries that were poor, some of which were landlocked, and some of which had governments that were unable to govern their territories. Poor governments are challenged by both domestic and foreign actors as they attempt to extend their control, and remain heavily dependent on the international community to govern at all.

As dependencies became countries, they inherited the international boundaries defined by colonialism, and in some cases their borders were defined by the boundaries of the colonial administrative units. French West Africa, for example, was defined by an international border, and within was divided into eight administrative units that on independence became eight separate countries: Côte d'Ivoire and Benin (Dahomey), Burkina Faso (Upper Volta), Senegal and Guinea (French Guinea), Mauritania and Mali (French Soudan), and Niger.[136] Togo (French Togoland) was a former German colony and so was administered separately by France under a League of Nations mandate and then a United Nations trusteeship.

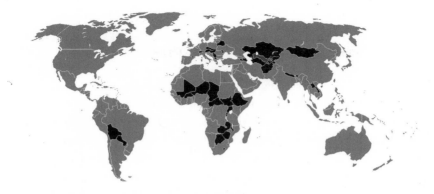

Figure 3.3. Landlocked Countries. Poor landlocked countries are Afghanistan, Burkina Faso, Burundi, Central African Republic, Chad, Ethiopia, Kyrgyzstan, Laos, Lesotho, Malawi, Mali, Mongolia, Nepal, Niger, Rwanda, Tajikistan, Uganda, Uzbekistan (doubly landlocked), Zambia, and Zimbabwe. (Courtesy of Wikimedia Commons)

Because colonialism began in most cases with European forts and settlements on coasts, followed by penetration into the interior, none of the colonial dependencies were landlocked; they had access to the sea as part of a larger polity. However, because internal administrative boundaries later became national boundaries, some landlocked administrative units became landlocked countries, and even worse, landlocked countries surrounded by other poor countries. French Equatorial Africa, for example, emerged as Gabon, French Cameroon, the Republic of Congo, the Central African Republic, and Chad; the last two are landlocked.

Landlocked countries are economically disadvantaged. About 90 percent of world trade is carried by ship.[137] Today there are thirty-one landlocked developing countries,[138] and as economists have observed, "nearly all of the world's landlocked countries are poor; the exceptions in Western and Central Europe are closely integrated with the regional European market and able to trade at low cost."[139] Nineteen landlocked developing countries are among the poorest.

Notwithstanding concerns about the economic and political viability of some former dependencies, as there was no obvious salient way to redraw colonial borders, the risk of conflict that could come with opening the issue was so great that one of the first moves of the newly formed Organization of African Unity was to agree that all members would respect each other's territorial integrity based on the preservation of the colonial boundaries.[140]

A preservation of existing borders was also in the interest of the new elites who had risen to prominence within those territories. They had little incentive to either surrender their authority by joining into a large entity, or to surrender their territory by agreeing to subdivision by allowing parts of their new country to secede.

The process of colonization and decolonization created states on paper, but the governments of some of these states have yet to achieve territorial control. While some new countries derived from preexisting states or had historically been governed as a single political unit, many of today's poor countries have no such prior history. Colonial borders were drawn without regard to the people who lived in the territories or their languages, religions, ethnicities, or political units, about which colonial powers were often ignorant in any case.[141] Colonial and, later, national borders enclosed hundreds of small political groupings speaking hundreds of languages. In Africa in particular colonial borders drove through ethnic groups, splitting them and assigning them to different dependencies and sometimes to different empires; in other cases, they locked different groups with historic grudges in the same borders.[142] Colonial policy did little to build national identity. On the contrary, it was sometimes colonial policy to maintain control by creating ethnic identities and stoking rivalries.

The problem, however, is not simply one of drawing arbitrary borders. A colonial effort to draw boundaries in such a way as to be mindful of ethnic, linguistic, and political factors would likely not have turned out any better, given the fluidity and plurality of precolonial ethnic identities and the fact that allegiances were not sharply defined.[143] The Soviets attempted to draw boundaries to accommodate existing ethnic groups to create national states in Central Asia. The effort took decades and involved ethnographers and statisticians. The process itself helped shape identities.[144] Notwithstanding the Soviet effort, ethnic tensions in post-Soviet Tajikistan resulted in civil war.[145]

Instead, the problem remains one of centralization. The territories of many poor countries have never been governed as a single polity, before the colonial period, during the colonial period, or afterward. Scholars studying state formation in Europe have argued that interstate war played a central role in centralization, nation building, revenue raising, and building state capacity as stronger states absorbed smaller and weaker ones.[146] Modern poor countries, however, were born in an era where the international system forbids wars of aggression and conquest and frowns on secession. There have been few interstate wars among poor countries, and most do not face significant external threats. There have been almost no involuntary boundary changes.[147] Some scholars have argued that by taking wars of conquest off the table as a way to consolidate the state and fix boundaries, a new phenomenon was created—that of "permanently weak states."[148]

But this focus on interstate warfare is a misleading one. European warfare was interstate during the process of European state formation because states were political entities under the control of governments; they were actual states, not simply states under law. Today's poor governments were given the unprecedented backward task of building states within a sandbox of internationally recognized borders. The struggle for state consolidation has therefore been taking place within, rather than across, those borders. Within two decades after independence, a number of today's poor countries were embroiled in civil war. For example, Vietnam and Laos both entered civil war in 1960; the Democratic Republic of Congo entered civil war the same year that it gained independence in 1960; Sudan, independent in 1956, was in civil conflict by 1963; Rwanda, independent in 1962, was in civil conflict by 1963; Uganda, independent in 1962, was in civil conflict by 1966; Chad, independent in 1960, was in civil conflict by 1966; Nigeria, independent in 1960, was engulfed in the Biafran War by 1967; Burma, independent in 1948, was in civil war by 1968.[149] Since 1950, civil war has been the most common form of war, and most civil war takes place in poor countries.[150] This is one reason why military spending is an important part of the budget of many poor governments, although there are others, such as the use of nontransparent security budgets for discretionary spending, patronage, and embezzlement.

Statehood was conferred on the new states by the international community with the expectation that poor governments would "grow into" their new national borders, becoming states in fact. Many of today's poor governments have yet to establish effective government across the breadth of their allotted territories. The capital and its environs are under governmental control, with some portion of the remainder of the country under the government's sphere of influence—just as in the colonial era. Where the government's sphere of influence wanes, there may be competing political forces that exercise aspects of sovereignty such as the operation of private prisons by local rulers[151] or the extraction of "protection fees" by local militias. At the extreme, a competing political organization can erect a state within a state, such as Azawad in Mali, Somaliland in Somalia, or Touba in Senegal.[152]

Humanitarian and development NGOs know that government permission to operate, while strongly advisable, is usually not enough. They stress the importance of obtaining "acceptance" of their presence and programs as a way of ensuring the personal security of NGO staff and the success of their programs. Obtaining acceptance involves negotiating with those who have the power to harm the NGO or block its activities, including host governments, local government officials, religious authorities and traditional leaders, militant groups, and the community at large.[153]

Some challengers to government do not seek to govern territory but instead want to pursue activities that are incompatible with the government's rule, such as terrorism or organized crime. In West Africa, tiny Guinea-Bissau has become a preferred hub for Colombian drug cartels.

> A senior official at the US's Drug Enforcement Agency (DEA) with a long record of fighting transatlantic drug trafficking, explained how and why the capture of Guinea-Bissau took place, and the trail to Europe. "Geographically, West Africa makes sense. The logical thing is for the cartels to take the shortest crossing over the ocean to West Africa, by plane—to one of the many airstrips left behind by decades of war, or by drop into the thousands of little bays—or by boat all the way. A ship can drop anchor in waters completely unmonitored, while fleets of smaller craft take the contraband ashore.
>
> "A place like Guinea Bissau is a failed state anyway, so it's like moving into an empty house." There is no prison in Guinea-Bissau, he says. One rusty ship patrols a coastline of 350km, and an archipelago of 82 islands. The airspace is un-patrolled. The police have few cars, no petrol, no radios, handcuffs or phones.
>
> "You walk in, buy the services you need from the government, army and people, and take over."[154]

Modern poor countries also continue to be dependent on foreign powers and subject to international influences. Just as the moment when colonial powers asserted legal claims to territories did not mark the beginning of their engagement in those territories, legal independence did not mark the end. The interventions and impositions that continued after independence have caused some to argue that colonialism has continued in a new form and to refer to this relationship as "neo-colonialism."[155] In many cases, expatriates stayed on long after formal independence to run key ministries due to the lack of local, trained manpower. Foreign companies continued to operate and foreign countries continued to seek secure supplies of strategic goods such as oil, rubber, or uranium. Preferential trading relationships between dependencies and their former colonizers continued, and former colonies were still considered to be in the sphere of influence of their former colonizers. France, for example, has been extensively engaged in former French colonies after independence, weighing in on transfers of government leadership, signing treaties with secret clauses that promised military support to existing regimes, paying bribes to government leaders in return for contracts for the national oil company, and receiving kickbacks from the same leaders as campaign contributions to French politicians.

Because most poor countries were recognized during the Cold War, many became proxy battlegrounds in the fight between the West and the Soviet Union. The West intervened in poor country governance in order to ensure that poor countries remained in the Western, rather than the communist, sphere of influence. For example, the Democratic Republic of Congo, with its rich mineral reserves of diamonds, gold, uranium, and copper, has been the subject of constant and intense foreign interest and intervention, beginning with U.S. and Belgian complicity in the assassination of the first elected prime minister, Patrice Lumumba, in 1961.[156] American support helped secure his successor, President Mobutu, whose thirty-two years of governance are most often described as a "kleptocracy"—rule by thieves.

Stronger states and their nationals continue to jockey for access to the natural resources of poor countries, such as oil and arable land. In the four years leading to South Sudan's independence, foreigners purchased 9 percent of its arable land for biofuels, ecotourism, agriculture, and forestry.[157]

At the same time, foreign aid is often essential to the maintenance of any government in poor countries. In 2010, foreign aid was about 20 percent of central government expenditures in The Gambia, 53 percent in Laos, 100 percent in Burkina Faso, and 190 percent in the Democratic Republic of Congo.[158] In some countries, foreign aid dwarfs the country's economic activity. In 2010 it was 12 percent of gross national income in Ethiopia, 40 percent in Burundi, and 177 percent in Liberia.

Conclusion

The creation of the modern state system was accomplished through legal fictions, and it is finished only on paper. The colonial powers allowed each other to mark off their spheres of influence and to claim the territories within even if they didn't govern them and, in some cases, hadn't even explored them. Colonization had not sought to create new states and so colonial powers had not invested much in nation building, whether in the form of creating a national identity, building industries, a revenue base, infrastructure to link the interior, or setting a precedent for accountable democratic government. On the contrary, colonial policies were often the opposite—preventing industrialization, disempowering and brutalizing colonial subjects, and pitting groups against each other.

In the era of decolonization, poor states were recognized and their governments were allowed to claim territories, although they did not govern them either. They inherited economies organized to service the colonial power, the remnants of the lightly staffed colonial administrations, a revenue model that in the case of poor dependencies had required external subsidies, and formal institutions and laws imported from much richer countries.

Statehood in fact became divorced from statehood in law, and the political maps that we draw changed from maps of power to maps of international legal claims. The assumption was that the recognized states would become states in fact in relatively short order. New states had the historically unprecedented task of building a state out to the borders allocated to them by the international community. Some succeeded. However, some have not. Surprisingly, this disjuncture between legal rights and actual control is not taught as an ordinary part of the school curriculum. Many Westerners are under the mistaken impression that the world is divided into states in fact, and that the state boundaries shown on political maps represent areas under the effective control of a government.

For many poor governments, the top priority is still to consolidate their control of their territory. The security community has named areas that are only nominally under the control of an internationally recognized government "ungoverned spaces." Entities that are recognized as states in international law, but that lack key prerequisites of governance capacity and territorial control, are often called "weak states."[159] Where this lack of capacity for control has resulted in internal armed conflict, they are more likely to be called "fragile states" or "failed states." While it is certainly possible for an established state to collapse, for most of today's poor countries the failure in question is the failure of the government to ever consolidate governance of its territory. It is the failure of a state to be born.[160]

It is impossible to pronounce on the permanent viability of any particular state. With the rapid advance of technologies and increasing global interconnectedness, new economic activities may become possible for them. Who knows what resources will be demanded by the global economy of tomorrow, or what current constraints will become negligible? Tomorrow may bring a technology that allows the effective conversion of sunlight into electricity, and sunlight is something that many poor countries have in abundance.[161]

But at the same time, the cost of government is rising with changing global aspirations. The requirement under international law that a state must have a government is usually given as requiring that a government have effective control of its territory and command the habitual obedience of its population.[162] The law does not say what type of government this must be; there is no requirement for "good governance."[163] However, as Enlightenment governance norms spread, and as globalized communications allow rich countries to set the world's aspirations for governance, governments that fail to deliver "good governance" may lack the legitimacy to command the habitual obedience of their people. The failure of the Malian government to deliver services was one of the core grievances that motivated Tuareg rebellions and the secession of the north of the country. Government corruption was one of the complaints that led to the rise of the Taliban in Afghanistan. While "good governance" may not be a legal requirement for statehood, it may soon become a political one.

4. Poor Countries, Poor Governments

One reason that some poor governments have not established effective governance of their territories, much less ideal governance, is that they are too poor to do so.[1] They have much less revenue per capita to spend, and unlike rich liberal democracies that are financed largely through taxation of citizens and businesses, poor countries must get their money from much less desirable sources.

At independence, poor dependencies became poor countries. Their new governments were charged with building a state to the limit of their international borders. However, they were equipped only with a colonial administration of limited ambition that may have been dependent on external subsidies to pay its expenses. One of the core challenges of poor governments—just as it was for Western governments when they were actively engaged in state building—has been to build an adequate stream of revenue.

Most people understand that poor countries have poor governments, and that because they are poor they govern less, but if the available data are even in the right ball park they suggest governments of much more limited means than people imagine. The consequences of government poverty are reflected in the quality and extent of offerings like public education and health, the inability to pay civil servants regular salaries, or the inability to establish territorial control when it is challenged.

But poor governments not only govern less; they govern differently. Unable to build a strong domestic tax base because their populations are so poor, poor governments rely on sources like foreign aid, printing money, or even criminal activities. All of these have undesirable side effects that further undermine their ability to provide public services or the rule of law.

The Poverty of Governments

It should come as no surprise that the governments of poor countries are themselves poor, too poor to offer the same basket of goods, services, and rights that rich governments do. They govern less. Yet the size of the gap and its implications are underappreciated. One reason is that we do not have either good data or an agreed-on way of comparing the wealth of governments. Perhaps that is why we don't usually think about poor governments as a group.

Absent a list of poor governments, this book focuses on poor countries. Poor countries have poor governments, but as was pointed out in chapter 1, the cost of governing any territory is likely to be variable, depending on factors such as area, population size and density, geographic challenges like deserts or being landlocked, or having poor or troublesome neighbors.

I mentioned Burundi and Democratic Republic of Congo as examples of two poor countries facing different governance challenges. However Burundi, which is slightly smaller than Maryland, with an estimated population of 10.4 million in 2014, has different challenges than does the Democratic Republic of Congo, which is roughly one-fourth the size of the United States with an estimated 77 million people.[2] The estimated 2013 GDP per capita, purchasing power parity is $600 for Burundi and $400 for the Democratic Republic of Congo. National wealth is at best a very crude way of getting at the poverty of governments.

A slightly better measure would be revenue per person, which would show how much per person a government has to spend.[3] But we lack good information about government revenue in poor countries, which makes use of any such measure problematic. Both the Government Finance Statistics Yearbook, produced by the International Monetary Fund (IMF), and the World Development Indicators, produced by the World Bank, have only spotty data on government revenue in low income countries. For example, as of 2012, the World Bank data set, World Development Indicators, offers data on government revenue for the Central African Republic only in 2004; Burundi from 1991 to 1999; and there is no data for countries such as Chad, Haiti, Malawi, Guinea-Bissau, or North Korea. Revenue can be teased out from another indicator that is offered: revenue as a percentage of GDP. The Central Intelligence Agency publishes government revenue for all countries in current exchange rates, but their numbers differ substantially from the numbers offered by the World Bank and the IMF. Data for some countries is available for current years, and for others the available data is a few years old. The CIA data also does not seem to properly account for the revenue of federalist states, reporting only the revenue of the national government.

There are several reasons why the data is spotty. One reason is that poor governments themselves may not know how much revenue they have. It costs money to hire educated people, keep and maintain good records, control corruption, and audit and publish government accounts. In some cases, it may also be because governments do not want their finances to be public. And finally, it may also be difficult to tell what should be counted as government money and what should not. Some governments intermingle public and private money, or get money from unauthorized or criminal sources that are not part of the public accounts.

Nor do we usually have good data on the population of poor countries. It costs money to conduct a census. They are conducted every number of years, and the results are highly political and sometimes subject to influence. Most population data for poor countries is an educated guess, an interpolation from the last conducted census.

With those very large caveats, table 4.1 shows back-of-the-napkin estimates of revenue per capita of poor governments based on available data. By way of comparison, in 1902 in the United States total government spending at federal, state, and local levels was about $438 per person per year in 2011 dollars. In 2013, it was $13,782 per capita.[4] This is for everything that government does, at all levels of government, including debt service, paying the civil service, national defense, and public health and education. Using the CIA data, which is in current exchange rates and so does not account for price differences in different countries, revenue per capita was about $109 in Niger in 2014, $75 in the Democratic Republic of Congo, $73 in Afghanistan, and $74 in Burundi.[5] It is easy to see how important aid is to the poor governments that receive it. Using 2012 data on official development assistance from the Organisation for Economic Co-operation and Development, in Niger, foreign aid bumps the revenue per capita up from $109 per person per year to $161. Uganda had about $89 per person; with aid, it rises to $135. Afghanistan, with $73 per person, has $285 per person with development aid, reflecting large aid flows to support the government as the war continues. These numbers look a little better if we attempt to compensate for the different prices of goods in different countries by using purchasing power parity—but not that much better.

TABLE 4.1 Revenue Per Capita for Select Countries

	PPP		Current Exchange Rate (2014 US$)	
	GDP per capita PPP 2013 est.	Revenue per capita 2012 PPP	Revenue per cap in 2014 US$	Revenue + ODA per capita in 2014 US$
Norway	55400.00	37672.44	56878.76	
Denmark	37800.00	24312.14	32572.72	
United Kingdom	37300.00	14632.44	15797.82	
France	35700.00	19339.58	21280.12	
Uruguay	16600.00	6476.98	5142.56	
China	9800.00	2690.56	1523.21	
Vietnam	4000.00	1323.35	458.35	502.41
Papua New Guinea	2900.00	806.05	665.22	766.70
Yemen	2500.00	811.39	298.20	325.43
Tajikistan	2300.00	754.00	302.55	351.49
Korea, Dem. People's Rep.	1800.00		128.76	132.71
Rwanda	1500.00	343.16	147.04	218.28
Uganda	1500.00	228.19	89.09	135.17
Haiti	1300.00	428.97	198.97	326.53
Afghanistan	1100.00	202.11	73.31	284.64
Niger	800.00	244.48	109.41	161.05
Burundi	600.00	237.73	73.77	124.05
Congo, Dem. Rep.	400.00	131.44	75.12	112.05

Note: GDP per capita PPP, revenue, and population from Central Intelligence Agency, *World Factbook 2014*, www.cia.gov/library/publications/the-world-factbook/; 2012 purchasing power parity from World Development Indicators, World Bank, "PPP conversion factor, GDP (LCU per international $)," http://data.worldbank.org/indicator/PA.NUS.PPP; official development assistance 2012 from Organization for Economic Co-operation and Development, "Query Wizard for International Development Statistics," http://stats.oecd.org/qwids/.

We can conclude that there is no data that suggests that poor governments can afford to provide the kind of public goods and services to the entire population that rich liberal democracies now do, or even the much more modest basket that the United States provided to a subset of the population at the turn of the twentieth century. The gap appears to be monumental. According to this data, in 2013 the U.S. government still had more than 100 times the amount to spend per person than Uganda had, even counting the development aid that Uganda receives.

When a government is poor, it governs less in every way. Poor governments struggle to hire and pay an adequate number of literate or skilled workers, and the government is often woefully understaffed, particularly in areas outside of the capital. By far the largest complaint of government workers is inadequate and irregularly paid salaries. Although the question of the adequacy of salaries is a difficult one in countries where much of the population lives in extreme poverty and private sector employment opportunities are limited, there is a large gap between official salaries and government worker aspirations to a stable, middle-class lifestyle. Much of the civil service lives below the poverty line, with official salaries that are inadequate to pay for basic family needs. Salaries are not only meager, but also may be paid irregularly. Some workers may not have received their wages for months or even years. In 2005, for example, Liberian civil servants went on strike to attempt to reclaim eighteen months of unpaid salary.[6] Junior government employees in Liberia earned between $9 and $13 per month.

The inadequacy and irregularity of government wages means that if lower-level government workers are to survive, they must either find additional, more lucrative work or find ways to turn their government job to personal profit. Similarly, the inadequacy and irregularity of the payment of government pensions also motivates some government workers to think of how to profit from their jobs while they still have them.

A World Bank study did spot checks of schools and clinics and found that teachers and doctors were often missing from their posts during times when they were supposed to be working. In Uganda, 27 percent of primary school teachers and 37 percent of doctors were missing. "In poor countries, substitutes rarely replace absent teachers, and so students simply mill around, go home or join another class, often of a different grade. Small schools and clinics are common in rural areas of developing countries, and these may be closed entirely as a result of provider absence."[7] Sometimes absent workers are busy tracking down their missing salaries; sometimes they are engaged in other economic activities like farming, petty trading, or running private businesses.

It is not only salaries that are in short supply, but funds to pay for supplies of every kind. This leads to a familiar sight in poor countries— schools with teachers, but no desks or chalk, hospitals with doctors, but no medicines, a government official without a desk, a chair, or paper and a pen. In Bangladesh,

> numerous officers complain of a lack of funds for basic materials such as radios, fuel for vehicles, bicycles and even stationery to write reports. This

makes it difficult, if not impossible, to respond to crimes and other instances of disorder. Many officers are often forced to pay out of pocket to complete even the most routine police functions. Expense claims are sent from the districts to Dhaka and reimbursements often follow months later—and not always in full, which further drives corruption. One inspector, while based in Rangpur district, described an all-too-common situation:

"A man came to me in the middle of the night and said that a murder had been committed in his village. It was my duty to investigate. I asked the man to drive me to his village because the station vehicle was in disrepair; it had been broken for days and we had no money to fix it. The villager didn't have a car so we had to hire a taxi, which was a few hundred taka. An autopsy had to be done on the body, and I had to take it to the morgue. But the driver refused to put the body in his taxi. So, I then had to pay—with my money—for another car, which was another few hundred taka. The coroner would not perform the autopsy on the corpse without some alcohol to drink. So I had to buy a few bottles for the coroner. . . . In the end I had to spend Tk2000 or Tk3000 ($30 or 40) out of my pocket to do my job."

The inspector said, "You tell me, who is going to reimburse for me this. No one."[8]

In Cambodia, before the government began to partner with international nongovernmental organizations to run clinics, much or all of the operating budget of the clinic disappeared before it reached the clinic, as the money wended its way through layers of bureaucracy.[9] Doctors were paid $20 per month and nurses were paid $15; accordingly, they spent almost all of their time away from the clinic running private practices.

Sokong Lim, 34, then a paramedic, said he saw only two patients for treatment in the two years before [they began to partner with NGOs]. But he also admitted that he was usually working at his own clinic near a ferry crossing on the Mekong River.

"Nobody was willing to work at that time," he said. "Even the chief of the hospital had his own business. Nobody blamed anybody."

The hospital was like a stolen car stripped of its parts. . . . The equipment had simply disappeared, probably into the staff members' private practices. Thermometers, stethoscopes, speculums, obstetrical instruments—all were missing.[10]

Without workers or supplies, poor governments cannot provide qual-ity goods and services to their citizens, whether they are roads, schools, hospitals, electricity, access to clean water, or justice. In 2009, only about 23 percent of people in low-income countries had access to electricity.[11] In 2008, about 35 percent had access to improved sanitation facilities, and 63 percent had access to improved water sources (compared to more than 99 percent in high-income countries). About 14 percent of roads in low-income countries were paved, compared to 87 percent of roads in high-income countries. In poor countries, there was only one telephone line for every 100 people; in rich countries there were 47.

Delivery of public goods and services is very unequal, concentrated in city centers. But in poor countries, most people live in rural areas.[12] Even within cities, service delivery is uneven. Rapid urbanization has overwhelmed city services, giving rise to slums and shanty towns where many people do not have access to basic water and sewerage services. Slum dwellers make up a large percentage of urban dwellers for a number of poor countries—for example, Central African Republic (95 percent), Chad (90 percent), Niger (82 percent), and Mozambique (80 percent).[13]

Poor governments have been under both international and domestic pressure to increase services, to divide the same limited resources more thinly among more people. For example, the Millennium Development Goals, a set of goals agreed on by a number of governments in 2000, set universal primary education as a goal for the world to achieve by 2015.[14] As the prescient British parliamentary under-secretary of state for the colo-nies observed in 1965 regarding African independence,

> The moment you get fully representative government—one man, one vote—any political party, any government, is going to be under terrific pressure to spread education universally, but very, very thin. And noth-ing eats money more rapidly than universal free primary education. And yet, you may say, it's the inalienable right of every child to have it.[15]

In the face of this pressure, many poor country politicians have declared the abolition of school fees and free universal primary education—repeatedly. Such declarations need to be made repeatedly because they fall short in practice. The resources to implement them are lacking. An analysis by the World Bank found that, in order to meet the goal of universal primary education by 2015, forty-seven developing countries would have to increase their education budgets from \$8.5 billion to \$21 billion; it concludes that "these countries, as a group, would not be able to achieve the goal without sustained and significant external financial support."[16]

Without this increase in resources, while children will not be turned away for lack of school fees, neither are they guaranteed a teacher, a classroom, or a textbook.[17] Many countries have met the increased demand by having students come in shifts, halving the duration of the school day for each student. In Conakry, Guinea, eighty-five students come to the classroom for morning classes; then they go home to make room for the afternoon shift. There are no bathrooms; no clean drinking water; no fans. Crammed four to a desk, there is no place to write.[18] In Zambia,

> Many years of over-use of school buildings, through multiple sessions and large classes, coupled with the near-absence of public funds for school maintenance and repairs, have left most schools in an unacceptably poor physical condition. Almost half the rural schools do not have their own source of safe drinking water, while urban schools have grown well beyond their planned size, but without any commensurate increase in sanitary facilities.[19]

In Kenya, the declining quality of public education has led to a mass exodus from the system:

> The [Ministry of Education] is aware that the quality of education has taken a nose-dive with the rapid quantitative expansion of primary education. . . . Consequently, parents who can afford to pay fees in private schools have removed their children from public schools and put them in private schools that have moderate class sizes and where teaching and learning is visibly taking place.[20]

Uganda adopted universal primary education in 1997 as the fulfillment of a popular campaign promise.[21] The surge in enrollment from poor families previously excluded by school fees was not matched by the resources to ensure that children had schools, teachers, and books. While the worst of the overcrowding was eased by donor-financed classroom construction, teacher morale plummeted and teacher absenteeism rates are among the highest in the world.[22] One early observer commented that, taking the deterioration of quality into account, he could not tell if the cost of education had changed at all.[23] The director of a small NGO in Uganda that is focused on children's education wrote:

I have seen how the great idea of free primary education has fallen short and in many cases failed because the framework was not in place for it to succeed. Picture this: you get hired to work as a teacher at a free government primary school. You are placed at a school in a remote village that is not your own. You show up to teach only to find that three of the other teachers aren't there and haven't shown up for weeks. You get to your class and the room is packed, with uniform-less (in Uganda all primary school students wear uniforms), shoeless, bookless, hungry children. Your classroom should only have 40 children, yet one hundred have come. Now because the other teachers have not shown up all of the other classrooms are looking to you as well. You wanted to help children learn but when the majority of the children in your classroom do not have a pencil or books it is very hard. Then you add in random attendance, where a child is there for a few days then not for a few weeks. You've been teaching for three months now but you haven't been paid, there is some problem with salaries being paid out, but it was stated that this would be solved quickly (that was three months ago).

Here's what often happens:

• The teacher gets fed up and goes and finds another job, keeping the teaching job but only showing up sporadically
• The teacher starts forcing children to pay school fees, even though the school is supposed to be free
• The teacher turns away children who do not have the necessary attire and school supplies
• The teacher decides to focus on six of the best pupils with school supplies, ignoring the rest

Do you blame the teacher?[24]

Uganda went on to adopt free universal secondary education in 2007.[25]

While politicians like to point to rising enrollment rates, such a measure overlooks the fall in the quality of education that can result, for example, in high dropout rates. An expert emphasizes: "Overall, it seems that nearly a quarter of children in Commonwealth Africa do not stay in school long enough to acquire permanent literacy and numeracy skills—a tragedy for them and a poor use of public resources. *Any claims to have reached [universal primary education] based on figures for initial enrollment will be bogus.*"[26] It also overlooks the question of whether high enrollments will be domestically sustainable. Foreign aid plays a significant role in financing the expanded offer of education. The United Nations estimates that in 2008, Liberia, Mali, Rwanda, and Zambia financed more than 50 percent of their education budgets from external sources.[27]

Public health systems are similarly underequipped, dependent on foreign aid, and under pressure to expand their offer of services. Whereas the United States has one doctor for every 413 people, and Sweden has one doctor for every 265 people, Somalia has one doctor for every 28,571 people, Liberia has one doctor for every 71,428 people, and Tanzania has one doctor for every 125,000 people.[28] The government of Niger, a country about twice the size of Texas, is planning to double the number of doctors in its employ—in 2011 there were fewer than 300.[29] In 2011 in Sierra Leone, there were only four gynecologists and two pediatricians in a country of five million people.[30] In 2010, foreign aid financed 24 percent of public health spending in Cambodia, 38 percent in Haiti, 47 percent in Rwanda, and 64 percent in Malawi.[31]

Clinics may also lack electricity, water, basic equipment, medicines, or regular operational funds. A survey of health facilities in Al Jawf governorate in Yemen found

a considerable shortage in Al Jawf public facilities with respect to the availability of basic infrastructure items such as clean water, electricity, toilets, ground telephone lines, and sewage systems. No facility in the governorate had any means of transportation including the two hospitals and the eleven health centers. Ground telephone lines were non-existent in 96% of all facilities; only 18% of health centers had ground telephone lines, and neither of the two hospitals had phone lines. All public sector hospitals and health centers had toilets available, compared to just 50 percent of health units. Electricity was also limited, with 66% of health units and 27% of health centers having no electricity.

Clean water was also scarce—44% of health units and 36% of health centers lacked this crucial service. The most significant observation was in Barat Al-anan rural hospital which lacked water although it was using 22 of 34 rooms (65%) to provide health services for 6 hours a day, working 30 days per month as emergency days.[32]

With few trained personnel, and limited access to clean water or electricity, poor sanitation and sterilization practices, such as reuse of needles and syringes, are common in poor countries.[33] The Al Jawf survey found two public health facilities disposing of medical waste by throwing it in the street.[34]

These shortages have tragic consequences for the quality of care, and make it difficult to tell when unofficial fees are necessary to make up for equipment shortages and missing salaries or are profiteering. In Uganda,

> When Ms. Nalubowa, 40, a peasant farmer and a mother of seven, arrived at the decrepit hospital in Mityana, said her mother-in-law, Rhoda Kukkiriza, nurses demanded a bribe of about $24 and more money to buy airtime for a cellphone call to the doctor, accusations the nurses have denied. Ms. Kukkiriza said she had less than a dollar left after spending $2.40 to buy a razor blade, gloves and other items the hospital lacked. Unable to pay the bribe, Ms. Nalubowa was taken to the maternity ward and left unattended, her mother-in-law said.
>
> "As she pushed with the labor pains, all that came out was blood," Ms. Kukkiriza said. "Sylvia called out, 'I'll sell all my pigs, I'll sell my chickens, my goats—please, nurses, come help me.'"[35]

Unable to pay the bribe, she was left to bleed to death, but, in any event, there was no doctor on duty, and not enough blood in supply.

Prison conditions in poor countries are life-threatening. In windowless overcrowded cells without beds, toilets, or medical care, with little food or water, prisoners suffocate or, often aided by malnutrition, succumb to tuberculosis, cholera, HIV, and other diseases. Abuse and torture are common. A *New York Times* article described the life of a prisoner in Malawi:

> He eats one meal of porridge daily. He spends 14 hours each day in a cell with 160 other men, packed on the concrete floor, unable even to move. The water is dirty; the toilets foul. Disease is rife.
>
> But the worst part may be that in the case of Mr. Sikayenera, who is accused of killing his brother, the charges against him have not yet even reached a court. Almost certainly, they never will. For some time after November 1999, justice officials lost his case file. His guards know where he is. But for all Malawi's courts know, he does not exist.[36]

The prisons in Zimbabwe have been described as "death traps" where "even a short prison sentence could mean death."[37] Guinea-Bissau has recently finished constructing its first prison. Previously, detainees were kept in an old colonial house in the center of the capital. While there were no beds, electricity, or running water, the good news for the prisoners was that they easily escaped by climbing onto the roof and jumping to a neighboring house.[38]

Poor democracies may be too poor to pay the cost of their own elections. Internationally, the cost of organizing elections varies from $0.70 per voter in Ghana, to $7.50 in Russia, to more than $20 per elector in Afghanistan during ongoing war.[39] The 1994 elections in Mozambique cost $65.5 million, and the 1996 elections in Nicaragua cost $45 million. The bulk of these costs were financed by donors.[40] Cambodia spent $24 million on its national elections in 1998, $15 million in 2002 on commune elections, and another $11 million in 2003 on National Assembly elections for a total of $50 million on one election cycle, or in total more than 10 percent of the government's budget in 2003.[41] In many cases, foreign aid underwrites the cost of elections in poor countries—because poor governments cannot afford to pay for these elections themselves. The United States has pledged $30 million for the Democratic Republic of Congo's elections in 2016.[42]

Finally, poor governments can even be too poor to deal effectively with organized challengers to their claims of territorial control. Mali is a poor, landlocked, West African state about the size of Texas and California combined. Mali was a darling of foreign aid donors, frequently touted as a model of democratic governance. However, the government has never had firm control of the north, or been able to supply the north with public goods and services. From Bamako, Mali's capital in the south, to the northern-most parts of the country is a distance of more than 850 miles. The north of Mali includes portions of the Sahara desert. It has a harsh climate and a population of one to four people per square kilometer living in abject poverty, including, among others, the nomadic Tuaregs.[43] The periodic rebellions in the north rose to the level of civil war in January 2012. In March 2012, just three months before the scheduled Malian presidential elections, the Malian military staged a coup, on the grounds that it was being called on to fight in the north without adequate equipment.[44] Tuareg rebels took advantage of the confusion in Bamako to seize large sections of northern territory, and on April 6, declared the independence of the new state of Azawad. The government of Mali was unable to prevent the rebels from abusing the population, fighting among themselves, and destroying ancient monuments. An international military operation, led by the French, was needed to reclaim key towns such as Gao, Timbuktu, and Kidal.

Scraping Up Revenue

Poor governments govern less than rich liberal democracies. They also govern differently. One important difference is where they get their revenue. It is not only the amount of revenue, but where the revenue comes, from that can make public service delivery and rule of law more difficult.

Poor countries lack the capacity to implement individual income tax, and most poor country citizens are so poor that the amount of taxes they could pay would not offset the cost of collecting them.

> All countries can make some use of the individual income tax, but it can be a major revenue source only if certain prerequisites are satisfied. A list of conditions proposed in 1951 included the following: (1) the existence of a predominantly money economy; (2) a high standard of literacy; (3) prevalence of honest and reliable accounting; (4) a large degree of voluntary compliance on the part of taxpayers; (5) a political system not dominated by wealthy groups acting in their self-interest; and (6) honest, reasonably efficient administration.[45]

To these prerequisites, several more can be added, including a citizenry that is sufficiently wealthy and has a sufficient population density that the taxes collected more than cover the cost of collecting them, a system for the resolution of disputes that is effective, accessible, and perceived as fair, and a system for finding and identifying people and businesses and tracking their income and tax payments. Poor countries lack all of these.

Income taxes make up about 36 percent of revenue in poor countries (compared to 54 percent in rich countries), and most of this is corporate income tax, levied on a relatively small community of registered businesses.[46] Many businesses evade taxes, staying unregistered to avoid taxation and government harassment. Even the registration process itself can be expensive, difficult, and harassing. According to the World Bank's "Doing Business" survey, in 2011 it took 100 or more days to register a new business in Laos, Haiti, and the Republic of Congo, and more than 200 days to register in Guinea-Bissau. Each administrative step and each delay is an opportunity for a government official to extort a bribe. Accordingly, many businesses prefer to remain in the shadows, forming part of the "shadow" or "informal" economy—where much of a poor country's economic activity takes place. By one estimate, the shadow economy makes up on average 26 percent of poor countries' GDP, compared to 14 percent in wealthier countries.[47] In Pakistan, "fewer than three million of Pakistan's population of 175 million pay any income tax. A huge and buoyant informal (underground) economy, estimated to be anywhere from 30 to 80 percent of the real economy, goes untaxed and unrecorded."[48]

For those that are registered, evasion is rampant through underreporting. Poor country economies operate on a "cash" basis—credit cards and checks are rarely used. Many people and businesses do not have bank accounts, although the spread of cell phone technology is also expanding access to mobile banking in some countries. One of the important features of a cash economy is that financial transactions leave no paper trail. This makes it difficult to calculate the basis of taxation or to enforce laws against tax evasion. "It is said in Vientiane [Laos] that businesses keep three sets of books: one for the tax office, one for the tax office when it says it wants to see the real set of books, and the real set."[49] The rich and politically powerful are often able to use their influence to avoid paying taxes, while the violent and dangerous are able to draw on a different set of evasive tactics.

One approach that poor governments use to try to collect taxes is to get businesses to collect taxes for them. A chief source of revenue for poor countries is taxes on consumption and production, including value added taxes (VATs), which many poor countries adopted in the 1990s with the encouragement of the International Monetary Fund. One estimate is that such taxes are responsible for about 43 percent of government tax revenue.[50] A VAT is a tax on the final consumption of goods and services and is an alternative to the retail sales tax.[51] Under a VAT, taxed businesses must register, and the sellers collect taxes from purchasers that they must remit to the government. However, the seller is allowed to offset this remittance by any VAT tax that the seller paid when acting as a purchaser. In theory, the ultimate impact of this is that intermediate businesses will not pay any tax, and instead the entire tax burden will rest on the final consumer of the good or service.[52]

The VAT system hopes to reduce tax evasion because purchasers who hope to claim a VAT credit will insist on properly documented transactions with receipts and because even if a business down the chain fails to collect the tax from its purchasers, taxes will have already been collected from that business.

> In practice, however, both propositions are optimistic, if not fanciful. What often happens in practice is that dishonest merchants register, claim all input tax credits, and then record only a fraction of sales, keeping sale to final consumers (who do not request tax invoices) hidden. In practice, thus, there is no paper trail all the way through the system.[53]

Another source of domestic finance is taxes on imports and exports. Taxes on international trade are an important source of government revenue in many poor countries. In Benin, Nepal, and Togo, taxes on trade made up more than 15 percent of government tax revenue in 2010, and in Bangladesh they made up 24 percent.[54] Taxes on trade are easier to collect than income taxes because they are collected at customs checkpoints where taxpayers present themselves and have an incentive to pay in order to ensure that they can move their goods across the border. Political resistance to such taxes is lower because the cost of taxes can be passed on to the ultimate consumer of the good, who, if annoyed by high prices, will not know where to place the blame. With taxes on trade, the complicated problems associated with monitoring income levels are absent; the goods are physically present, their nature and quantity can be verified, and a single schedule of taxes is applied to the goods.

The ease of administering such taxes should not be overstated, however. The ability to extract tax revenue depends on the government's ability to stop goods at the border. Most poor countries lack the ability to police their borders effectively. Smuggling is lucrative, involves organized crime, and undermines government revenue collection.[55]

Moreover, revenue from taxes on trade fluctuates with global trade flows. The high volatility of government revenue makes planning and multiyear financial commitments difficult. This is a particular problem for poor countries, because many of them have been dependent on only a few exports such as cotton or copper since colonial times. This created booms and busts in revenue during the colonial period, and the same problem continues today.[56] In 2009, on average, a poor country's top three exports accounted for 60 percent of all of its exports. This percentage is higher for poor countries in Sub-Saharan Africa, and in some cases, such as Niger, Guinea-Bissau, Congo, and Sao Tomé and Principe, they account for more than 90 percent of all exports.[57] According to the World Bank, today the list of twenty least-diversified economies includes fourteen oil and gas exporters; if these are excluded, the bottom twenty is made up of countries that tend to be small, poor, landlocked, and African.[58]

Foreign aid is another important revenue source for many poor governments. While foreign aid is a small fraction of the budgets of rich governments, in a poor country it can double or exceed the government's public spending and finance a significant percentage of national economic activity. But aid flows are volatile and unpredictable—much more so even than the poor country's revenue flows.[59] This makes it difficult for poor governments to make multiyear commitments. The volume of foreign aid is high when the world economy is doing well, and low when it is doing poorly—which is exactly the time when poor governments most need it. Where aid is conditioned on the completion of policy reforms by the recipient government, the recipient government may not be willing or able to complete those reforms and aid disbursements may be slowed or halted.

Foreign aid is a mixed blessing. By definition foreign aid supports activities that the government itself cannot—and so projects are unsustainable unless they result in a reduction of government expenditures or an increase in government revenue. Donor projects may have hidden costs for recipient governments in the form of recurring costs, such as maintenance and operational costs. Donors are happy to send technical experts to help a poor government engage in law reform—or even to condition aid on law reform—but do not consider the costs of implementing the laws that they write. They assume that poor governments will ensure implementation from their own resources. This contributes to "the gap" between law on the books and law in action.

Donor policy preferences can overwhelm recipient government policy preferences. Aid can be conditioned on the recipient government's completion of specific policy reforms. The conditionality of World Bank and IMF loans has historically been very controversial. Many researchers today believe that attempts to force recipients to undertake policy reforms through the carrot of aid or the stick of aid withdrawal have not been very successful, whether or not they agree that the recommended reforms were a good idea. Aid earmarked for specific activities, such as improving school enrollment rates for girls or making credit available to the poor, may reflect intellectual trends in the West more than the recipient's priorities. An example is the intense focus of foreign aid donors on HIV/AIDS in Africa, including in countries where the rate of HIV infection is low. In Sub-Saharan Africa,

> HIV is the biggest single killer, contributing 17.6% of the burden of disease in 2001. But it received 40% of all health aid in 2004. . . . Why has this happened? One factor surely has been the success of HIV lobbies and activists in promoting HIV as exceptional. In rich countries, HIV has become the crusade of the famous, fashionable, and influential. In high prevalence countries, HIV affects the middle classes more than the poor and is of more concern to them: middle class children do not die from pneumonia or malaria and middle class women do not die in childbirth.[60]

Some observers worry about the economic consequences of aid—that poor countries will engage in unsustainable spending, or that the presence of aid will reduce the incentives for poor governments to build robust tax systems to solve their revenue problems. Still others have raised the question of the economic impact of large inflows of foreign currency, which can cause local currency to appreciate, benefiting importers but harming exporters.[61] Development experts worry about whether poor governments are receiving money faster or in higher volumes than they can sensibly manage and spend it given their limited capacities.[62]

Others are concerned with the political impact of aid. Governments that get money from sources other than taxation of the citizenry may be less accountable to their populations and have less incentive to grant civil and political rights and provide public goods, while their populations may lack a sense of entitlement and a right to accountability.[63] Some are concerned that the involvement of foreign donors in providing public services and goods may marginalize recipient governments and undermine their legitimacy, although there is as yet little empirical evidence that this is true.[64] Foreign aid flows may be distributed as patronage, propping up leaders who otherwise would not be able to remain in power. Indeed, sometimes foreign aid is given for just this purpose.

Poor governments also borrow domestically. While richer countries might float bonds, inviting investors to lend them money in return for interest, poor governments have a history of defaulting on loans and difficulty borrowing from private investors. Instead, they "borrow" by simply not paying their bills for wages, goods, and services. These "domestic arrears" can be considerable. Guinea-Bissau, for example, financed its entire budget deficit in 2003 through domestic arrears, which is a fancy way of saying that it declined to pay its bills.[65] This strategy has a number of unpleasant side effects, however. The first class of creditors who don't get paid on time are civil servants who don't receive their wages and are then forced to find other income. Suppliers to government may raise their prices in anticipation of finding themselves unwilling holders of government debt or of having to bribe government officials in order to get paid.

Poor governments also borrow internationally. In the late 1990s, forty-one poor governments had been dubbed "heavily indebted" by the World Bank and the International Monetary Fund, meaning that they were effectively bankrupt, owing more than they could ever repay. A coalition of Western nongovernmental organizations, organized under the umbrella organization Jubilee 2000, played a key role in lobbying for rich countries to "drop the debt" of the heavily indebted poor countries. Through debt relief initiatives, the original debt stock of those countries was largely erased, although poor governments continued to borrow during and after debt forgiveness.[66]

To prevent poor countries from once again becoming heavily indebted, the International Development Association, the arm of the World Bank that provides aid to poor countries, shifted from issuing only loans to issuing grants or a mix of the two. Countries with the most risk of becoming heavily indebted are only eligible for a lesser amount of grants; those with an intermediate level of risk are eligible for a mix of grants and loans.[67] However, these efforts can succeed only if other creditors also refrain from lending, and after debt relief, the improved financial position of poor governments has once again made them attractive to lenders. China, Kuwait, Brazil, India, South Korea, and Saudi Arabia have all begun to lend into Africa.[68] In 2007, China announced $3 billion in low-interest loans, in addition to interest-free loans for Africa.[69] Vulture funds are also buying up old debt and suing the newly solvent governments for payment, diverting the benefits of debt relief.[70]

Finally, there are money-making strategies of desperation. Some poor governments find that the best way to make money is . . . to make money. When they want money, they simply print more. By issuing money to pay debts, governments get something for the price of a piece of paper, a profit called "seigniorage." The only problem is that increasing the supply of money can cause inflation—a general rise in prices. Everyone who holds money suddenly finds that his or her money does not go as far as it used to. In this sense, seigniorage is like a tax—the government exchanges paper for goods and services, and everyone else pays.

All governments print money and so all governments get the benefit of seigniorage. However, poorer countries (who have more trouble borrowing) make use of the power of printing money more often. On average, poor countries get about 22 percent of their revenue by printing it, compared to 1.7 percent of revenue for rich countries.[71] Where governments overindulge in this benefit, people become aware that the value of their money is eroding and exchange their money for other assets with more stable values as fast as they can. At the same time, they expect the value of the currency to continue to erode, and they raise their prices for goods and services in anticipation. Like everyone else, the government finds that its purchases have become more expensive, and it prints larger amounts of money to cover them. The result can be "hyperinflation"—where all confidence in the currency is lost and its value plummets through the floor.

In Zimbabwe, President Mugabe printed money to fund the implementation of government projects for his increasingly shaky government.[72] In February 2007, the rate of inflation had reached 1,594 percent, rendering a new issue of national currency obsolete before a single bill was spent and leaving mounds of it piled in warehouses.[73] As of June 5, 2008, Zimbabwe's currency was trading at an average of one billion to the U.S. dollar; analysts claimed annual inflation rates of 1.8 million percent by May.[74] In a desperate attempt to rally political support in advance of presidential runoff elections, the government promised free education, health care, and food for the needy and free fuel for the transportation sector, and ordered the central bank to print the money needed to cover these programs.[75] A loaf of bread cost 600 million in Zimbabwean currency; a two-liter bottle of cooking oil about five billion.[76] Finally, the Zimbabwean unity government was forced to abandon the local currency altogether.[77] One hundred trillion dollar notes in Zimbabwean currency are now for sale on Ebay as collectors' items.

Poor governments also rely on sources of revenue that never show up in budgets and cannot be audited, which renders their finances opaque and undermines both the rule of law and government accountability. This is part of the reason why it is difficult to say how much money poor governments have. Government money is sometimes commingled with private money. To be sure, such comingling should not disguise the fact that the greater flow is of government money into private pockets and bank accounts, but the flow in the opposite direction, the use of commingled or private funds for government expenditure, also occurs, although it is not as well documented.[78] For example, in some communities, local leaders call community meetings and assign contributions of money or labor to households in order to build roads, water and sanitation systems, schools, health centers, dams and irrigation systems, and electrical systems, or to organize cleaning of public areas.[79] Large surveys in a number of developing countries have suggested that 20 to 50 percent of households contribute to these local works. In Indonesia, this type of informal tax is an important source of local public finance, about half as much as budgeted amounts.

Many government service providers also request extralegal private payments from service users, such as when the police demand gas money in order to investigate a crime or a court clerk requests paper in order to produce a judicial decision. Because government workers may be without the tools and supplies to do their jobs, the necessity of these levies and the distinction between these private payments and bribes are often unclear.

Governments may also finance themselves through criminal activities. Government positions can be leased or sold; government authority and discretion can be sold; government property can be stolen or used for personal benefit. While individuals and small networks can certainly engage in such activities on their independent initiative, governments at the highest levels may permit such activities both as a way of financing the government wage bill and of rewarding political supporters by giving them government posts and allowing them to turn them to personal profit. Government actors are permitted to supplement their often meager and unpredictable salaries with whatever they can beg, bully, extort, or fleece from citizens or each other, or can capture by stealing or borrowing the government resources in their charge.

The amounts that government officials obtain through bribes can so far surpass their official salaries as to render salaries superfluous. People are willing to work without salary in government positions that offer the possibility of deriving good income through bribery, sale of influence, or embezzlement, and government agencies have people working in them who have no official position but have been allowed to volunteer their labor in return for a share of the profits. A former director of customs of one poor Sub-Saharan African country was banking about one million dollars a year from his post; customs agents up and down the hierarchy helped themselves to revenue, before the remainder trickled into the treasury.

The new director of customs was able to substantially increase revenue, not only through personal restraint, but through urging his subordinates to restraint. He explained, "I don't tell them not to take," an impossible request to enforce and an unreasonable expectation when official salaries are low and irregularly paid, "I tell them to take less." As a public servant in the Democratic Republic of Congo said, "With our average salaries of less than US$30 a month, how can we survive without accepting bribes? We know quite well that it is forbidden by law, and that we are harming our country. But if we don't do it, then we can't have food for ourselves and our children, and we can't send them to school."[80]

Allowing government officials to supplement their salaries in this way means that the returns of corruption, at least in part, help finance the government wage bill. If these flows were stopped tomorrow, so that the government could only attract the workers that it could pay, there would be an exodus from government service, and it might even be difficult to fill some skilled positions.

Poor governments also finance themselves by counterfeiting currency, cigarettes, or pharmaceuticals; trafficking in drugs, illegal arms, and technology; money laundering; smuggling; or looting and plundering neighboring countries. The proceeds go to private pockets but can also be used to finance government activities. Typically, both government and nongovernment actors are involved in the network and reap benefits from the activity, as in illegal logging in Cambodia, or smuggling in Laos, which involves "collusion between importers, customs officers and local Party members . . . with the savings in tariffs shared between the importer and the officials (who may have to pay a portion up the local Party hierarchy)."[81] The Lao military has been implicated in the drug trade as well as the illegal wildlife trade, although the government denies it.[82]

The United States has long been concerned about North Korea's financing activities, which have included "drug trafficking, gold smuggling, illegal sale and distribution of endangered species, trafficking of counterfeit U.S. currency, and rare earth metals."[83] The United States has accused the government of North Korea of counterfeiting Federal Reserve notes and circulating them abroad.[84] The counterfeiting "apparently helps fund travel abroad, meet 'slush fund' purchases of foreign goods, and subsidize the lifestyles of the privileged class in Pyongyang."[85] North Korean diplomats and government officials have been arrested repeatedly for drug trafficking, while drug traffickers engaged in the shipment of heroin and methamphetamine to Taiwan and Japan reported that the goods had been loaded onto their boats by uniformed North Koreans.[86] According to the U.S. State Department, "These reports raise the question whether the North Korean government cultivates opium illicitly, refines opium into heroin, and manufactures methamphetamine drugs in North Korea as a state-organized and directed activity, with the objective of trafficking in these drugs to earn foreign exchange."[87] One consequence has been a North Korean addiction to crystal meth of epidemic proportions.[88]

The Congressional Research Service notes that:

> Areas of DPRK criminal activity commonly cited include production and trafficking in: (1) heroin and methamphetamines; (2) counterfeit cigarettes; (3) counterfeit pharmaceuticals (for example "USA" manufactured Viagra®); and (4) counterfeit currency (e.g., U.S. $100 bill "supernotes"). Media reports also indicate that North Korea may be engaged in insurance fraud as a matter of state policy.... Conservative/mainstream estimates suggest North Korean criminal activity generates as much as $500 million in profit per year, with some estimates reaching the $1 billion level.[89]

In this context, it is a relief to see North Korea exploring other revenue-raising opportunities like opening a chain of foreign restaurants—although these also seem to be used for money laundering.[90]

Some countries can raise government revenue by plundering their neighbors. Ugandan and Rwandan involvement in the conflict in the Democratic Republic of Congo gave their armies access to the gold-producing regions of that country. A panel of experts appointed by the United Nations concluded that the conflict was instigated by a network of government, military, and business elites for the purpose of exploiting Congo's natural resources. The 2002 report identified key actors.[91] Among the named members of the Ugandan network were senior government and military officials, including the Chief of Military Intelligence and Lieutenant General (Retired) Salim Saleh, President Museveni's younger brother. Human Rights Watch notes that notwithstanding the results of a Ugandan investigation that recommended further investigation of criminal charges against Salim Saleh among others, no action by the Ugandan government has been forthcoming.[92] In 2006, he was appointed minister of state for microfinance, an important area of programming for foreign aid donors.[93]

The Rwandan involvement in the conflict was reportedly managed by the Congo Desk of the Rwandan Patriotic Army:

While revenues and expenditure in the Congo Desk are considerable, they are kept strictly separate from Rwanda's national budget. A reliable source associated with the Congo Desk has calculated that income to the Desk provided 80 per cent of all RPA expenditure in 1999. . . . This comes to 20 per cent of GNP for 1999 and approximately 150 per cent of recurring budget expenditure for that year.[94]

Because of reliance on these commingled, extralegal, or criminal funding sources, the official data on government revenues and expenditures is incomplete. Governments also cannot be held accountable for the way they manage or spend such funds. More fundamentally, perhaps, the reliance on these sources means that "government revenue," as a separate pot of legally obtained public funds may not exist or, at best, is fuzzy, with some funds that are clearly public and others that are harder to categorize. This makes it difficult to say what actions, actors, or resources are governmental, or how much revenue the government really has. As a consequence, transparency, public accountability, and the rule of law are undermined.

Conclusion

Independence governments were given legal claims on territory out to the limits of the colonial boundaries and left with the task of state building—including in some cases exploration, pacification, and conquest—and governance. To accomplish these tasks they need revenue. However, poor governments have little revenue, and what revenue they have is from less stable and desirable sources than the revenue of rich liberal democracies. They cannot afford to staff their own governments, pay their own workers, build or maintain government infrastructure, arm their soldiers and police, or equip their civil servants. They cannot afford to deliver universal public goods and services such as public education, public health, or social safety nets for the poor, or even to assure law and order. The strength and quality of their governance is an inverse function of the distance from the capital. Most of their populations live in rural areas with little access to government services, but even in the capital, public goods and services are insufficient for the number of people and of poor quality by global standards. Poor governments must, of necessity, govern less.

They also must govern differently. They must rely on different strategies for raising revenue than do rich liberal democracies. The revenue sources on which they rely are more unpredictable and have undesirable side effects such as foreign dependence, inflation, weakening public accountability, undermining the rule of law, or even, in the case of North Korea, national drug addiction. The lines between governmental resources and private resources are fuzzy at best, making it difficult to decide what standards to apply to an actor, a resource, or an action. This includes the quiet dependence on government employees to pay themselves, either by keeping more lucrative jobs on the side or finding ways to make their government jobs pay.

At a deeper level, if poor governments cannot provide public goods and services to their citizens, why should their citizens support them or, at the very least, not challenge their authority? Is simply holding a democratic election enough to give the government authority? It doesn't seem so. Without the legitimacy that comes from providing public goods and services impersonally to all citizens, without the rule of law, without a way to directly control their territory, poor governments must make heavier use of alternate cheaper strategies of governance—the same set of strategies on which poor governments have always relied.

5. Governing Cheaply

"Great, so the state helps the state, but what does the state do for us? What does the state do that is of any use? Our kids don't study, they are undernourished, what does the state do for us? We don't actually know what the state does."

—CONGOLESE WOMAN AT BORDER CROSSING[1]

The poverty of poor governments means that they provide fewer and lower quality services to their populations, whether in terms of security, justice, health, or education. Many people pay no income taxes, receive no services, and have only occasional contact with the government. How then can poor governments maintain the acquiescence, if not gain the support, of such people? How can poor governments govern territories where they have no ability to maintain much presence?

We often imagine that simply organizing a democratic election will be sufficient to create popular support for a government; in fact, this was one mistake the Coalition made in Afghanistan. But for those who are very poor, it is not clear that democratic idealism will be enough. It is interesting to note that in a survey of Africans asked to identify the single most essential characteristic of democracy, about a quarter of respondents picked "Government narrows the gap between the rich and the poor," roughly the same percentage as those who identified democracy with freedom of expression.[2] It was the most common answer given by people who had no formal schooling.

In chapter 1, I argued that poor governments, like all governments, use a variety of strategies to win support or compliance. However, constrained by poverty, the mix of strategies that poor governments use is different than the mix used by rich liberal democracies. They rely on older, cheaper strategies than the twentieth-century conception of governance that relies on the legitimacy conferred by democratic elections, rule of law, and the supply of public goods and services to the entire population.

Three common strategies on which poor governments rely are patronage, clientelism, and repression. Patronage is a personal relationship in which a patron offers a client protection, status, and economic benefits in return for loyalty and favors. Clientelism is a less personal relationship in which politicians in democracies offer private benefits to supporters in return for their votes. Repression involves the use of force to suppress dissent or compel obedience. There is an abundant literature in political science and regional studies analyzing these and other strategies of governance, and it is not my intention to summarize the literature here. Interested readers can find some key works in the notes.[3] Instead, this chapter gives a little bit of the flavor of what these strategies can look like on the ground, with an emphasis on patronage.

Just as the reliance on disfavored strategies of raising revenue has undesirable side effects, so does reliance on these strategies of governance. Reliance on patronage puts people in government jobs who do not have the skills or the incentives to perform them, encourages and facilitates monetization of government positions, and undermines the government's ability to implement policy. Reliance on clientelism makes politics a winner-take-all contest, sidelining public policy and the public interest. Reliance on repression to govern inevitably involves human rights violations. And to the extent that these practices are illegal under domestic law, reliance on these strategies is in tension with the rule of law, a tension that will be explored more thoroughly in chapter 6. People who must then engage the government to obtain a service must navigate through the resulting informality and illegality.

Patronage and Clientelism

The patronage relationship is a voluntary personal relationship of mutual obligation in which a more powerful patron provides protection and support to a client who responds with loyalty and obedience. It is more than an impersonal economic exchange. The word "patron" has its roots in the Latin "pater," or "father," and echoes a familial relationship even where there is no tie of kinship.

Except where displaced by impersonal government institutions—a historically recent and geographically limited development—patronage relationships are one of the basic building blocks of human society. The same person may be a client of a more powerful patron, while also acting as a patron to his or her own clients. These interconnected relationships can form patronage networks spanning government, business, religious institutions, and other civil society organizations. Together with other social relationships such as family relationships, social networks form a structure of power that is an alternative to and in the case of poor governments, often more important than the formal organizational structure of government.

Under the Western governance ideal, the public goods and services provided by the government are allocated to all citizens according to clearly defined impersonal criteria, such as income, disability, or place of residence. Citizens receive benefits under clearly defined procedures because they are entitled to them. The receipt of benefits does not imply any reciprocal personal obligation by the recipient to the government actors who supply them. To get service, you don't need to know the government officials' names, and you don't expect to see them again or owe them anything.

By contrast, governance through patronage is a government of individual deals based on the distribution of private benefits. It allows leaders to leverage the power of elites who in turn deliver the support of their own clients. Refusal to accept a patron's offers of protection and favors can be seen as an insult, if not a challenge to the existing governance structure. Those who are courted with offers by the existing regime and refuse to participate may be excluded from any form of government job or benefit, imprisoned, or threatened with violence.

Patronage is a very old strategy of governance. The words that we use for this relationship—"patron," "client," and for the benefits given by the patron to the client, "patronage"—date from the Roman Empire. European feudal governments were built on this type of personal relationship, in which the king was the ultimate patron.

> The king kept his nobles sweet by grants of honours, lands, pensions, appointments, and the power to distribute minor appointments to their followers. In their turn these great nobles dispensed these favours to their dependents, high and low, like so many Mafia "Godfathers," and so guaranteed the Crown their allegiance and service.[4]

Powerful leaders may be able to concentrate the authority to distribute patronage in themselves in order to deny potential rivals a power base. Because it was imperative that recipients of favors understand to whom they were beholden, King Louis XIV of France made sure that "he and nobody else would grant the favours, and they had to be asked for. . . . When somebody asked him to favour an individual who failed to court him, his reply would be: 'I never see him. . . . Everything that is a favour must be asked for personally."[5] In poor governments, however, leaders often lack the capacity to do this, and so every actor with resources or favors to dispense has the ability to use them strategically.

Modern poor governments continue to rely heavily on this strategy of governance. In Yemen, "in distributing patronage, the President considers a variety of factors, including the type of elite under consideration (tribal, technocrat, merchant, etc.), an elite's grassroots influence and proven loyalty, and the tactical needs of balancing tribal, family, and regional alliances."[6]

In Central Asia,

> today's presidents, like the khans of the past, exercise personal control over all public affairs. In theory, there is a division of institutional functions and powers. In practice, senior figures in the state apparatus are selected by the presidents, generally from among their own networks of dependents and clients; these in turn surround themselves with loyal subordinates of their own. This pattern is repeated at every level of the administrative hierarchy, thereby creating chains of interlocking personal loyalties that can readily circumvent proper procedures. Such a system inevitably fosters jealousies and rivalries between individuals as well as government departments. Partly as an antidote to these negative tendencies and partly in order to strengthen their own hold on power, the leaders frequently reshuffle ministers and other senior personnel. The high turn-over rate ensures that they alone represent continuity and authority and remain the ultimate dispensers of patronage. . . . However, this constant movement has exacerbated the sense of personal insecurity and created an atmosphere in which individuals at every level of the administration seek to "milk" their office for private gain.[7]

In Laos, "powerful families thus functioned as patronage networks, the more ambitious leaders of which established their own political parties. Patronage took the form of financial assistance, obtaining jobs in the civil service or private sector, or promotion in the army or bureaucracy, in return for political support."[8] After the revolution, "senior Party members soon began to dispense patronage in the traditional Lao way, rewarding extended family members and loyal retainers with jobs for which they were often poorly qualified, in order to build a political support base."[9] Wives and families "became conduits for requests for favours and preferences."[10] Similarly, in Cambodia, powerful families span the police, the military, the

Red Cross, the ministries of commerce, agriculture, and the interior, the legislature, and the party. The *Phnom Penh Post* published a diagram of elite family relationships and their relationships to power.[11]

In poor societies, people with access to money or authority find themselves subject to strong demands for support by their less fortunate relatives and network members. Government actors at all levels are faced with demands by family, friends, and acquaintances for money, contracts, jobs, favorable government decisions, school fees, or a place to stay. When mid-level government workers go home, favor seekers are waiting for them in their houses and courtyards. Combined, their demands far exceed government salaries, and yet the reputation of government as a fount of wealth is such that many government officials find it difficult to plead their limited resources. A refusal to accommodate such demands risks social sanctions such as isolation and exclusion, while granting them brings status and elevation to the role of patron.

Some government actors cite these social pressures as one of the principal catalysts for using government offices to make money. President Bongo explained this system in the context of the upper-middle-income country of Gabon:

> We have not attained your degree of political maturity. In Africa, the notion of the state is unfortunately often fuzzy, although that of chief is clear. He has his role and his privileges. Here, if one thinks that the chief doesn't have money to redistribute, he can't be respected or considered. He is thought to be selfish. Our culture is different. But it is not inferior to yours. In Africa, the demands are such that one can't be chief and be rich, because you have to redistribute. . . .
>
> Sharing is inherent in African society at all levels. Not only the head of state, but also the ministers, the senior civil servants, as well as all those who have a little bit of money or power. One has to pay the school fees of a cousin, furniture for a nephew who is getting married, hospital expenses for a relative, etc. Africans will not accept that a big brother keeps everything for himself. The chief who doesn't redistribute loses all credibility. We don't trust him. This is why the money that I have, I have to give not only to one of my secretaries whose child has special needs but also to Gabonese I don't know. When you go the interior of the country, people ask for a hearing, they wait all day. There is missing equipment, poverty. The president comes with sacks, he gives 20 million here, 30 million there.[12]

PATRONAGE GOODS. Patrons dispense patronage goods to clients. Anything of value, or anything that can be used to make money, can be used as a patronage good. Two of the most important patronage goods in government are government positions and government contracts. Jobs are especially important patronage goods in poor countries where there are limited employment opportunities. A government position may carry with it a salary or benefits; perquisites such as a government-provided office, car, driver, or telephone; and government authority that the office holder can use to make money by selling government decisions or access to government services.

Where government positions are used as patronage goods, the government has a strong incentive to make more of them in order to have more political currency to spend. As long as they do not come with attendant salaries, they can be minted for free. The monarchy of France, teetering on the edge of bankruptcy and unable to borrow, manufactured government positions so that they could be sold or gifted:

> King Francis I created new government offices simply for the purpose of selling them; as a consequence, in 1515 there were 8,000 persons in the service of the state; in 1665, there were 80,000.[13] Having sold the offices and therefore having lost control over the income that they represented, the French government established an office to tax the sale of offices as well as offices passed by inheritance. At its peak, in the first half of the seventeenth century, these taxes provided 40% of the Crown's revenue.[14]

Similarly, in poor countries "public employment becomes an instrument for political patronage and social welfare. Governments distribute jobs to supporters and spread the limited wage envelope across a large number of workers."[15] In Zimbabwe, the International Monetary Fund pointed out that "the wage bill in Zimbabwe is one of the highest in sub-Saharan Africa.... A recent public payroll audit identified 38,000 staff positions with significant irregularities, including possibly 14,000 ghost workers."[16] (Ghost workers are those who are paid despite the fact that they never report to work.) Alternately, poor governments distribute patronage positions by cycling supporters through existing jobs, leading to rapid turnover, including at the senior or ministerial level.[17] Because office holders do not have security in their offices, this rotation can prompt office holders to seek to make money from their positions more zealously, as the opportunity is likely to be short term.

As foreign aid donors pressed for government decentralization, in the hope that it would bring government closer to the people and make it more accountable, some politicians saw the opportunity to expand the number of patronage positions they would be able to dispense. Uganda created more than forty new districts in less than a decade, creating a host of new parliamentary positions, "each one a patronage opportunity,"[18] as well as a number of technical staff positions at the district level. These included:

> six executive secretaries, a Chief Administrative Officer (CAO), Resident District Commissioner (RDC), deputy CAO, deputy RDC, and a District Auditor, Clerk (and Assistant Clerk), Community-Based Services Manager, Education Officer, Engineer, Extension Coordinator, Finance Officer, Director of Health Services, Information Officer, Inspector of Schools, Land Officer, National Agricultural Advisory Services Officer, Personnel Officer, and Planner, among others. Second, the payroll must include a new district chairperson and a new set of district councilors representing special-interest groups such as women, the youth, and the disabled, which in total average out to around 13 per district. The result of all of these new jobs at the district level is a cascading effect as lower-level officials are promoted upwards, thereby creating new job openings at all levels of local government. Indeed, when asked about the benefits of district creation, sub-county councilors in Nakaseke primarily answered by noting the new jobs and promotions for local citizens who formerly had been unemployed by the previous Luwero district administration.[19]

Another important government patronage good—and one that receives the most attention—is the public contract. Contracts may be awarded to friends, families, political supporters, and party members. The contract winner need not have any capacity to perform the contract; instead the winner acts as a prime contractor and subcontracts the actual work, after taking a percentage of the value of the contract. Large contracts are valuable because they are potentially more profitable. Contracts whose performance cannot be easily monitored are also valuable for the same reason. These include contracts in infrastructure (which is built in layers, with each layer concealing whatever defects might lie beneath) and contracts in the national security sector (which are usually protected from disclosure and public oversight).

Monopolies are also a historic patronage good. In England under Queen Elizabeth, the grant of a commercial monopoly was a favorite patronage good. Recipients of royal monopolies sold their privileges to merchants and manufacturers.

> There was scarcely a commodity that was not the object of a monopoly. On one occasion, when a long series of concessions was recited in Parliament, a member exclaimed, "Is not bread in the number?" And to the astonished cries of "Bread!" he replied, "Yes, I assure you, if affairs go on at this rate, we shall have bread reduced to a monopoly before the next Parliament."[20]

In modern Yemen, President Salih "issued import licenses to favored shaykhs who then sold the licenses to traditional merchants for a profit," while the state-run Yemeni Economic Corporation "received lucrative access to commodity and private sector imports."[21] The president also distributed oil concessions and the right to sell oil to clients, and he allegedly allowed a favored few to buy subsidized diesel and sell it on the international market.[22] Finally, a number of sheikhs simply received stipends from the state in order to purchase their loyalty.[23]

> Those sheikhs collaborate with the government in keeping security and stability in their areas, said Mohamed Hussein Taher, an officer at the Sana'a-based Tribal Sheikh Affairs Authority. "If the cabinet cuts their stipends, they will let their fellow tribesmen attack oil pipelines, power grids and other vital installations that contribute much to the state's budget."[24]

CLIENTELISM. "Clientelism" is used more narrowly to describe democratic politics in which politicians deliver private economic benefits to their voters, such as jobs, contracts, or cash for school fees or medical bills. It is sometimes used to include local public goods such as schools or roads delivered to supporters (in the United States, "pork barrel politics"). Because each politician has many supporters, the personal aspects of the relationship are not as pronounced as in a patronage relationship, but even here it can be more than an impersonal economic exchange. By addressing supporters' personal and material needs, politicians show themselves to be generous and caring leaders. Weber, lecturing about patronage in Europe and the United States, said that

> With the development of the money economy, perquisites and prebends especially are the typical rewards for the following of princes, victorious conquerors, or successful party chiefs. For loyal services today, party leaders give offices of all sorts—in parties, newspapers, co-operative societies, health insurance, municipalities, as well as in the state. *All* party struggles are for the patronage of office, as well as struggles for objective goals.[25]

In the 1990s, many poor authoritarian states became at least nominal democracies with regular elections. When governments are too poor to provide public goods and services, the impact of democratization is a change in the way in which patronage is wielded, rather than reducing or eliminating it. Previously, a seemingly immovable political leader ("big man") was the ultimate dispenser of patronage and favors, but with democracy, candidates and parties could now contest for the popular vote; one way to do this was by distributing benefits to their supporters.

In Papua New Guinea,

> electoral politics is primarily a competition for access to the state. In the Highlands province of Simbu, for example, "people have come to regard the government as the major, or only, source of opportunity and finance. Having a friend in national government is seen as necessary for economic success. . . ." Aspiring candidates make (often optimistic) calculations of their electoral prospects based on the number of voters in their own clan or tribal group. Once elected, the expectation is that the successful candidates will use their position to extract resources from the government and deliver them back to their supporters, but not necessarily to the electorate as a whole.[26]

Political candidates are expected to distribute material goods to voters or to make substantial contributions to local public goods such as schools, roads, or churches. In Kenya, according to the Coalition for Accountable

Political Financing, the average parliamentary candidate spent about $33,000, over 40 percent of their total campaign expenditures, on the distribution of cash and gifts to voters.[27] The 2005 Afrobarometer survey asked respondents in nine poor Sub-Saharan African countries, "In your opinion, how often do politicians do each of the following: Offer gifts to voters during election campaigns?" Seventy-four percent of respondents in Mali, Benin, Kenya, Madagascar, Malawi, Mali, Mozambique, Tanzania, Uganda, and Zimbabwe answered "often" or "always."[28] It may be a mistake, however, to see these interactions as an impersonal economic exchange of "vote buying." Instead, it may be a signal of a candidate's wealth, personal concern, and generosity—all important characteristics of good patrons.

Because politicians preserve their power by distributing patronage, they must have access to government resources to distribute. After elections, there is rampant party switching as supporters from the opposition seek to gain access to the patronage benefits now controlled by the majority. In francophone Africa, this type of party switching is called "political nomadism"; it has been decried in countries such as Burkina Faso,[29] Mali,[30] and Niger.[31] In former British colonies, it is known as "party hopping." Some countries have passed laws or amended their constitutions to prohibit this behavior. Senegal, Bangladesh, and Papua New Guinea are examples; a constitutional reform in this direction was proposed in Mali.[32] While the presence of such laws may suppress legislative party switching, the need for such laws is a strong indication of the relative importance of patronage and clientelism.

The administration is also affected by elections, with sweeping replacements of lower-level government workers as the new party in power allocates jobs to its supporters. While one might expect that more senior political appointees would also be replaced—as happens today in the United States—there is, paradoxically, often less replacement at the higher levels of government in poor governments because the group of elites is so small that new governments have no choice but to consolidate their position by paying off the same elites and incorporating them into the new power structure, even after having accused them of corruption while campaigning. In Nepal, Pramanada Jha was demoted from the Supreme Court on the grounds that he accepted a bribe to free a convicted drug smuggler. But this did not prevent a political party from advancing him for the vice presidency—a position that he ultimately won.[33]

In Benin,

> politicians are elected not to defend policy issues, but to ensure that government resources are channelled to their region of origin. In fact . . . personalities are more important than parties, and it is more common for prominent people trying to hedge their status to join a political party or, more often, create one, than for politicians to gain national prominence through a party career. Thus, it is not surprising that most parties have no political programme and no technical capacities in terms of policy analysis. In addition, parties and individual MPs that find themselves in opposition after an election tend to gravitate towards the government. As one notorious party-hopping MP declared: "Opposition does not feed a man."[34]

When political parties are organized to capture state resources for their members, they do not need—and typically do not have—distinct ideologies, platforms, or policy agendas. Shared ideologies and policy goals can bind parties together, but patronage politics is a zero sum game. The larger the share that goes to a person, group, or party, the smaller the share for the rest. Coalitions and parties tend to be unstable. Unless prevented by electoral law, poor democracies tend to attract large numbers of candidates and parties with small constituencies. In 2007 in Kenya, more than 2,500 individuals ran for 210 parliamentary seats.[35] (It should be noted that due to a self-awarded pay raise, Kenyan parliamentarians earned $147,000 per year.[36] They subsequently reluctantly agreed to accept a salary cut in return for a number of other perks, such as a grant for the purchase of a car.[37])

Monetizing Government Positions

There are a number of reasons why people in poor countries seek to translate government jobs, authorities, and contracts into maximum financial gain. These include salaries that are often inadequate and irregularly paid, weak rule of law and law enforcement, the absence of social safety nets, and networks of dependents and favor seekers laying social claims for support. Where government jobs, authorities, or contracts are dispensed as patronage goods, they are expected to be used as personal property rather than for the public welfare. Historically, they have been bought and sold, leased, bequeathed, and inherited. As President Mobutu of Zaire put it:

> In a word, everything is for sale, anything can be bought in our country. And in this flow, he who holds the slightest cover of public authority uses it illegally to acquire money, goods, prestige or to avoid obligations. The right to be recognized by a public servant, to have one's children enrolled in school, to obtain medical care, etc. . . . are all subject to this tax which, though invisible, is known and expected by all.[38]

The importance of government positions as a way of generating personal profit is reflected in popular metaphors in Sub-Saharan Africa and in Melanesia that link government to eating or food.[39] In Nigeria, "I chop, you chop" ("I eat, you eat") was a political slogan and an attitude toward government brilliantly spoofed by the Mama G song "National Moi Moi" (in which she sings, "you chop your own, I chop my own, my government will not chop alone"). Ugandans speak of making a corrupt official "vomit up what he has eaten." In the francophone countries, officials eat or wolf down government money and resources ("manger," "bouffer"). Similar metaphors can be found in Melanesia ("big man" as a political leader, the "national cake" and analogies of corruption to eating food).[40] In the Solomon Islands,

> many close to the tendering process say that the word corruption has been replaced by less "demeaning words." "Everybody is calling it lunch money nowadays. . . . It's not a bribe, so it is not corruption, just lunch money," said a senior government officer who preferred to remain anonymous. "Those in most of these tender boards have a system where they predetermine who gets a contract, and this is based largely on what they could offer board members, or a selected few, . . . lunch money, that is," the officer said. "Many board members have people on the outside who, in most cases, approach contractors and basically find out how much lunch money they are willing to fork out."[41]

The value of government jobs as patronage goods is not defined by their low and irregularly paid salaries or their bewildering array of official salary supplements. Instead, the value of the position is defined by the extent to which a position carries authority that can be monetized. At the highest levels of government, schemes for enrichment are elaborate, more sophisticated, and certainly more rewarding. In Kenya, the government paid subsidy payments for nonexistent exports of gold and diamonds to Goldenberg International, to the tune of $600 million; Kenyan president Daniel Arap Moi was implicated.[42] In Liberia, former president Charles Taylor gave control of the Bureau of Maritime Affairs to family friend Benoni Urey.[43] The BMA runs Liberia's lucrative ship registry, through which the country earns revenue by providing "flags of convenience" that allow ships to travel international waters. It was later shown that Urey diverted about 20 percent of the registry's annual income; he is now under a United Nations travel ban for economic crimes. (This has not prevented Liberian president Sirleaf from appointing Urey as a mayor, notwithstanding her anticorruption stance.)

The ways to profit from a government position are limited only by human imagination, but certainly one of the most common is to charge fees to render government services. Whereas just 0.5 percent of Americans reported an encounter with a bribe-seeking public official in a 2003–2004 survey, 30.5 percent of those surveyed in Mozambique and 29 percent of those surveyed in Cambodia reported such an encounter in the previous year.[44] Police demand payment to respond to a crime scene or to investigate, secretaries demand payment to schedule meetings with their bosses, clerks demand payment to process files. "Teachers expect to be 'rewarded' for raising marks, or awarding diplomas; health workers charge for 'free medicines.'"[45] In Vietnam,

> the situation in hospitals can be galling: nurses will arbitrarily write anything on your admittance sheet: heart rate, pulse, blood pressure. They will only take your pulse and blood pressure and record them in your patient's intake form if you pay.
>
> "They make it painful for you," says Nghiem Thi Thu, a woman in her late 40s who works as a caregiver. "You pay, and the nurses will give you shots without hurting you." Indeed, it is a frequent complaint that otherwise the nurses make it physically painful.
>
> Within my first year of living here, I fell and cut myself deeply. At the hospital, I sat in the emergency room for more than an hour before a visiting neighbor asked, "Did you give them an envelope?" That's when I learned that in an emergency, you pack envelopes to take with you to the

hospital. You put a few bills inside and hand them to intake clerks, nurses and doctors if you want to get any service.

Visiting a friend in a hospital recently, I saw a short woman getting in and out of bed every few minutes to pace the room, stepping over and around the mass of people. These people from the countryside had come into Hanoi seeking better medical care related to their reproductive system. The woman was cursing out the nurses, the doctors and her husband in turn.

"I'm just a second class citizen," she said. "It's been five hours and they won't give me my shots."

The room had four beds—two patients per bed—and scores of relatives acting as caregivers. Several people kept reminding her to hand over an envelope. She refused, and everyone else received their shots and medicines. Alone, she kept pacing the room and cursing.[46]

In Bangladesh, primary school teachers must bribe the local government education officials in order to obtain training, transfers, monthly pay orders, and retirement benefits.[47] Along with school officials, they receive a share of funds that were intended for student scholarships and food. Teachers and administrators also demand bribes from students and their parents for admission to school or even to be allowed to sit for exams.

Shafayet Ullah, an examinee at the higher secondary level, claims that his geography teacher forced him to pay 2,200 taka (US$3232) to secure passing grades in the practical session of examinations. "The teacher did not teach a single class, but we still wanted to take the test and submit our practical sheets, but the teacher forced us to pay the money. This happens in every educational institution. I am really ashamed at how some teachers commit such sins and pollute a noble profession."

Interviews with a number of students in several schools reveal that even students at the secondary education level have to pay bribes to the school authorities in exchange for selection for the lengthy secondary school certificate examinations. If they fail the test examinations, they have to pay 1,000 taka (US$15) to 1,500 taka (US$2222) for each subject to ensure that they will be allowed to take the next round, the public examinations. Students are also required to bribe their teachers for the required marks in the practical examination sessions.[48]

Payment may also be demanded by government actors or offered to them for faster service. Those who do not pay may find that they do not receive service, as government actors invent delays or those who pay are repeatedly prioritized above them. In courtrooms in Sierra Leone,

> there are posters that remind people that bail is free. Nevertheless, human rights groups continue to draw attention to the fact that people still pay illegal fees every day to court officials to secure bail. I myself learned recently that it is a common practice in the Magistrates Court for clerks and police prosecutors to encourage a defendant in minor cases to plead guilty at the start of their trial.
>
> One lawyer told me that the defendant can then negotiate and secure a lighter punishment by illegally paying a fee to the court officials. In cases of corruption at government hospitals, nurses' handbags are used as illegal pharmacies from where prescription drugs are sold to patients. An extra payment to officials at relevant government departments will lead to faster processing of an application for various services including passports, drivers' licenses, property title registrations or utilities.
>
> People have little option but to pay incentives to public officials in order to secure faster processing of an application for most public services. This is because there is no functioning complaint and redress mechanism to discourage officials from delaying or refusing to process an application for a public service without being paid a bribe.[49]

Even aid donors are sometimes taxed by government actors who are monetizing their offices. In Myanmar,

> a lay Catholic who spent a year working on the church's relief effort on the ground—and who with a few others spoke more frankly about the aftermath—said that junta officers rarely missed an opportunity to enrich themselves in a storm's wake. They regularly forced church officials to pay bribes just for permission to deliver basic aid.
>
> Permits for construction projects, ranging from rudimentary chapels to larger housing units, also required hefty bribes to officials. Other times, authorities would simply deny permission to build. One brother said his order had to abandon plans to expand a hostel for poor boys because it lacked funds to bribe the requisite officials.[50]

A recently passed antibribery law in the United Kingdom raises concerns for nongovernmental organizations (NGOs) trying to reach populations in need.

It is well-known that NGOs may make "facilitation payments" to gain access or ensure the delivery of aid in emergency situations. The new UK Bribery Act stipulates that any act of bribery by a UK organisation or nationals, anywhere in the world, breaks the law in the UK and that "facilitation payments" come under this. This represents the clearest obstacle to NGOs.[51]

Payment may also be required for protection from government coercion. Auditors and inspectors require payment so that they do not engage in harassment. Health officials charged with ensuring that incoming travelers have proper vaccinations threaten to administer missing immunizations on the spot with a dirty needle, unless a bribe is paid. Police and immigration use their powers to extort bribes by threatening violence or jail. In Somalia,

Ali Isse, a local businessman, had firsthand experience of being detained at Mogadishu's Adden Adde International Airport while coming back from a business trip to the United Arab Emirates.

"The security at the airport took me to a room and questioned me for an offense I did not understand. They threatened me with arrest if I did not pay them 1,427,000 Somali shillings (US$1,000), but I refused to pay because I knew I was innocent," Isse said.

Isse was taken to a secret prison in Mogadishu's notorious presidential palace where he was held in solitary confinement for a month and allowed to speak to no one. After being repeatedly interrogated by anti-terrorism squads, he was finally released after his relatives paid a bribe of 2,854,000 Somali shillings (US$2,000).

"They paid the money without my consent because they knew I might never get any justice," Isse said. "Here, we have to pay just to be alive."

At the seaport, merchants importing goods into Somalia say that even after they pay the regular tax, which they maintain is already prohibitively excessive, importers and exporters are required by port officials to pay "facilitation fees." This means they must pay bribes to be allowed to take their imported goods out of the port or face indefinite delays that involve undue inspections for illegal weapons, explosives or drugs.

"We have to cooperate or else we lose everything we have in the stores of the port or in containers," Yusuf Musse, a rice importer, said. "If we dare report this to higher officials we would wind up fighting for our lives."[52]

One woman explained why she prefers the less comfortable shared compartments when traveling by train from Kyrgyzstan to Russia:

"It takes four days to get from Bishkek to Moscow, and the journey feels like torture, but it's cheaper and safer than individual compartments for four people—it's more difficult to harass people in front of others," says Lydmila, who regularly travels back and forth between the Kyrgyz Republic and Russia. Several months ago, she enrolled her daughter in a Russian university and regularly visits her.

Being an experienced traveler, Lydmila quickly arranges a seat for herself and retrieves a small digital camera from her pocket. "My little savior," she calls it. "When they start their raids they are cautious around people who have the means to document the abuse."

Lydmila explains that during her last trip the officers behaved rudely as they inspected the passengers and rummaged through their luggage. After finding that Lydmila and her daughter were carrying nothing illegal, the officials became frustrated and began to bully them. The officials asked for papers that, by definition, could not be obtained before arriving in Russia. "It was obvious they wanted a bribe. They threatened to unload our luggage and force us out of the train in the middle of nowhere. I asked them 'How much?' and they told me to pay 5,000 Russian rubles (US$200). It was literally all I had on me at that point. I replied I couldn't afford this and they lowered the tariff from 5,000 to 2,000 rubles (US$200 to US$80)."

When the officials started bargaining, Lydmila figured she needed to be blunt and resist the pressure. She took out her digital camera and warned she'd be taking pictures of their actions. They backed down immediately and dropped their demand to 200 rubles (US$10).[53]

It is not only the public who pays; government actors may also be compelled to pay. Those with the authority to fill government positions may choose to sell or lease positions, instead of giving them to their clients. The more potentially profitable an office is, the higher the price it can command. "No jobs in Laos are simply advertised and then filled on the basis of experience or talent. Every applicant knows that they will need someone to speak for them: not just a referee, but someone who will actively attempt to ensure they get the job, and keep it. . . . But this support has to be paid for; and the more the job permits the holder to extract benefits, the greater the payment."[54] Where government offices are sold or leased, those who paid to be appointed must find ways to make their offices profitable in order to recoup their initial investment or to make regular payments in order to continue to hold their office. For police, "getting a job issuing traffic tickets can be lucrative, but to get this job a cop needs to have connections and pay some dues. He also has to share what he takes with his superiors and colleagues."[55] This practice creates hierarchies within government in which funds flow upward from lower-level employees, who demand payments from the public to those responsible for appointments, assignments, and promotions, and to those responsible for the distribution of paychecks and benefits.

Any position with the power to award large contracts for the purchase of government goods and services can be a very lucrative position. Those with procurement authority may allocate contracts to themselves, to their relatives and friends, or to those willing to pay, so a position on a tender board is a prime patronage good. In 2012, for example, the World Bank canceled a credit to Bangladesh for the construction of a bridge over the Padma River, citing "credible evidence corroborated by a variety of sources which points to a high-level corruption conspiracy among Bangladeshi government officials, SNC Lavalin executives, and private individuals in connection with the Padma Multipurpose Bridge Project."[56] The executives of the Canadian engineering firm SNC Lavalin were charged with corruption in Canada.[57]

Contractors routinely factor the need to pay bribes to obtain contracts and to receive payment, as well as the delay and hassle of "walking their payments through," into the prices that they charge government for goods and services.[58] As a consequence, poor governments pay above market value for goods and services. Military purchases, infrastructure construction, or natural resource extraction all give rise to high-value contracts, with an incentive for competing contractors to pay bribes to get contracts and for government actors to pocket them. When a new government was elected in Kenya, ending Moi's decades-long presidency, it was promptly tarnished by the involvement of senior government officials in procurement scandals, such as the Anglo-Leasing Scandal.[59] The government then reported that up to $47 million in foreign aid for textbooks and medical

supplies had been stolen between 2005 and 2009 by officials in the education and health ministries.[60]

Because poor governments are often dependent on foreign aid, positions managing the stream of aid are valuable. "When I was prime minister,
people used to come see me—not to ask to be made minister, but to ask to
be put in charge of an aid project," confided a former prime minister of an
impoverished government.

Every other attribute of government office is routinely turned to personal use. Official cars and drivers are seen on the weekend ferrying
relatives on shopping and personal chores. Computers, generators, air con-
ditioners, fans, chairs, and stationery are stolen from government offices.
Those in charge of government money embezzle it or lend it out at interest.
In Zimbabwe,

> one of the most scandalous cases involved the controversial governor of
> the Reserve Bank of Zimbabwe, Gideon Gono, who illegally withdrew
> money from the foreign-currency accounts of nongovernmental orga-
> nizations, individuals, companies and embassies, allegedly to bankroll
> Mugabe's electioneering as well as to fund his operations. Gono, who,
> rightly or wrongly, is also mentioned as one of the most corrupt individu-
> als in Zimbabwe, publicly admitted that the Central Bank raided accounts
> of nongovernmental organizations to the tune of about US$1 billion.[61]

It is impossible to unpack this flow of funds and to separate out money
that goes for personal enrichment, money that is used for political purposes, money that is redistributed to personal networks, and money that
is used to pay for the ordinary expenses of rendering government services
that should normally be paid with budgeted funds, such as supplying necessary but missing equipment or substituting for unpaid salaries. Those
who profit from this system are quick to deny. Asked if this system was simply "a convenient excuse for enriching oneself," President Bongo of Gabon
replied: "Don't fool yourself. For the head of an African state it is very
difficult to enrich himself because he is subject to so many pressures, coming from the entire country."[62] However, the criminality of self-enrichment
through the state, the social unacceptability of amassing wealth without
sharing, and the disapproval of those who embrace Enlightenment governance values, including the donor community, make it unlikely that any
government actor would publicly and candidly confess to having amassed a

fortune using his government office. According to the *Guardian*, President Bongo's family (at the time his son was minister of defense, his daughter was head of the cabinet, and his son-in-law was head of the Ministry of Finance), with forty years of access to his country's oil wealth, "may be one of the richest first families in the world," with multimillion dollar mansions in Gabon and France.[63]

While Gabon is not a poor country, and leaders of poor countries have less ample opportunities for wealth accumulation, there are also reports of multimillionaire leaders of poor countries. According to a leaked U.S. diplomatic cable, the chief prosecutor at the International Criminal Court told U.S. diplomats that Sudanese president Al-Bashir had nine billion U.S. dollars in foreign bank accounts, although Al-Bashir has denied these claims.[64] In Haiti under "Baby Doc" Duvalier,

> while international aid organizations tried to help, Duvalier pocketed much of the relief money for himself. According to documents, shortly after the International Monetary Fund granted $22 million to Haiti on December 5, 1980, $20 million of that money was withdrawn from the government's bank accounts. Former U.S. Secretary of State Alexander Haig received a cable saying that approximately $4 million may have been diverted to Haiti's secret police, the Tonton Macoutes, while the remaining $16 million disappeared into Duvalier's personal accounts.
>
> At the same time, Duvalier was making lavish purchases, like the eighty-six foot luxury yacht, named "Nikki," that he bought for $1 million. Even after he fled the country in 1986 to escape an imminent coup, the spending continued. In 1988, a journalist from the St. Petersburg Times in Florida described Duvalier's luxurious villa in the French Riviera (monthly rent: $40,000) as having "Ferrari sports cars parked in the driveway."
>
> While it is hard to link specific bank accounts or purchases to specific incidents of corruption or bribes, the rate at which money flowed out of the public coffers was staggering. All told, Jean-Claude Duvalier, his ex-wife Michelle Bennett Duvalier, and three people acting as agents are believed to have taken $504 million from the Haitian public treasury between 1971 and 1986.[65]

THE VIEW FROM THE BOTTOM. Most governments engage in redistribution of wealth. In theory, this should be accomplished through public policies with transparent and impersonal eligibility criteria (such as social safety nets for the poor). However, patronage systems use government itself as a good to redistribute, and its offices and consumption of goods and services as an instrument of redistribution; in contrast with program eligibility defined by objective and transparent criteria, the redistribution of patronage systems is opaque and hinges on personal networks. It is an unequal system of redistribution that favors government actors, their families, friends, and supporters—a narrow elite.[66]

The unequal treatment generates substantial frustration. Some, however, benefit indirectly, when government resources and income streams are shared. Others hope to benefit, patiently waiting their turn.[67] For them, government is a lottery and they can dream of becoming winners. Still others accept that they are in a system that is beyond their power to change and strategize accordingly. As Steven Pierce related:

> A highly educated friend with a professional, public-sector job, someone who has been eloquent in condemning corruption in government and Nigerian society, one day surprised me by going on at length about his desire to gain government office in order to provide for his children. Failing such a job, he wanted to be given a government contract. Public works are generally assigned to contractors, but many of these contracts are handed out because of one's proximity to government officials and do not reflect any actual capability to fulfill the assignment on the part of the original contractor. Getting a contract therefore is a lucrative opportunity to get paid by the firms that will actually perform the services, which can recoup their money (and then some) with substantial cost over-runs. My friend saw nothing hypocritical in the disparity between his political beliefs and his ambitions; it is an imperfect world, and life is full of compromises.[68]

At the same time, there is vocal condemnation of corruption. In a 2005–2006 Afrobarometer survey of eighteen Sub-Saharan African countries, a strong majority of people answer that for a government official to give a job to a relative without adequate qualifications is wrong and punishable, although a significant number of respondents answer that it is either "not wrong" or "wrong, but understandable"—for example, 45 percent in Madagascar and 36 percent in Uganda.[69] A higher percentage think that it is wrong and punishable when "a government official demands a favour or an additional payment for some service that is part of his job;" although here too there are similar minorities that answer that it is either "not wrong" or "wrong, but understandable"—40 percent in Madagascar and 37 percent in Uganda.[70]

There are two common interpretations of the disconnect between practice and expressed attitudes. They are not mutually exclusive, and both explanations are probably true. The first is that people do not find corruption as reprehensible as they say they do when asked, and that corruption complaints are actually complaints of unfair sharing and exclusion. Anders writes that "the general rejection of 'corruption' does not imply a clear and unequivocal rejection of practices considered to be corrupt among average Malawians if we investigate this vernacular."[71] He notes that in Malawi, bosses who fail to share properly with their subordinates are likely to have corruption allegations lodged against them.[72] In French West Africa, "actors simultaneously condemn the practices that they justify" by justifying corruption as long as one doesn't "overdo it."[73] One justifies and defends one's own behavior; it is only corruption when someone else does it.

The second explanation is that in a system in which no one else is following the rules, it becomes much more difficult and costly for any individual to follow the rules. Failure to "go along" with the system could not only mean forgone opportunities, but also the inability to access government services and vulnerability to extortion and abuse. As one report of police corruption in Hong Kong in the 1970s put it, the choices of young police officers confronted with the existing system of corruption were to "get on the bus" or "run alongside the bus," but "never stand in front of the bus."[74]

There are individuals willing to pay such a high price in defense of their principles, but they are exceptional. As King Louis XIV explained:

It seems that, in this general disorder, it would be impossible for the most just person not to become corrupt; because the average person would swim alone against the tide of all the others, and curb his tendency to pursue his self-interest, while those that should prevent it cause it by their example.[75]

The king's observation echoes in the frustration of an anticorruption campaigner in Zimbabwe:

John Maketo, an official with an anti-corruption watchdog group in Harare said that corruption in Zimbabwe was so deep-rooted and institutionalized that some people accept it as their sole means of survival. Acknowledging that corruption is on the increase largely due to the economic crisis, Maketo says that Zimbabweans have begun to actually celebrate the most corrupt among them. Only "small fish" are prosecuted for petty corruption; big fish are immune to prosecution as they are cash-rich. "As a country and a people, we have become [so] morally degraded that we accept corruption as a normal practice. If you are not corrupt, people laugh at you," says Maketo.[76]

This suggests that changing such a system would require changing the behavior of many people at the same time. But if the government is poor, and relies on patronage and clientelism as governance strategies, it is worth asking what governance strategy it would use instead.

THE IMPLICATIONS OF PATRONAGE GOVERNANCE. For a poor government, patronage is an important and necessary strategy of governance, and so to the extent that government is a benefit, the strategy can be seen as beneficial. From the perspective of the government, the advantage of patronage as a governance strategy is that upfront costs are low, which makes it an attractive strategy for cash-strapped governments. Many patronage goods can be created and distributed for free. These include exemptions from laws or regulations, such as a license to open a business, import, or export. Government posts can be cheaply created, provided that they don't come with much in the way of salary. And when scarce goods must be allocated, such as government contracts or travel opportunities for government workers, allocating them to clients or to one's own network has no upfront cost. As a political strategy, patronage and clientelism also have the benefit of allowing government actors to allocate scarce resources for maximum political payoff, whether this is to purchase political or electoral support, neutralize opposition, or to leverage the influence of elites in a form of "indirect rule." In the words of one scholar of Africa considering the democratization of the way in which governments hold power,

> Fiscality constitutes the Achilles heel of poor democracies. . . . The advantage of the kind of elite clientelism practiced in authoritarian Africa is its cheapness, and the more ambitious expenditures of a more democratic clientelism will bring with it huge economic risks, particularly in the absence of rapid economic growth.[77]

And of course patronage systems reward those at the top of the system generously, in wealth, power, and social status. Because patrons are supposed to be wealthy and generous, their accumulation of wealth is tolerated as long as it is seen to be matched by their generosity. No wonder that patronage continues to be a common system of rule not only when countries are too poor for alternative strategies of governance, but even as they become wealthier.

But as a governance strategy it also has a number of undesirable side effects, which lead to the marginalization of this strategy in rich liberal democracies. The distribution of private goods is a zero sum game—more for you means less for me. Rather than campaigning for policies to grow the (economic) pie, under patronage and clientelism individuals and groups contest for a slice of the national cake. Government becomes a prize to be shared out rather than a means to an end of improved public welfare. Although patronage does involve redistribution, as a system of redistribution it is neither transparent nor fair. Insiders and their circles are rewarded; others less so, their rewards fading with their distance from power.

Moreover, patronage may enable governance by creating a coalition with an interest in upholding the current government, but the coalition is fluid and unstable. The support that is purchased is support for the current sharing arrangement, not support for government in the abstract or a set of rules that determine how government should operate.

Because patronage uses government itself as a reward, and its apparatus as an instrument of personal profit, the government's ability to make and implement policy is undermined. Neither government contracts nor government positions are given to those best able to carry out the associated duties. In the United States before the establishment of merit-based hiring in the federal civil service, the "spoils system" produced regular mismatches between jobs and the qualifications of those who held them:

> Before 1883 the spoils system largely prevailed, with politicians dictating appointments. Consequently, civil servants had varied and irrelevant backgrounds. In 1867 employees of the Treasurer's Office numbered in previous occupations "7 accountants, 13 bankers, 18 bookkeepers, 27 clerks, 1 detective, 2 druggists, 1 editor, 5 farmers, 1 hackdriver, 1 housekeeper, 1 hotel steward, 16 laborers, 1 lawyer, 1 machinist, 1 manufacturer, 8 mechanics, 14 merchants, 2 messengers, 1 minister, 1 page, 1 porter, 1 postman, 2 salesman, 1 sculptor, 12 students, 1 surveyor, 24 teachers, 2 telegraphists,

1 county treasurer, 1 waiter, 1 washerwoman, 1 watchman, and of no particular occupation, 112."[78]

Government contracts are not given to those best able to implement them,
resulting in inflated costs and uncompleted public works. Poor countries
are pocked with abandoned or collapsing infrastructure projects—half-built
buildings and collapsing roads. Governments may even be motivated to
adopt policies that are not in the public interest for the purpose of generating
more patronage to distribute, such as creating unneeded government positions, contracting for unneeded work, passing regulations whose principal
purpose is to allow the distribution of exemptions, or creating monopolies.

Under patronage systems it is impossible to draw a clear boundary
between public and private actions, roles, or resources. Because corruption
is often defined as "the use of public office for private gain," it is possible to
characterize these countries as suffering from systemic corruption, but the
definition of corruption assumes two clear and distinct spheres, the public
and the private, and a norm that public office is to be used only for the
public benefit. Neither of these exist under patronage systems.

A final downside of patronage as a strategy of governance is that it
makes rule of law impossible, weakening state-made law as a system for
coordinating behavior or predicting the actions of government. This is both
because patronage is a system of opaque individual deals, and because use
of public office for private gain is usually criminal under both domestic
and international law. This important implication is explored more fully
in chapter 6.

Repression

The use of force is another strategy of governance common in poor countries, whose armed forces tend to be deployed within their own territorial
boundaries. Some poor governments are battling insurgents for territorial
control. Others use repression of unarmed civilians as a routine tool of
statecraft, suppressing speech and association, and imprisoning, tortur-
ing, or killing political opponents. Highly repressive poor governments
include Central African Republic, Somalia, Sudan, Eritrea, North Korea,
Uzbekistan, and Turkmenistan.[79] Accordingly, some poor governments
have sizeable military expenditures as a percentage of the budget. In 2008,

according to World Bank data, military expenditure made up 27 percent of Ethiopia's central government expenditure and 20 percent of central government expenditure in the Kyrgyz Republic; in 2009, it was 16 percent of Cambodia's central government expenditure. (The use of opaque security budgets as a cover for diversion of funds and patronage goods should also be kept in mind.)

Although the ill-trained, ill-equipped, underpaid, and under-motivated security forces of poor governments may be adequate to control unarmed civilians, they may crumble in the face of armed opposition. The same poverty, patronage systems, and self-dealing that compete with public policy objectives in civilian administrations undermine military capacity. A special operations trainer with the 2009 U.S. effort to train the Malian military reported on conditions found. The unit was equipped with obsolete rifles, as well as rifles without stocks, hand guards, or with missing or broken sights.[80] He found that a number of Malian soldiers reported that prior to training they had not shot 1,000 rounds in their entire military careers, and that they had abandoned vehicles after an ambush because the drivers had been killed, and only the drivers knew how to drive vehicles.[81] Soldiers were apathetic and lacked initiative, while officers did not conduct training or seek to address and correct obvious problems.

Many poor governments have poor human rights records. Just as poor governments lack the capacity to centralize the distribution of patronage, poor governments also lack the capacity to control and discipline their own security forces. Civilian control of the military may be tenuous or illusory; chains of command may exist in name only. Poor governments also lack the ability to deliver adequate justice, to maintain prisoners in humane conditions, or to protect citizens from abuses. This is particularly likely when the government is engaged in violent conflict to extend or maintain its control over contested parts of its territory. This can make it difficult to distinguish between repression as a deliberate strategy of governance and abuses that occur due to a lack of capacity to prevent them. From the standpoint of a citizen, however, it may be a distinction without a difference.

The U.S. State Department produces annual reports on the observations of human rights in foreign countries that help direct U.S. policy toward those countries. In Burundi,

> The main human rights abuses included torture and extrajudicial executions of detainees, particularly members of certain opposition political

parties, by police, military, and intelligence services; prolonged pre-trial detention of detainees, often without formal charges; harsh and sometimes life-threatening prison conditions; and a lack of judicial independence.

Other human rights abuses included interference with and intimidation of government officials and political opposition members by certain members of the CNDD-FDD and the intelligence and police services. The political rights of certain opposition political parties—including the right to hold party meetings—were restricted arbitrarily, and members of these parties were detained, threatened, and intimidated. Some journalists and members of civil society and nongovernmental organizations (NGOs) who criticized the government and CNDD-FDD were harassed and intimidated.[82]

In North Korea,

Public executions, death by starvation and torture are common in North Korean political prisoner camps, according to testimony given to human rights group Amnesty International. . . . According to testimony, every former inmate at one camp had witnessed a public execution, one child was held for eight months in a cube-like cell so small he couldn't move his body and an estimated 40% of inmates die from malnutrition.

Tortures included placing a plastic bag over the head of a victim and submerging them in water, sleep deprivation, bamboo slivers under the fingernails, and suspending prisoners whose feet and hands have been bound behind them, witnesses said.[83]

Repression of dissent operates through a number of channels. Governments may act to restrict the freedom of speech, or association, or to imprison or torture opponents. According to Freedom House, an NGO focused on promoting human freedom, in 2013 in Eritrea,

The law does not allow independent media to operate in Eritrea, and the government controls all broadcasting outlets. A group of journalists arrested in 2001 remained imprisoned without charge, and the government refuses to provide any information on their status. Reporters Without Borders said in August that it had received confirmation of the deaths of three of the journalists detained in 2001 as well as a fourth, held since 2009. Eleven members of the Asmara-based broadcaster Radio Bana, who were detained in 2009 on suspicion of collaborating with exiled opposition groups, remained in custody without charge. According to the Committee to Protect Journalists, at least 28 journalists were in prison in Eritrea as of December 2012. The government controls the internet infrastructure and is thought to monitor online communications. Foreign media are available to those few who can afford a satellite dish. . . .

Freedoms of assembly and association are not recognized. The government maintains a hostile attitude toward civil society, and independent NGOs are not tolerated. A 2005 law requires NGOs to pay taxes on imported materials, submit project reports every three months, renew their licenses annually, and meet government-established target levels of financial resources. The six remaining international NGOs that had been working in Eritrea were forced to leave in 2011. The government placed strict controls on UN operations in the country, preventing staff from leaving the capital.[84]

Repressive governments may use the justice system instrumentally to suppress regime opponents. Ironically, because poor governments rely on patronage to govern, and patronage is criminalized, accusations of corruption are often used to discredit or disempower political opponents. While they may be true, enforcement is selective and the same activities of regime insiders are ignored. Military tribunals, which operate under rules that provide fewer protections to defendants, are sometimes used to judge civilians, a hallmark of repressive regimes.

At the extreme, some poor country governments simply gun down opponents. In Zimbabwe in 2008, opposition supporters "were tortured, beaten and killed. That campaign of violence was organized and directed by a clique of military commanders and senior politicians close to Mr. Mugabe."[85]

As regional leaders push for free and fair elections in Zimbabwe, a high-ranking general in the country's army has vowed that the security services will ensure that President Robert Mugabe, 87, remains in power, calling his chief political opponent a "national security threat" who "can only be dealt with by people in uniform."

"President Mugabe will only leave office if he sees it fit or dies," a state-controlled newspaper, The Herald, quoted Brig. Gen. Douglas Nyikayaramba as saying in an article on Thursday. The general added, "We will die for him to make sure he remains in power."[86]

In May 2011 the government of Yemen responded to a peaceful protest of unarmed civilians outside a government building by shooting into the crowd, killing four and wounding sixty.

Then the real assault began. Armored vehicles, tanks and bulldozers began converging on the protesters' tent city from all sides. They fired tear gas and water cannons into the square and began shooting protesters at point-blank range. They doused the tents, which extended for hundreds of yards in every direction, with gasoline and lighted them on fire. None of the protesters had weapons.[87]

In postgenocide Rwanda, the ruling party

has imposed various legal restrictions and informal controls on the media, and press freedom groups have accused the government of intimidating independent journalists. In February 2011, Umurabyo newspaper journalists Agnès Uwimana Nkusi and Saïdati Mukakibibi were sentenced to 17 and 7 years, respectively, for denying the genocide, inciting civil disobedience, and defaming public officials based on a 2009 article criticizing President Paul Kagame. Nkusi and Mukakibibi appealed their case in January 2012, and in April, the Supreme Court reduced their sentences to four and three years, respectively. In July, Idriss Gasana Byiringiro, a reporter for the private weekly Chronicles, was detained for 30 days shortly after he submitted a police request to investigate an incident of state security agents interrogating him about his reporting and confiscating his telephone and laptop. In November, the editor of the Kinyarwandan-language paper Umusingi, Stanley Gatera, was fined and sentenced to one year in prison for gender discrimination and inciting "divisionism" in a June opinion piece.

Rwanda's repressive media environment has led many journalists to flee the country and work in exile. In November 2011, Charles Ingabire, editor of the Uganda-based online publication Inyenyeri News and an outspoken critic of the Kagame regime who had fled Rwanda in 2007 due to threats, was shot dead in Uganda. His murder remained unsolved at the end of 2012. There are increasing indications that e-mail and other private communications are being monitored. In August 2012, the lower house adopted a constitutional amendment expanding the surveillance and interception capabilities of security authorities.[88]

More recently, Rwanda has been accused of sending assassins after regime opponents living in South Africa; the government has denied it.[89]

Repression cannot be the only strategy of governance, however. At a minimum, the government must maintain the voluntary support of its enforcers. The frequency of military coups in poor countries demonstrates that this support cannot be taken for granted, particularly given the absence of any long tradition of constitutional rule or civilian supremacy. Scholars studying coups have long noted the relationship between national poverty and coup attempts.[90] Recent coups and coup attempts in poor countries include those in Mali, Madagascar, Niger, Guinea-Bissau, The Gambia, Sri Lanka, Burundi, Togo, Lesotho, Guinea, and Ethiopia.[91]

Conclusion

Patronage and clientelism are not strategies that are reserved for use by poor governments. In the context of the United States, we can think about the practice of appointing as ambassadors campaign finance "bundlers" who lack even a minimal understanding of the country to which they wish to represent the United States.[92] Alternately, we might think of the reported practice of Hillary Clinton of keeping a spreadsheet and points system of supporters as "an improvement on what old-school politicians called a 'favor file.' It meant that when asks rolled in, she and Bill would have at their fingertips all the information needed to make a quick decision—including extenuating, mitigating and amplifying factors—so that friends could be rewarded and enemies punished."[93] It is not that the governments of rich liberal democracies do not ever use patronage, clientelism, or repression as strategies of governance; it is that they rely on them less. Their wealth gives them additional options, including the ability to hold democratic elections, provide the rule of law, deliver universal public goods and services, and enjoy the popular support and legitimacy that comes from providing them.

As rich liberal democracies created more impersonal rule-based government institutions, they stigmatized the older, personalistic strategies and more sharply defined the distinction between public and private roles and spheres. "Corruption" is commonly defined as "the use of public office for private gain," a definition that implies the existence of two separate spheres: the existence of a public office, and the existence of a public benefit for which such public offices should be used. From this vantage, poor governments are often termed "systemically corrupt." But this is a misnomer. Corruption, in the context of a rich liberal democracy, is a deviant and criminal act in a system that strives to provide services according to impersonal criteria. For poor governments that rely on patronage and clientelism, however, the monetization of government office is a consequence both of the way in which public power is exercised and of the incapacity of poor governments to displace personalistic social insurance mechanisms by providing the rule of law, regular and adequate government salaries, and adequate impersonal means of public service delivery. "Corruption" is system-wide, common, and even expected. Many poor governments' positions are routinely monetized; there is a secondary market in lucrative government positions; and such behavior is considered unsurprising and rarely punished. This sharing out of government wealth is the glue that holds poor governments together and makes it possible for them to govern. There may be better ways for poor governments to govern, but it will not be from the popular legitimacy that comes from democratic elections, the rule of law, and the wide delivery of public goods and services because poor governments cannot afford to provide them.

Understanding the way in which poor governments hold power is necessary if we wish to understand or predict their behavior. For example, the demands of patronage systems often dictate government actions that would be inexplicable if one assumed that the primary purpose of government was to make public policy or to deliver public goods and services effectively under the rule of law. Such actions might include, for example, a strong preference for easily monetizable infrastructure projects; a refusal to fire people who are obviously not working; the creation of a host of new ministries; or the adoption of burdensome regulations that can then be used to allocate discretionary exemptions to favorites.

As we discarded these disfavored strategies of governance we criminalized them and used our international influence to press for their criminalization worldwide. The monetization of government offices is illegal under domestic law in most countries. As a consequence, where patronage and the monetization of government authority and office are a central strategy of governance, law cannot rule. The criminalization of one of the government's principal strategies of governance leads to a divorce between the formal rules and institutions of government and the actual routine operation of government. In chapter 6 we will consider the weak rule of law in poor governments in more detail.

6. The Rule of Law

"In all that we do, we must remember that what sets America apart is not solely our power—it is the principles upon which our union was founded. We are a nation that brings our enemies to justice while adhering to the rule of law, and respecting the rights of all our citizens."

—PRESIDENT OBAMA (2011)[1]

"We have before us the opportunity to forge for ourselves and for future generations a new world order—a world where the rule of law, not the law of the jungle, governs the conduct of nations."

—PRESIDENT GEORGE H. W. BUSH,

ANNOUNCING OPERATION DESERT SHIELD (1990)

"What's the constitution among friends?"[2]

—SENATOR GEORGE W. PLUNKITT, TAMMANY HALL (1905)

Poor governments govern differently. They do not get their revenue from the same sources, they do not use the same strategies of governance (and in particular do not rely as heavily on the legitimacy that comes from democratic elections and the supply of public goods), and they do not use state-made law as a coordinating mechanism for government and society to the same extent that rich liberal democracies do.

There is always a "gap between law on the books and law in action," but when governments are poor that gap is especially wide. Enforcing laws costs money that poor governments don't have. The governance strategy of patronage is incompatible with rule of law, because patronage rests on individual deals, while the rule of law involves transparent rules impersonally applied. The adoption by poor governments of laws from rich liberal democracies also makes rule of law more difficult. They may assume the existence of institutions that poor governments can't afford. They criminalize the strategies of governance on which poor governments rely, such as repression or patronage, making governments into criminal organizations. There may not be much demand for rule according to state-made law, particularly when it clashes with local norms.

As a consequence, rule of law—by which a government derives its authority from its compliance with the law and governs according to law—is weak, and the law is not a reliable guide to government processes or a predictor of government action. In the same way, legal reform is not a powerful tool for changing either government or social behavior. Interactions with government, even for routine services, must often be individually negotiated according to local norms, which makes government action opaque and less easily predictable.

Weak Rule of Law

Both because they believe in the rule of law as part of the governance ideal and because law occupies a central social role in coordinating behavior, Americans tend to reach for the law and formal institutions when seeking to understand the operations of a foreign government. These instincts serve them poorly when dealing with poor countries. To be sure, no country fulfills the rule of law ideal. As early as 1910, Roscoe Pound remarked on the gap between "law on the books and law in action" in the United States.[3] But in poor countries, state-made law is less powerful and plays a less important role; the connection between law and behavior is more tenuous. The day-to-day operation of government may have little to do with the formal laws and policies. The organizational chart of government may have nothing to do with the actual allocation of governmental authority. Laws are selectively or sporadically implemented or enforced, or not at all. Human rights are not effectively guaranteed, and government actors are frequently engaged in illegal behavior.

Assessments of the rule of law in poor countries repeatedly emphasize the powerlessness or irrelevance of laws and the impunity of government actors. In Yemen,

> On paper, Yemen has an elected parliament and president, a multi-party system, an independent judiciary, and the framework for a democratically elected local government. In reality, however, these institutions do not produce or transfer political power. Instead, power and wealth are produced and transmitted through a highly informal, yet deeply patterned web of tribally- and regionally-based patronage relationships.[4]

According to another assessment,

> Yemen's political elite views the country's formal laws as generally quite well developed on paper, but lacking in implementation. In practice,

however, ordinary citizens do not feel they have access to justice through the formal state system. . . . Previous [USAID Democracy and Governance] assessments have noted that the administration of justice in Yemen is among the most underdeveloped in the Arab world.[5]

An assessment of the West African country of Benin stated:

There was constant reference to the fact that virtually all needed laws exist, and the courts are there to enforce them, thus indicating a perception of relatively few shortcomings in the formal structures of the rule of law. Nonetheless, there were also frequent references to the widely held belief that "impunité totale" marks legal and political life in Benin. The notion of total impunity was articulated equally by outside observers and critics of the government . . . as well as those who might have interests in being less critical, including representatives of the state, the judicial sector, and numerous donors.[6]

In Nepal,

Though the courts are functioning and the legal framework seems adequate for a judiciary to function, the ongoing conflict and the current political crisis render the term **"rule of law"** almost meaningless. The vast majority of citizens do not rely upon the law—and the state's ability to uphold laws—to secure their rights and ensure their security. Much of this is a direct impact of the conflict: the state is not capable of providing security, or upholding law and order in its conflict-affected areas. At times the state itself is a threat to personal security.[7]

The same kinds of observations are made by sectoral specialists, focusing not on countries, but on their areas of expertise. A tax specialist, for example, writes:

Although differences between law and practice exist in industrial countries, the set of tax statutes by and large approximates the actual tax system. For many developing countries, however, the gap between tax law and actual taxation is so wide that one bears virtually no resemblance to the other. A reading of statutes relating to personal and company income tax, capital gains, customs duties, and general sales taxes in a given developing country might lead the observer to believe that the country's legislative tax system was close to European or North American models. The actual workings of the system, however, are determined by administrators who collect a core group of easy-to-administer taxes.[8]

A public administration expert writing about Bangladesh concludes:

Our focus . . . has been on formal structure [of the public administration], but gaps between formal structure as reflected in legal instruments and regulations, and "real world" operations of such structures are commonplace in the politics of most nations. In Bangladesh, the gap is especially wide.[9]

Weak rule of law is manifested in human rights abuses, corruption, and other forms of government illegality. The legal codes of poor governments guarantee human rights, but poor governments are unable to protect their citizens from abuses; often, they are the abusers, particularly in countries with more authoritarian governments, and in countries in conflict. All poor governments practice torture at least occasionally, and most practice torture frequently.[10] With untrained and unaccountable security forces that lack the basic equipment to carry out their functions, torture can often seem like the most accessible and least expensive investigatory tool. In 2009, the U.S. State Department summarized the state of human rights protections in the Central African Republic, offering a laundry list of human rights violations:

Government abuses included security forces continuing to commit extra-judicial executions in the north; torture, beatings, detention, and rape of suspects and prisoners; impunity, particularly among the military; harsh and life-threatening conditions in prisons and detention centers; arbitrary arrest and detention, prolonged pretrial detention, denial of fair trial; official corruption; occasional intimidation and restrictions on the press; and restrictions on freedom of movement and on workers' rights. Mob violence resulted in deaths and injuries. Societal abuses included female genital mutilation (FGM), discrimination against women and Pygmies; trafficking in persons; forced labor; and child labor, including forced child labor. Freedom of movement remained limited in the north because of actions by security forces, armed bandits, and armed groups.

Sporadic fighting between government forces and armed groups continued to internally displace persons and increase the number of refugees.

Armed groups, some of which were unidentified, continued to kill, beat, and rape civilians and loot and burn villages in the north. Armed groups kidnapped, beat, raped, and extorted money from local populations. There were reports of children as young as 12 serving as fighters in armed groups.[11]

While government actors continued to kill suspected bandits, bandits continued to kill citizens, and citizens continued to kill persons suspected of witchcraft, which remains a crime under the penal code.[12] Even government officials are not safe:

> On February 5, Lieutenant Olivier Koudemon, alias Gbangouma, and two other members of the presidential guard confronted Commissioner of Police Daniel Sama over the commissioner's right to carry a firearm in Bangui while off duty. An altercation ensued and the commissioner was beaten to death. The permanent military tribunal (PMT) heard the case in April and found sufficient grounds to try the three. At year's end, Gbangouma and the other two remained free. No additional information was available.[13]

Poor governments are frequently involved in criminal behavior. The most visible to the public is corruption. The monetization of government office, discussed in chapter 5, is criminalized in the domestic laws of poor governments. Yet the bribes that citizens must pay to those charged with rendering public services or who are given coercive authority—nurses and doctors, tax collectors, utility providers, police officers, and school teachers—frustrate them daily. In a survey of twelve Sub-Saharan African countries, when asked how many civil servants are involved in "corruption" defined as "bribes, gifts or benefits" (and not including favoritism or nepotism), on average 38 percent of respondents said that "almost all" or "most" civil servants were corrupt; in Zimbabwe, 65 percent gave these answers.[14] The monetization of contracting authority is a violation of law and results in the visible failure of public works and infrastructure projects. Many poor government actors are engaged in other forms of organized crime, including embezzlement, smuggling, banditry and looting, counterfeiting, and human and drug trafficking. In Vietnam, for example, where illegal logging resulted in a loss of a third of its forest cover between 1985 and 2000, the chief perpetrators are reported to be senior members of government, including the military in Vietnam and Cambodia.[15]

While the criminal behavior of government actors is exceptional in rich liberal democracies, and the threat of punishment of such behavior is a credible one, in poor countries many if not most government employees are engaged in some form of criminal behavior, and the likelihood of punishment is minimal. Where the criminal activity is organized, government actors who refuse to participate may be punished by being fired, demoted, denounced, imprisoned, or killed, in part because of the potential threat they represent to the system. On the other hand, when government actors enter the system, they can be controlled with threats of selective criminal prosecution.

Why Law Doesn't Rule

There are several interrelated reasons why rule of law is weak in countries with poor governments. Poor governments have limited resources to implement and enforce laws. Patronage, a frequent governance strategy of poor governments, is in tension with the rule of law. This is especially true because poor governments have laws modeled on those of rich liberal democracies, criminalizing the use of public office for private gain. Finally, there may not be much demand for rule of the existing law, particularly when it is imported.

TOO POOR. Some studies have pointed to a strong relationship between weak rule of law and national poverty.[16] Poor countries have poor governments that lack the resources to draft, disseminate, implement, and enforce laws. Most laws are passed without the benefit of any fiscal analysis that would allow the government to determine if it has the resources to enforce the law. There may be no resources to ensure a law's implementation or to enforce it once enacted. Police, lawyers, prosecutors, clerks, judges, prison officials, and guards are few in relation to the population and poorly trained, equipped, and paid. Police have no functioning radios, no gas for their cars, and no cartridges for their guns. Judges run out of paper with which to write opinions halfway through the year. Prisons do not have food for their prisoners, space to house them, the ability to provide them with medical care, or the ability to prevent prison breaks.

Nor does the government have the capacity to ensure legal consistency and coherence. Poor governments' legislatures are unable to undertake the work of systematically repealing conflicting legislation. The legal systems of poor countries are a jumble of conflicting and poorly disseminated laws. As a consequence, the laws of poor countries are like rings of a tree; one set of laws may date back to the colonial period; a second set of contradictory laws mark postindependence periods of socialism or military dictatorship; a third set mark subsequent shifts to the market economy and democracy, some passed as specific conditions of the receipt of foreign aid. Some countries have, in addition, multiple legal systems, such as religious or customary legal systems, with customs varying by location or ethnic group. Citizens are unable to learn what the law is, and few can afford to avail themselves of legal counsel.

Determining what the law is and what law applies is a challenge further complicated by the difficulty of obtaining copies of the law, whether in hard copy or electronic form. Lower court judges in particular may not have law books. Different law may be applied in different cities simply because a different subset of law books is available. This is a particular issue in conflict environments, as government archives and libraries do not fare well in war. The result is that it is often not easy to say what law applies or what actions are legal or illegal.

Poverty is one reason why poor governments fail to honor treaties, particularly those that require affirmative government action.[17] One scholar found that more children survive in countries that ratified the Convention of the Rights of the Child, which commits a country to invest in children's primary health care—except in poor countries.[18] Similarly, a scholar looking at the implementation of environmental treaties in the Pacific Islands points to lack of capacity, information, and funding as chief impediments to implementation.[19]

PATRONAGE. Just as a patronage strategy of governance undermines the ability of the government to implement policies or deliver public goods and services more generally, it also undermines the ability of the government to deliver rule of law. Patronage is based on personal relationships and individual deals that span government, business, and social arenas. This is the opposite of governance according to a set of impersonal rules impartially and universally applied. If a benefit is provided equally to everyone, then it cannot be used as a patronage good. Moreover, personal exemptions from the law, such as exemptions from customs or taxes or queuing, are one of the cheapest patronage goods that a government can hand out; they cost the government nothing up front. But such exemptions undermine the impartial and universal application of rules.

Justice personnel—prosecutors, judges, clerks, police, and prison staff—are themselves part of the patronage system, monetizing their positions, which undermines the impartiality of justice. In surveys on the perception of corruption, citizens routinely report the police and the judiciary as the most corrupt sectors of government. For example, in Afghanistan one study found that the most common type of bribe paid was for police protection and disposition of a court case.[20] In Bangladesh

the most startling findings of the baseline survey revealed that about one-half of the complainants (49.5%) made prior arrangement with the police for disposal of their cases; a majority (55%) of the prior arrangements was not to send the disputes to the court, while nearly two-fifths (38%) of the arrangements was to send the complaints to the court for disposal. About 71% of the respondents reported that police deliberately delayed sending the cases to the court.

More than two-thirds (68.1%) of the complainants reported to have payments to the police for filing complaints as First Information Report (FIR). Payment to the police was made directly by the complainants (40%), followed by payments through office employees (34%) and through local dalal (26%). It is, therefore, not surprising that the public opinion of the police is very low. The survey revealed that 96.3% of the total households expressed the view by way of their complete agreement or general agreement with the assertion that it was almost impossible to get help from the police without money or influence. . . .

The other startling piece of information is that the standard of the legal system, particularly the legal profession, has plummeted. More than three-fifths (63%) of the households involved in court cases reported that they had to bribe the court officials. The proportion of rural households paying bribe money to court officials was 63.6% compared to that of 57.1% of urban households. Cash for bribe was paid to the court employees by 73.1 of households, followed by 16.3% of households to opponent's lawyer. Majority of households (53.3%) made payments for bribe directly, i.e., in person, and 28.1% of households through the lawyers.[21]

LEGAL TRANSFERS. Another reason for weak rule of law is the nature of the law itself. Much of the formal legal system of poor countries is imported from, copied from, or heavily influenced by rich liberal democracies. These transfers are often not a good fit for local norms or conditions, with the consequence that people do not know them, do not want them, or cannot comply with them.

The transfer of laws from rich liberal democracies to poor countries has proceeded through a number of different channels. The first was the inheritance of the colonial legal and political system by former colonies on independence.[22] A second channel is imitation. Elites in poor countries are often educated in rich liberal democracies, and elites from former colonies are likely to have been educated by the former colonizing power. A third mechanism of transfer is global integration and foreign aid. Accession to international organizations such as the World Trade Organization, for example, may require specific legal changes that usually follow the model of rich liberal democracies. Foreign aid donors may condition the receipt of foreign aid on the passage of specific laws; foreign technical assistants hired to help poor countries reform their laws are likely to replicate the legal systems with which they are familiar.

Legal imports may also be incapable of implementation because implementation depends on the existence of other structures or social conditions that are present in rich liberal democracies but are missing in poor countries. For example, some poor governments have enacted laws against outside employment for government employees, imitating richer countries that sought to ensure that government employees are not subject to conflicts of interest. However, in rich countries, government employees receive regular salaries, and in poor countries they may not be paid for months.

Compliance with law is more likely if the law accords with peoples' sense of morality and obligation.[23] However, where laws conflict with existing norms and existing structures of power, compliance is less likely. An example of this type of failure is the challenge of using law reform to improve the social position of women and children. For example, the Social Institutions and Gender Index attempts to rank countries according to the social institutions that obstruct women's access to resources, evaluating the family code, civil liberties, physical integrity, preference for sons, and ownership rights.[24] In its ranking of 102 non-OECD (Organisation for Economic Co-operation and Development) countries, twelve poor countries are in the bottom twenty. Notably, among the bottom five, four have ratified the Convention on the Elimination of All Forms of Discrimination Against Women: Afghanistan (2003); Sierra Leone (1988); Mali (1985); and Yemen (1984).[25] Although the legal campaign against child marriage has been largely successful, the practice continues in secret, particularly where people are poor.[26] According to the United Nations in 2005, in Southern Asia, 48 percent of young women are married before they are eighteen; in Africa, 42 percent; in Latin American and the Caribbean, 29 percent.[27] In Chad, tradition and the penal code set the minimum age for marriage at thirteen (and even this is not regularly enforced).[28] A proposed bill that provided for equality for men and women was blocked on religious objections.

A critical problem for the transfer of laws from rich liberal democracies to poor governments, however, is that these legal codes reflect modern good governance values. Although Western governments relied on patronage and repression to govern when they were poor, as they became richer they relied less on these strategies and more on the provision of public goods and services to citizens. They then criminalized these strategies of governance, on which modern poor governments depend. Western-financed anticorruption campaigns have attempted to criminalize monetization of government positions worldwide. Poor governments are incapable of complying with these legal codes if they are to govern.

By definition, the criminalization of the governance strategies used by poor governments makes them criminal organizations. The blatant contradiction between the legal system and the routine operation of government deprives both of moral authority. As an opposition leader in Cambodia put it, considering the delayed passage of the anticorruption law, "Thieves can't catch thieves. . . . They cannot approve the corruption law. They will lose their income and their opportunities."[29] As the Ghanaian rice smuggler explained to his interviewer, "I wish there was a level playing field for all importers, but if I don't smuggle, somebody else would do it anyway. So tell me: Why should I miss the opportunity to get more money when even state institutions themselves aid us in making these corrupt deals?"[30] Or as a taxi driver in Kenya put it: "Who will follow the law if the executive cannot uphold it?"[31]

The tension between laws criminalizing corruption and the operation of patronage politics is illustrated by the difficulty in catching and prosecuting "big fish." In 2001, while awaiting debt relief estimated at $3 billion, the government of Tanzania purchased a military radar system from BAE, the British arms company, for 28 million pounds. Tanzania has no air force.

However, as the *Guardian* reported, "it was claimed the Commander system, which was portable and festooned with anti-jamming devices, could also be used for civilian air traffic control."[32] The deal was called "corrupt" and "useless" by British secretary of state for international development Clare Short. It was investigated by the United Kingdom Serious Fraud Office, and the results of its investigation were passed to the head of Tanzania's anticorruption bureau for prosecution. BAE may have paid a commission of 31 percent of the contract value into Swiss bank accounts to secure the contract.[33] But a U.S. diplomatic cable released by WikiLeaks detailed a 2007 meeting between the senior Tanzanian anticorruption official and U.S. diplomats regarding the prospects of prosecution of those implicated in the deal done under the previous administration of President Mkapa. In a cable titled "Big Fish Still Risky Catch in Tanzania," the U.S. Deputy Chief of Mission reported that the official was receiving threats and feared for his life:

> He called the deal "dirty" and said it involved officials from the Ministry of Defence and at least one or two senior level military officers. . . . He noted that President Kikwete does not appear comfortable letting the law handle corruption cases which might implicate top level officials. . . . President Kikwete is hesitant to pursue cases which may implicate former President Benjamin Mkapa: "Kikwete is soft on Mkapa. He does not want to set a precedent by going after his predecessor." . . .
>
> In our January 2007 meeting with [the prosecutor], he said his primary goal as the newly appointed Director General of the Prevention of Corruption Bureau would be to prosecute "big fish." He told us point blank, however, that cases against the Prime Minister or President were off the table. Now, he has revealed that former President Benjamin Mkapa and certain members of Mkapa's inner circle may also be untouchable, many of whom have ministerial or sub-ministerial posts in Kikwete's government. Thus, while President Kikwete's talk against corruption might be tough, he is clearly treading carefully and the jury remains out on his commitment to tackling high-level corruption.[34]

Widespread government criminal activity transforms the function of legal enforcement. Because so many people are violators, enforcement becomes discretionary and selective, as where anticorruption campaigns are used as a means to attack political opponents. The ability to arrest any government actor on a corruption charge at any moment gives the executive a powerful political tool. Outside observers have been fooled into seeing an exercise of judicial independence in the arrest and trial of members of government who are out of favor, members of a former government by a current government, or members of the opposition, as frequently happens in anticorruption campaigns when the West is clamoring for convictions.

Alternately, the executive can block enforcement of judicial decisions. The judiciary depends on the executive branch for the implementation of its decisions, whether it is the arrest and imprisonment of an individual criminal or an order to cease an illegal executive branch practice. Where the executive branch is not interested in enforcement or implementation, it does not happen. This not only results in a lack of enforcement of judicial decisions, but it also has a chilling effect on judicial decisions themselves. Some savvy judges avoid issuing decisions and orders that will have no practical effect, except to annoy the executive and call attention to the impotence of the judiciary.

DEMAND. Finally, it is not clear that there is strong popular demand in poor countries for the rule of law. Most disputes are handled through alternative mechanisms, such as customary or traditional justice systems, which may not have legal status, apply rules of the formal legal system, or be formally recognized in the country's justice system. The British aid agency estimates that "in many developing countries, traditional or customary legal systems account for 80% of total cases."[35] In Afghanistan,

> traditional justice mechanisms have the advantage of being familiar to the population and are less costly and more accessible than courts. Decisions made by local shuras and jirgas are generally consensual, and therefore reach a final resolution much faster than state courts. They focus more on making the parties whole through equitable outcomes rather than adversarial courtroom processes that have winners and losers or that punish wrongdoers. Also, traditional justice resolutions are more likely to be enforced than those of state institutions because disregarding decisions of respected local leaders can be disruptive to social harmony.[36]

A number of factors influence how people choose to resolve disputes, including cost, distance, familiarity, time spent, complexity, and the type of dispute.[37]

There may not be demand for the existing body of state-made law, particularly when the law is an alien import. People may prefer to be governed by rules that coincide with their own sense of justice, administered by institutions that are local and familiar. In some poor countries, to the extent that there is demand for the rule of any one law, it is a demand for shar'ia, Islamic law, not secular state-made law. Yet because the West objects to shar'ia, it sees this demand for the rule of law as retrograde.

There may not even be demand for rule of law in the abstract. Impersonal rules are necessarily imperfect and blunt instruments, which, when applied impartially, work injustices in the individual case, and they often reflect the interests of those in power. As Anatole France said, "The law, in its majestic equality, forbids the rich and the poor alike to sleep under bridges, to beg in the streets, and to steal bread."[38] People may prefer less justice and more equity or mercy, fewer rules and more situational justice and personal treatment, especially if the law is not seen as impartial. A story from Niger illustrates that perspective:

> Two old women in a Nigerien village, Kouli and Kouti, were in charge of selling the water from the foot-operated water pump by the bucket. They were appointed by the committee for the management of the pump. They were both given nicknames. Kouli, who refused any favours and did not allow a woman to take water without paying, was nicknamed "ceferia," the ungodly one, and Kouti, who was more flexible and accommodating, became known as "alsilaama," the believer.[39]

In rule-based systems, some people find the very idea of strategic or utilitarian friendships distasteful, and find the effort to win favorable personal treatment to be dishonorable and therefore demeaning. In relations-based systems, the impersonal application of rules can be seen as unfair, as an insult to individuality, and a repudiation of friendship and social obligations. The preference for the former is by no means universal in any country. Families, for example, do not operate through impersonal rules. The shift from a personal system to a rule-based system advantages some and disadvantages others. Not surprisingly, those who are favored by the rules are more interested in the rule of law.

As long as non-state mechanisms are doing a passable job of preserving the peace, and as long as people do not have much interaction with the government, there may not be much demand for the government itself, much less for government-backed rule of law, even though traditional dispute resolution mechanisms can be biased and unfair. Compared to village-level or local-level dispute resolution, the formal court system is very slow, more complex, less transparent, more expensive, and applies rules that are alien or counterintuitive. It also requires trusting the judgment of strangers who may have different values, who do not know any of the persons involved, and who might, in the eyes of the litigants, have limited moral authority because of their gender, age, religion, ethnicity, or clan.

Even where existing means of rule enforcement are feeble, and people suffer from insecurity and conflict, they may not demand the rule of law, a benefit they have never known, but instead may adapt their behavior to reduce their risk. In Madagascar, for example, grain traders slept with their merchandise at night in order to protect it, hired fewer employees than they might like in order to control theft, inspected all merchandise personally, and did not do business on credit.[40] In choosing people with whom to interact or transact, people may avoid strangers and instead interact and transact with people about whom they have information, with whom they have long-term relationships, or whose behavior is likely to be constrained because of common interests, dependencies, and social circles. They rely on membership in common groups as a vetting process and on such groups to help with dispute resolution should any disputes arise. This is one reason why family and ethnic networks play such an important role in facilitating trade in poor countries.

Less Transparent, Less Predictable

In countries with stronger rule of law, interactions with the government are usually impersonal, and people expect to receive government services as of right. Social connections and even bribes are still sometimes used, but they are used in an effort to get more favorable treatment than the law allows. In countries where the rule of law is weak, whether rich or poor, even routine government services must be individually negotiated with money, favors, and connections. Relationships with those in power become a form of currency, deliberately cultivated. In Laos,

> two extra-legal factors commonly influence cases of law: conformity with current policy of the Party, often pointed out by Party officials

seeking a particular outcome; and attempts by interested parties to bring extra-legal pressures to bear in the form of personal visits, telephone calls and written notes (less often, as these can be incriminating) from politically powerful friends or relatives. As the Lao say, winning a legal case, especially in a civil dispute, depends on who has "the strongest string."[41]

Even those businesses that have cultivated good political contacts have to make regular payments to their protectors, and perhaps also the Party. Political contacts are not to escape payment, but to minimise it and to avoid additional payments demanded by lower level officials or other ministries or Party branches. Additional payments also have to be made for special favours, such as the awarding of a contract.[42]

In Vietnam,

It's about who you know. A business owner's visit to the tax office will be smoother and faster if it's accompanied by someone who can guide you to a connection—an official who will "sort things out" for you after receiving an envelope.

Sometimes, an envelope is handed over with a discreet muttering about a "gift" to the children. Other times, prices and "fees" are discussed directly, in the open. No matter what, you can expect to pay lower taxes if you know the right people and offer the right amount.

State utility employees will change your wires or fix your power meter after you make an initial "investment" of about US$60, but your monthly bill will be a third of what it was before.

If you wish to keep your shop open past official business closing hours, or if you want to use the sidewalk to park customers' scooters, a few envelopes passed into the right hands will do the trick.[43]

In the Democratic Republic of Congo, a journalist reports:

Mary-Ann can't get over it. She paid US$7,500 for customs services at the Ruzizi border station, which separates Bukavu, a city in eastern Democratic Republic of Congo, from the Rwandan city of Kamembe. In return, she received a receipt for only US$1,500 of her payment for the six containers of goods she imported from Dubai. The rest of the money was shared among customs officers—before her own eyes in that very office.

"We're not going to change this country. The example comes from the top," the customs officers' boss told her.

But Alphonso (who, like Mary-Ann, declined to use his last name while talking about corruption) never pays to bring his goods into the country, and he is one of the richest businessmen in the east of D.R. Congo.

"Why should I give money earned with difficulty to the government? I have relatives and friends at all levels of the province and the country. I can easily get all the false invoices that I want," he said. "In addition, I pay customs officers better than the state pays them. Consequently, they turn a blind eye and do not even check my goods."[44]

In Ghana, instead of taxing importers, the customs service is an organized bribe collection agency. One author describes the smuggling of rice into Ghana from neighboring Côte d'Ivoire:

Asare had arrived at midnight the night before we spoke with a bus full of smuggled rice. "I came in the company of over 13 smugglers last night from Abidjan through the Anyamaah barrier to our secret routes that lead us to Kofibadukrom. Overall, over 10,000 bags of rice entered into Ghana illegally just last night alone." This crime, he added, is perpetrated against the state every day.

According to Asare, the first and most crucial step in the smuggling process is paying an agent to introduce the importer to the CEPS [Customs, Excise and Preventive Service] boss. Once the agent clears the way, the two set up an appointment to negotiate the bribe. "Also, before we meet, there's a good old tradition of giving the CEPS boss one sack of rice to appease him and help soften his negotiating stand."

Asare himself negotiated with the CEPS boss over the amount of rice they would allow him to bring in and what the price would be. At the conclusion, Asare paid the CEPS boss 50 cedis (US$40). The CEPS accountant collected the money, but did not issue any receipt as is usually done with legitimate imports.

"He just told me to go with my truckload of rice," Asare said with a broad smile, "No paying of duties, not even Value Added Tax (VAT)! I smiled, thanked him and shook his hand for a job well done. That 50 cedis (US$40) was not even close to the usual price for a bag of rice."[45]

Those doing business in China depend on cultivating *guanxi* (personal connections or relationships) with government officials.[46] "If you do not have connections to look after you at different levels of government, they can find excuses to suspend your business," said one interviewee to Xin and Pearce in their study of guanxi. A story told to them by another interviewee is illustrative and worth repeating in its entirety:

My company had bad luck. We were audited for income tax fraud. The Auditing Bureau has Red Eye Disease [jealousy]. Whenever they see a private company making money, they come and find trouble.

The tax auditor just showed up one day and wanted to see company books. There are no standardized rules on how to keep books in China, especially for private companies like ours. If they want to find fault with your income tax, they will always find something wrong. If we had been found guilty of tax fraud, we could have faced thousands of yuan in fines and the possible suspension of our business license. All our hard work would have been gone like the wind. Our accountant was very worried. I called my administrative assistant, X, into my office and told him the situation. He smiled and said, "Give me a 2,500 yuan allowance [equivalent to a middle managers' six-month salary] and I will take care of everything." I had no choice. So I said, "I will give you 2,500 yuan, but you will lose your job if you cannot handle this crisis."

By noon, my phone rang. X asked me to go to lunch with the auditors, at the best restaurant in the city. We hired a Mercedes Benz and went to lunch. The auditors kept saying that they only needed a working lunch. I was worried that X had gone overboard, but X was right. After expensive drinks and Peking duck, the head auditor started to praise our accounting system, saying how good and efficient it looked. This lunch lasted three hours and cost plenty, but it saved my company. After lunch the head auditor left me a notice requesting a 2,500 yuan income tax supplement. The reason he had to force us to pay the supplement was that he had to report to his boss on what he accomplished that day. Later on I found out that X's father is a good friend of the head auditor.

There are too many threats for small companies like mine. There are no laws to protect you. The only way we can protect ourselves is through personal connections, trust, and being flexible. I hired X, a high school graduate, with his father's connections in mind. It does not sound right but everyone does it; you have to be open-minded.[47]

Xin and Pearce wrote "In China, it is difficult to find executives willing to talk about their *guanxi*." Accordingly, to complete their study, they used some guanxi of their own: "To overcome this problem, the first author drew the sample from the business connections of a close relative who is an executive for the state owned insurance company in that city."[48]

Daniel Smith, an American anthropologist married to a Nigerian woman, described his own attempt to get a vehicle registration and a driver's license in Nigeria. He did not know anyone in the office personally, and so attempted to establish a personal connection through common ground. The entire episode is so torturous that it can only be summarized here; Smith's blow-by-blow account runs for several pages. He went armed both with his intent to pay any reasonable "extra fee" and with Frank, a Nigerian friend. After explaining his need to Mr. Okonkwo, the official in charge of the vehicle registration,

> Mr. Okonkwo's face grew somber. "Unfortunately," he continued, "there are no number plates. Imo State plates are finished." Frank immediately jumped in, knowing from experience that scarcity, whether real or faked, was a typical ploy for a bureaucrat to seek a bigger bribe. "Mr. Dan is our in-law," Frank announced. "He is just as much Nigerian as you or me. You should treat him as a brother. We need the registration and plates as soon as possible." With these few words Frank had communicated with Mr. Okonkwo both that I was willing to "put something on top" of the official fees and that he should not try to take undue advantage of my being a foreigner.[49]

Smith then reinforced this message by chatting with the office workers in Igbo, the local language, about his wife, her village, and his own familiarity with local foods. They then contracted with Mr. Okonkwo to handle their transaction, which would include paying bribes to the other officials whose cooperation would be needed to obtain all of the official documents. Mr. Okonkwo was able to obtain the license plates, but not the driver's license.

> Frank was irate. He suspected that Mr. Okonkwo had simply pocketed the extra money for the urgent processing of the driver's license rather than settling whoever operated the machine. He demanded that Mr. Okonkwo accompany us to the office where driver's licenses were issued.

There, Smith explained to the woman in charge that he had applied for a driver's license and that Mr. Okonkwo had promised to bring it. She explained that the office had no electricity to produce driver's licenses, and no gas for the back-up generator. Frank then asked to meet with the woman alone, where he told the woman that

> we had already paid enough money on top to get the license urgently, and that it was up to Mr. Okonkwo to settle her and assure that my license was issued immediately. She was apparently irritated with Okonkwo for "eating alone" and promised Frank that the license would be ready the next day. I have no idea how much Mr. Okonkwo had to pay to assuage the licensing officer. [50]

When Smith returned the following day to get his driver's license and asked for Mr. Okonkwo, he was directed instead to Mr. Okonkwo's supervisor. "Holding my plastic driver's license in her hand she asked, 'So Mr. Smith, you wanted to collect all your papers and your license without ever seeing me?'"[51]

OPACITY AND PREDICTABILITY. When even routine interaction with government must be individually negotiated, the operation of government becomes opaque. The rule of law ideal assumes that the law is public, accessible, and understandable. In theory, in a government of laws anyone can learn how government power is likely to be wielded by consulting the law. In countries with weak rule of law, where government is based on personal relations, those seeking information must consult government actors personally. This is why when interviewees in Madagascar were asked whom they would consult for advice if they had a case in court, 40 percent said that they would go to the court building and ask for help from court personnel. The interviewees perceived the system to be one governed by people and personalities, rather than by general rules. This answer was given even by those who were the most educated, and even those who anticipated hiring a lawyer.[52] In Laos, "the workings of the party are opaque to outsiders, based as they are on networks of personal contacts, alliances and deals. Foreign representatives seldom know where to bring pressure to bear—with the exception of the Vietnamese, and they are happy to see the system continue."[53] Where power is decentralized, even government leaders may not know how the government is doing its business.

If criminality or illegality has any consequences, either through occasional enforcement of the law or in the court of public opinion, government actors may hesitate to explain some of the regular practices of government. This is another reason why the operations of governments with weak rule of law are opaque. The small circle of people who actually know how things are running may not want to share that information if it can be used against them. Bureaucrats may be afraid of being sanctioned, prosecuted, or compelled to share with competitors; politicians may hesitate for fear that they will give fuel to their domestic or international enemies; and governments may hesitate because the West (somewhat erratically) prizes rule of law and demands that at least lip service be paid to it.

For example, Liberia's much-abused Maritime Registry generates millions of dollars of revenue that have previously been embezzled, but this revenue has never been included in the budget or publicly reported.

> Maritime revenue is not reflected in Liberia's annual budget as it should be, and all transactions are secret. The [Bureau of Maritime Affairs]'s new chief, Beyan Kesselly, after long ignoring public outcry for accountability and openness in reporting the Registry's revenue, told the media that releasing financial information was a security threat. Finance Minister Augustine Ngafuan concurred.
>
> Ngafuan has warned national legislators against publicly disclosing the contents of the maritime bureau's contract and budget. He said in a legislative hearing on the draft budget for fiscal year 2009–10 that doing so would reveal Liberia's maritime secrets to competitors and hurt the country.
>
> The minister's warnings came after successful requests to exclude maritime revenues from the fiscal budget. President Sirleaf had promised to instruct BMA officials to release the budget, but that has never happened.
>
> "I want you, all members of the Ways and Means Committee, to get the information and to use it with the care it deserves. Otherwise, we shoot ourselves in the foot," Ngafuan told legislators.[54]

Lastly, where information is scarce, it becomes a valuable commodity, and people do not want to give it away for free. In the rule of law ideal, anyone could find out how a government office operates. Where bureaucracies are opaque, entrepreneurs often spring up to help the bewildered navigate the maze—for a fee. "Fixers" cultivate relationships with the government actors in a particular office, learn how the office operates, and offer their services to the public as go-betweens. The presence of fixers outside a government office or agency is a sure sign of a personal and opaque government system. In Afghanistan,

> There are people known as "employed on commission" who operate in front of government buildings. They approach us saying that they can solve any kind of issue in a short time and then they quote the price. For example, if you need a passport or driving license or are paying taxes and customs duties, they can give you the final receipt which has been processed through all official channels in a matter of days, a process which takes usually weeks. Then they will take the money and share it with those who are sitting inside offices.[55]

LACK OF PREDICTABILITY. The predictability of government action is claimed to be one of the principal benefits of the rule of law. Rule of law allows people to harmonize their behavior more easily and plan their activities based on their expectations of what the government and others will do. Even when the law is not applied or invoked, it can "anchor" private behavior, setting expectations about rights and obligations. In private negotiations, the parties may "bargain in the shadow of law," having in the back of their minds the result that they would get in the formal legal system if private negotiations fail.[56] This allows agreements to be reached more easily. It can provide the confidence needed to transact with strangers in the absence of a social guarantee of good behavior, such as a friend-of-a-friend relationship.

Perhaps one of the strongest proponents of predictability as an essential benefit of the rule of law was the free-market economist Friedrich Hayek, who saw this predictability as key to human freedom:

> The formal rules tell people in advance what action the state will take in certain types of situations, defined in general terms, without reference to time and place or particular people. . . . The knowledge that in such situations the state will act in a definite way, or require people to behave in a certain manner, is provided as a means for people to use in making their own plans. . . . If the individuals are to be able to use their knowledge

effectively in making plans, they must be able to predict the actions of the state which may affect these plans.[57]

The sociologist Max Weber argued that the rise of capitalism in Europe was facilitated by the unique qualities of its legal system, including the application of general, universally applied rules.

> It curbs the arbitrary action of the ruling groups, and is, partly as a result, highly predictable. Thus, under European law, the rules governing economic life are easily determined; this type of legal order reduces one element of economic uncertainty. This calculability of European law was it major contribution to capitalist economic activity.[58]

This historical analysis has been generalized to mean that the predictability provided by the rule of law is necessary for the efficient operation of markets.[59]

Western lawyers visiting poor countries often decry the lack of dissemination of laws and the lack of availability of legal texts. But while lack of dissemination undermines rule of law, it is government compliance with law that makes legal texts valuable and thus more likely to be disseminated. In 1897, Harvard Law professor and eventual Supreme Court Justice Oliver Wendell Holmes argued that the prediction of what judges would do was the reason to study or consult the law.[60] Where interactions with government are opaque and individually negotiated, government action is less predictable, government promises less credible, and legal texts less valuable because they provide less information about government behavior.

This is not to say that governments with weak rule of law are wholly unpredictable. In Laos, for example, although the government has a long tradition of secrecy, its operations are nonetheless "well understood and manipulated by Thai businessmen, who account for by far the majority of small-scale [foreign direct investment] projects in Laos. . . . And it is a system increasingly manipulated by expatriate Lao investing in Laos."[61] People do business and interact with these governments; they predict government behavior and plan strategically; they court those in power and exploit connections; and sometimes they even hire lawyers.

But predictability comes from social norms that are more guidelines than rules. A basic social norm is that of reciprocity—a person who helps you has a claim on you for a reward or for future help. Other norms come from the obligations that are owed to family and to friends or that define the patron/client relationship. Anthropologist Daniel Smith explained:

> When Nigerians seek a service from their government, they routinely expect that they will have to navigate corruption at all levels of the bureaucracy. Everything from obtaining birth and death certificates, to registering a company, to applying for a passport, to renewing a motor vehicle registration normally requires some sort of payment in addition to the official fee. Generally, the only way around paying extra money for routine government services is if one has a personal connection to someone with influence—a patron who will use their power to push on behalf of their client. But even then a relationship of reciprocity exists; the patron is helping with the implicit expectation that their act contributes to retaining and strengthening the loyalty of their client. Further, although a patron who helps a client navigate the bureaucracy may not expect payment, the client will nonetheless offer a "dash" (gratuity) to say "thank you."[62]

Writing about Africa, Goren Hyden posited "the economy of affection," which is summarized as "(a) whom you know is more important than what you know, (b) sharing personal wealth is more rewarding than investing in economic growth, and (c) a helping hand today generates a return tomorrow."[63] A scholar writing about the civil service in Malawi insists that although civil servants juggle several set of rules, of which the formal rules are just one, "nevertheless, there is a set of basic informal rules and codes, which can be found to some extent in all ministries and departments down to the smaller units of police posts, health posts and schools."[64] Civil servants discuss these rules as "the rules of the game," and they include respecting the boss and sharing the wealth with kin, while the boss in turn has the obligation to ensure that subordinates receive their share. Another scholar described the system of patronage in Yemen as "deeply patterned" and attempted to codify the informal rules that governed it: "Patronage is Distributed Broadly," "Elites Must Accept Inclusion [in the patronage system]," "The Type and Degree of Patronage Distribution Is Not Random," "In Return for Patronage, Elites Must Provide a Minimal Level of Support for the Authority of the President and the Corrupt Political Economy that Supports his Regime."[65]

At the national level, government policy actions can be more predictable with a better understanding of government political imperatives and constraints. For example, in countries with ethnic tensions, there may be established norms regarding the sharing of patronage among country regions or ethnic groups. In Nigeria, this is called "zoning"; in Cameroon, "équilibre ethnique" or "ethnic balance." The multiplication of government positions and its alternative, fast turnover in those positions are both predictable consequences of patronage governance.

LAW AS AN INSTRUMENT OF BEHAVIORAL CHANGE. Finally, weak rule of law means that law is a weak instrument for changing public or private behavior. As Professor Antony Allot observed in 1968:

> The making of laws is one of the governmental functions which is overtly carried out in the capital city. It is within the capital of each state that the legal draftsmen, and those who give them instructions, are clustered; within this limited circle the apparatus of law appears much the same as it did in colonial times, or as it does in the contemporary states of Europe and North America. Outside the capital, the facilities for administration are generally much weaker, however, and there is a natural temptation to bridge the gap left by lack of administrative capacity through the promulgation of still more laws. . . . A law is enacted, but the regional facilities for its application are as weak as are the administrative cadres generally, and nothing of significance happens. This is what I have termed "phantom legislation," the passing of laws which do not have, and most probably cannot have the desired effect. The illusion of progress, of doing something, is given, but the reality is far different. Such legislation is an expression, not of power but of the impotence of power. . . . Many of the laws so hastily passed in tropical Africa over the last decade or so fall into this category.[66]

Although some donors are aware of the limitations of state-made law and are working with customary law or supplementing legal reform programs with social action to bring about change, the mistake of thinking that law reform is sufficient to bring behavioral change in poor countries continues to the present day because it is a cultural mistake based on the stronger rule of law of Western governments. One scholar described the Lao response to donor pressure to take action on issues like corruption:

> A new law is promulgated, new regulations are introduced, a presidential or prime ministerial decree is announced (such as the 1999 Anti-Corruption Decree that "curtails activities that lead to a possible conflict of interests or an abuse of office"). But nobody takes any notice. Implementation is minimal, but the government can point to good intentions. Laos has some excellent environmental protection laws, for example. It is just that they are not enforced.[67]

Conclusion

Poor governments have weak rule of law because they are poor, but poverty means more than a lack of law books, inadequate prison space, or illiterate judges. Poor governments depend more heavily on the distribution of patronage to govern, on individual deals with individual power brokers, and on the strength of personal relationships expressed in business, politics, and social activities. Loyalties are personal. This is the opposite of the rule of law, which imagines a set of abstract rules applied impartially to everyone, that is at the same time the source of the government's authority, the way in which it exercises authority, and the bounds that limit it. The contradiction is heightened by the importation of law from rich liberal democracies that criminalizes the way the government actually operates.

Strengthening the rule of law would require a change in the underlying dynamic of power such that the population gives its allegiance to a body of rules and the government demonstrates its legitimacy by adhering to those rules. This is not impossible for poor governments, but the laws that they have are neither widely known nor deeply felt. This is perhaps one of the attractions of Islamic law for some countries, with its promise of a common orientation for government and society. And yet the West has been very uncomfortable with this movement toward the rule of law, because of the clash between Islamic law or its interpretations and other Enlightenment values, such as the equality of men and women.

Law that criminalizes one of the government's principal governance strategies is unlikely to be observed in any systematic way. On the contrary, enacting laws that cannot be implemented, whether because of this

contradiction or lack of resources, weakens the rule of law and marginal-
izes the legal system, making it a less effective reference point for individual
action. It widens the discretion of the government, which, because it cannot implement the law impartially, can choose when to apply the law, and
for whose benefit. Without a well-functioning legal system, the government is rudderless; all types of criminal behavior can go unpunished. Just
as the political map of the world does not reflect political power in poor
countries, the legal system does not provide good guidance to the organization or operation of government.

The last several chapters have sketched how and why poor governments
not only govern less, but also govern differently than rich liberal democracies. The processes of colonization and decolonization resulted in the
international recognition of a number of countries without effective governments and with formal institutions inherited from their much richer
colonizers. With fewer resources, poor governments cannot govern according to the governance ideal; cannot provide public goods and services to
all their citizens; and cannot implement or enforce their own laws. Some
cannot defend their territory from challengers, internal or external. Unable
to maintain government through the legitimacy that comes from providing
public goods and services to everyone or from the rule of law, they rely on
other, older, cheaper strategies, patronage being a common choice. Yet we
continue to engage them as if they govern the way we do (or would like to).
We continue to engage and manipulate the legal system and formal institutions without understanding how weak they are. We continue to engage
poor governments as if public service delivery and the establishment of the
rule of law were, or could be, their only priorities.

7. Governance as It Is

"Have you been to see the Ministry of Finance of the GoSS [Government of Southern Sudan]? It's a guy. In a trailer. Yet somehow everyone expects him to do everything that a ministry of finance does."
—WORLD BANK STAFF MEMBER (2008)

One of the key problems of American (and more generally Western) engagement with poor governments is unrealistic expectations about governance. Americans approach poor governments with the expectations that governments control their territories; that they do, can, or should provide the same types of services that their own, much richer, governments provide; that law is a central coordinating mechanism for government and social behavior; that the legitimacy of government comes from providing services, the rule of law, and democratic elections, as it does in large part at home; and that providing services and assuring the rule of law are therefore top priorities for poor governments. To the extent that any of these things is not true, they believe that they can be easily corrected, by training or other expert assistance, or at the extreme, by replacing government leadership. They believe that these governance values are universally shared, and this model of governance is universally achievable.

Because these beliefs are common to the culture, new entrants into aid, military, and policy positions tend to share these beliefs unless they are given the opportunity to unlearn them, leading us to make the same mistakes repeatedly. The three principal mistakes we make when engaging poor governments are failing to understand that they govern less; that because they are poor, they do and must govern differently; and that providing public goods and services under the rule of law is therefore not their top priority.

Part of our problem is cultural naïveté, a failure to understand the different circumstances of poor governments. But even though over the last twenty years we have paid increasing attention to the question of how poor governments govern, we have been strangely unable to take these insights onboard in policymaking. We do have a problem with knowledge and learning, but this is not the whole story.

Governing Less

Sometimes we demand that poor governments implement policies that they can't afford, asking them to spread thin resources thinner, instead of looking at the universe of options available to them. For example, when we insist that poor governments extend access to services, it can come at the further expense of quality. The fitful struggles of poor countries with universal primary education (UPE) have already been discussed. A declaration of a policy of UPE leads to a surge in school enrollments that overwhelms the government's capacity to deliver. The quality of the offer of public education deteriorates so seriously that families stop sending their children to public school. Fees creep back into the picture unofficially or under other names. While official enrollment statistics rise, many children do not receive enough schooling to learn to read. In a few years, the government declares a policy of universal primary education—again.

A similar story has unfolded in health care in the debate over user fees for medical services. User fees were introduced in the 1980s as a condition of foreign aid, in order to finance public health systems. The introduction of user fees provided a direct source of finance to local clinics. While doubtless some percentage of user fees went to line private pockets, they were also used to pay for medical supplies and staff salaries. However, according to the World Health Organization,

> making people pay at the point of delivery discourages them from using services (particularly health promotion and prevention), and encourages them to postpone health checks. . . . It has been estimated that a high proportion of the world's 1.3 billion poor have no access to health services simply because they cannot afford to pay at the time they need them.[1]

The introduction of user fees also presented the question of how to deal with indigent patients. Some hospitals in poor countries attempt to recover payment by holding patients hostage, in the hope that a relative or other sponsor will step forward to buy their freedom. In Kenya,

> the parents of one 11-year-old girl with kidney disease issued a public appeal in April to clear a $2,000 hospital bill. The girl recovered in January but has been detained since then by the government-run Kenyatta National Hospital here in Nairobi, the capital.

The same facility was pressured this month to release 44 new mothers after a TV station used a hidden camera to prove that they were being held in a padlocked room.[2]

Human Rights Watch reported the practice in Ghana, the Democratic Republic of Congo, Zimbabwe, and Burundi.[3]

"I had to come to hospital because I needed a caesarean delivery. When I got the bill, the doctor said to me, 'Since you have not paid, we will keep you here.' Life here is difficult. I don't have permission to leave with my baby. We are often hungry here," said an eighteen-year-old mother, held with her baby at Louis Rwagasore Clinic in Bujumbura, Burundi.[4] Healthy but detained patients occupied the limited rooms and bed space needed by sick patients, a situation called "absurd" by one hospital director.[5]

International organizations, activists, NGOs, human rights organizations, think tanks, and scholars called for the abolition of user fees for public health services in poor countries. Even the unions got involved. "The AFL-CIO told the Clinton administration, 'The IMF and World Bank should not condition one dollar of debt relief or development financing on the creation, expansion, or continuation of a user fee program by a borrowing country.'"[6] In 2000, the U.S. Congress passed a law that would require the U.S. executive director of the World Bank "to oppose any loan, grant, strategy or policy of such institution that would require user fees or service charges on poor people for primary education or primary healthcare, including prevention, care and treatment for HIV/AIDS, malaria, tuberculosis, and infant, child, and maternal health, in connection with such institution's financing programs."[7] This language has been repeated in subsequent legislation.

As of 2011, seventeen African governments had abolished user fees, partly in response to the international pressure and partly because, like universal primary education, it is a domestically popular measure.[8] According to some, the question is no longer whether to remove fees but how best to do it.[9]

Despite the enthusiasm for removing this source of funding for public health services, "an often neglected dimension in the user fee debate is how a government should compensate health facilities when it decides to ban user fees."[10] Those calling for the abolition of user fees were certainly not planning to make up the difference. Burundi is a landlocked

Central African country and one of the poorest countries in the world. The president announced the abolition of user fees for children under five and women giving birth in 2006.

> Before the President's announcement, little if no preparatory work was done to think over the aims of the policy and the operational dimensions of its implementation. First of all the policy to remove user fees was formulated in a hasty and incomplete way with little attention to: the ultimate objectives (whether equity in general or promotion of the [Millennium Development Goals]), the existing situation (no baseline study was undertaken) and the available financial resources. In this regard, no economic assessment of the impact of the reform was performed.[11]

This was not because Burundi's government had ample resources to pay for free public health. On the contrary, in 2007 health expenditure per capita was $17.40, of which out-of-pocket payments accounted for 38 percent and foreign aid for another 40 percent.[12] The government's share was less than $3.00 per person.

One hospital director detailed the impact of Burundi's changed policy.[13] Without user fees, hospitals quickly ran out of medicines and ran up unmanageable debt with pharmaceutical suppliers. They were then unable to implement the announced policy of free care for children under five. While the government was in theory supposed to reimburse hospitals for such expenses, the delay for reimbursement grew to a year. The hospital was unable to make planned investments, such as new laboratory equipment or computers. Other consumable items were quickly in short supply, including hygiene and cleaning equipment, gas, paper, or ink cartridges for photocopiers. Staff saw their workload increase because of the additional effort to get reimbursements from the central government for expenditures that had previously been paid for with user fees. Lacking medicine, hospitals had to charge fees for patients under five years old or require patients to purchase medicine outside of the hospital. "Quality of services decreased, as shown by the frequent drug stock-outs, the longer waiting times and the decreased duration of patients' contacts with health staff, while the private not-for-profit sector refused to comply with the law and managed to keep higher standards of quality (thus becoming more appealing to the population than public providers)."[14]

In the absence of an alternative source of financing, abolition of user fees does not mean that the poor receive care free of charge. In addition to official fees, in poor countries patients must usually pay unofficial fees for everything from being seen by a nurse or a doctor to getting an orderly to change an IV bag. According to a survey in East Africa by Transparency International, in 2011 more than 51 percent of respondents who had been to a public hospital reported that a bribe had been demanded of them.[15] It is reasonable to ask to what extent these unofficial payments are being used to pay the ordinary operating costs of providing public health services that can no longer be financed with official user fees.

Burundi's story can be considered as a policy failure that could have been avoided with better planning, implementation, and funding. However, poor governments do not generally distinguish themselves in the area of policy planning and implementation, because they lack the expertise, information, and resources, and because they have conflicting policy objectives. To say that the policy would have worked if only there had been better planning, implementation, and funding is to say that the policy would have worked if only Burundi had another (richer) government. In Uganda, the abolition of user fees was followed by a surge in the use of health services—up to 80 percent. Medical staff were overwhelmed and demoralized by the increased workload and the frequent drug shortages.[16] The government's effort to substitute for the user's share was not sustained over time, leading to drug shortages and difficulty in recruiting staff; patients are obliged to purchase medicine on their own and privately.[17] In Ghana, health facilities resumed charging patients when they ran out of money. In Senegal, some facilities never implemented the policy in the first place. And many patients are still required to pay informal payments, whether or not formal fees are required.[18]

The health impact of the abolition of user fees is unknown. A multicountry study of the abolition of user fees for the United Nations Children's Fund found that monitoring and evaluation were "appalling. . . . In a nutshell, these reforms have been launched without the prior establishment of a basic system to monitor their progress and their impact. . . . It is difficult to establish the proof of the impact of the reforms in terms of health outcomes. . . . It is doubtful that there will be any evidence, given the limited attention paid to evaluation."[19]

The sentiment behind the drive for expanded access to government services for the poor is understandable. The idea of the poor being unable to obtain an education or even life-saving health care because they are unable to pay is distressing, particularly because we have defined these services as human rights. That indigent patients would be ransomed by hospitals is shocking. But the problem is not solved by demanding that poor governments provide more services to more people, not only because poor governments do not have the resources to provide more services, but because the need to rely on other strategies of governance deprioritizes service delivery and makes it more difficult.

Governing Differently

A second mistake is failing to recognize that poor governments do and must govern differently. One of the clearest examples of this lack of understanding is the international campaign against corruption, which the United States has spearheaded.

As Western countries developed a norm that public office, authority, and resources should be used only for public purposes, they built meritocratic, politically insulated bureaucracies that were paid regular salaries. The older practices in which government offices were treated as private property and government actors were allowed to use their posts to pay themselves were abandoned and criminalized. Because the use of public office for private gain is equated with depravity even in academic discourse, it is difficult to talk about patronage and monetization of government positions in a morally neutral way, paving the way for tub-thumping campaigns against corruption in poor governments.

Following congressional hearings that showed that U.S. businesses commonly paid bribes overseas to get contracts, the United States passed the Foreign Corrupt Practices Act in 1977, criminalizing the payment of such bribes. American companies said that they would be at a disadvantage compared to European companies that were not subject to any similar law. The United States has campaigned to expand this type of criminal liability globally in an effort to level the playing field. International treaties now echo and in some cases go beyond the original U.S. legislation. The 1997 Organization of Economic Co-operation and Development (OECD) Anti-bribery Convention committed signatories to adopt similar legislation criminalizing overseas bribery, and the OECD monitors signatories for compliance.[20] While many countries criminalized domestic corruption, and some of these laws were transferred to poor governments, there is now explicit pressure to criminalize a range of behaviors considered corrupt. The United Nations Convention Against Corruption requires signatories to pass legislation:

> Each State Party shall, in accordance with the fundamental principles of its legal system, develop and implement or maintain effective, coordinated anti-corruption policies that promote the participation of society and reflect the principles of the rule of law, proper management of public affairs and public property, integrity, transparency and accountability.[21]

More than 140 countries are now party to the Convention, including many with poor governments such as Afghanistan, the Democratic Republic of Congo, Niger, Cambodia, and Yemen.[22]

Corruption has not only been criminalized, it has also been widely compared to a disease. In 1996, President James Wolfensohn of the World Bank made a speech in which he referred to "the cancer of corruption." The phrase caught on and became part of international anticorruption rhetoric. Secretary-General of the United Nations Ban Ki Moon stated, "All of us have a responsibility to take action against the cancer of corruption."[23] The United Kingdom's international development secretary Andrew Mitchell said, "Corruption is a cancer in developing countries and the Coalition Government has a zero tolerance approach to it. We are committed to rooting out corruption where ever it is undermining development."[24] The foreword to the United Nations Convention Against Corruption states, "Corruption is an insidious plague that has a wide range of corrosive effects on societies."[25] Accordingly, in 2006, the World Bank declared a "zero tolerance" policy for corruption.[26] In 2010, the World Bank launched the "International Corruption Hunter's Alliance." The United Nations has named December 9 International Anticorruption Day.

Poor governments have heard the message that the strategies by which they govern are unacceptable. Uganda announced a zero tolerance policy in 2006 (the same year that it was announced by the World Bank) and passed a 2009 law that created strict punishments for corruption.[27] Poor governments such as Angola and Kenya have also followed suit. The president of one of the world's poorest countries, Burundi, announced a zero tolerance policy for corruption, even though patronage is one of the government's key governance strategies.[28]

Back in the United States, corruption abroad continues to occupy our energy and our discourse, and prosecutions continue under the Foreign Corrupt Practices Act, but much of our attention is now focused on descrying corruption in foreign governments. In 2004, President George W. Bush issued a presidential proclamation barring corrupt foreign officials and their families from entry into the United States if their corruption has been detrimental to U.S. interests (although it has rarely been invoked).[29] The Millennium Challenge Corporation, a U.S. aid agency, funds compacts with countries that outperform their peers on a set of governance indicators. The most heavily weighted of these indicators is one that seeks to measure control of corruption.[30] And of course, the United States has focused on ensuring the control of corruption in Afghanistan, even as reports argue that its massive foreign aid inflows are in fact feeding the system.[31] The G-8 demanded to know how President Karzai was going to tackle corruption in Afghanistan, while a U.S. House panel voted to cut off aid to Afghanistan because of corruption in its government.[32]

Foreign aid donors invest heavily in anticorruption programs and projects in poor countries, which focus on developing codes of ethics, campaigning to moralize public servants, strengthening the capacity of the police to investigate white collar crime and of the judiciary to punish it, improving public financial management, and supporting broad public sector reform programs that aim to strengthen formal procedures, transparency, and accountability.

In poor governments, anticorruption efforts have had little success. As the International Crisis Group correctly noted about Burundi in a report titled "A Deepening Corruption Crisis," "as the core problem has not been correctly identified, this approach is doomed to fail. The solution is not to 'get the talk right,' to 'get the institutions right,' and to 'get the legal framework right'; it is to change the power relations that undermine good governance."[33] In Afghanistan, despite more than a decade of anticorruption efforts, the Department of Defense reported to Congress that there has been little progress, blaming the lack of "capacity and political will of the Afghan government."[34]

The World Bank's effort to reform the civil services of poor countries in order to create a meritocratic and technocratic civil service takes direct aim at patronage as a strategy of governance, while offering nothing that could replace it. Unsurprisingly, it has been one of the least successful areas of World Bank intervention. Civil service reform is the second most common public sector reform carried out after reforms to strengthen public financial management, but the World Bank's evaluation group reported that fewer than 45 percent of borrowers showed even temporary improvement.[35] The Bank has shifted away from civil service reforms in poor countries because of "the view that the poorest countries, and countries with the lowest civil service capacity, are less likely to benefit."[36] Similarly, the U.S. Agency for International Development has stated that in governments with high levels of corruption, "large-scale programs to address administrative weaknesses are not sustainable" and recommends working instead to create political pressure for change.[37]

An emerging body of work on corruption focuses below the national level, looking at practices in regions, cities, ministries, or sectors. It shows that within the same country or the same government, corruption levels vary substantially. This has given anticorruption campaigners hope that they can establish "islands of integrity" (a name originally coined by Transparency International to describe pacts between government and bidders to refrain from corruption in government procurement) under anticorruption "champions" and that given time these corruption-free zones will spread through a sort of demonstration effect. Like Diogenes' searching for an honest man, foreign aid donors have labored to identify champions who share their values and can make a difference, if only they have a little bit of outside support. But while there may be value in establishing, even for a moment of time, a space in which the rule of law triumphs, this approach has not resulted in the transformation of poor governments either, and islands of integrity tend not to be sustainable. One World Bank staffer likened fighting corruption to squeezing a balloon full of gas—the gas is simply displaced elsewhere. When foreign aid donors insist on "following the money" in the health sector, the government shifts the pattern to a sector that is under less scrutiny. Donors have short attention spans anyway.

The failure of anticorruption efforts in poor countries is typically blamed on "lack of political will," or, more cuttingly, greedy and exploitative elites. Sometimes it is blamed on lack of capacity, pointing to the underequipped and poorly trained police and prosecutors that are unable to investigate and prosecute white collar crime. Both of these explanations are true, but they overlook a core part of the problem. When governments are poor, the practices labeled as "corrupt" are used to pay the civil service. More deeply, they are often used to cobble together a fragile support for the government. Poor governments cannot, in good faith, promise to jettison the strategies they use to govern in the absence of alternatives, just as they cannot expand access to services without resources. But because their strategies of governance are so stigmatized, it is impossible to have an honest conversation about how such a transition can be effected or whether it is even possible.

Different Priorities

The failure to recognize that poor governments govern differently not only leads to attacks on the existing basis of governance but also to the mistaken assumption that poor governments see service delivery under the rule of law as their core function instead of one of several competing priorities. Because the governance strategies of poor governments are heavily stigmatized, poor governments have little to gain by correcting this assumption. Indeed, those that are aid dependent would certainly resist any suggestion that they do not share the priorities of donors. Yet actions often speak louder than words, and there are visible consequences of the diverging interests between rich liberal democracies and poor governments, particularly in the foreign aid arena.

Foreign aid donors identify improving the living conditions of the poor as the principal need of poor countries. This is captured in the Millennium Development Goals as well as in the slogan of the World Bank ("our vision is a world free of poverty"). Donors have often gone further to identify specific problems in aid recipient countries and to insist upon specific policy solutions and programs. This process of micromanagement has been criticized as undercutting poor government "ownership" of donor-funded projects and programs, with the consequence that poor governments do little to contribute to or sustain such efforts. Instead, donors are urged to allow poor countries to take the lead, meaning that poor governments should find their own way to reduce poverty by delivering public goods and services under the rule of law. This has led the World Bank and International Monetary Fund to require that poor governments develop "Poverty Reduction Strategy Papers" as a framework for funding. The problem, however, is not just a disagreement over means, but over objectives, including the principal donor objective of improving the living standards of the poor by delivering government services.

One signal of differing priorities is diversion of foreign aid. A substantial amount of U.S. and other foreign aid donor funding has gone into the health sector.[38] A 2004 World Bank study on the health sector in Chad found that only 27 percent of nonwage health spending allocated by the Ministry of Health reached the regions, and less than 1 percent reached local health centers. "It was estimated that if all public resources officially budgeted for regional delegations had reached the frontline providers in 2003, the number of patients seeking primary health care in Chad would have more than doubled during the year."[39] In Kenya in 2004, the Bank estimated that about 38 percent of funds transferred to health centers and 25 percent of user fees collected at health centers were diverted.[40]

While some of this loss can be attributed to sticky-fingered entrepreneurs, it can also be a signal that government is choosing to spend funds elsewhere. Poor governments commonly prefer construction projects, such as roads, schools, and clinics. Completed infrastructure projects are a tangible demonstration of government accomplishment, and construction contracts are favorite patronage goods. Of course, when they are used as patronage goods, the monetization of the project often means that it is poorly completed if it is completed at all. The Global Fund to Fight Aids, Tuberculosis and Malaria, a multibillion dollar fund backed by the Bill and Melinda Gates Foundation, has struggled to ensure that its funds are spent as intended. In Ethiopia, the government diverted grant funds for the renovation of existing health centers and the purchase of medications in order to construct new health centers. Of the seventy-seven newly constructed health centers visited by the foundation's inspectors, "71% of the sites visited did not have access to water; 32% did not have functioning toilet facilities; 53% had major cracks in the floors; and 19% had leaking roofs. . . . Only 14% of the HCs had equipment such as microscopes and delivery beds; only 12% had functional drug stores; and none of the laboratories had work surfaces."[41]

But clever aid recipients do not redirect donor funds, which can cause conflict with donors. Instead, they use aid to substitute for their own spending, freeing their own funds to spend elsewhere. One study concludes that the increased foreign aid for health programs has resulted in recipient governments lowering their own health expenditures—particularly in poor countries.[42] Another concluded: "We found that, on average, for every $1 of [development assistance for health] given directly to governments, those governments decreased their own health spending by a range of 43 cents to $1.14."[43] The largest reductions in government spending for health were in those countries with the largest HIV/AIDS epidemics and the most development assistance for health.[44]

Where does the money go instead? One place it might go is for defense spending, both because of security needs and because security spending is less transparent, allowing easier redirection of funds. Journalist Celia Dugger points out that while "Uganda put 57 cents less of its own money toward health for each foreign aid dollar it collected," it simultaneously "confirmed that it had paid more than half a billion dollars for fighter jets and other military hardware—almost triple the amount of its own money dedicated to the entire public health system in the last fiscal year."[45] The question of whether this is appropriate should be considered in light of Uganda's security issues, which include terrorist attacks and border clashes. On the other hand, it should be remembered that Uganda followed the grant of debt relief with the purchase of a presidential jet. Seven years later, in 2007, a British commitment to a ten-year, seven-hundred-million-pound poverty reduction program was followed within the month by a decision to scrap the first jet and buy another more expensive jet, on the grounds that the first was "outdated."[46]

Similarly,

Ethiopia is on another arms buying spree as millions of Ethiopians starve due to the worst drought in 60 years. According to Prime Minister Meles Zenawi, Ethiopia is purchasing 200 battle tanks from Ukraine for over $100 million. Was it a coincidence that the day before Meles' announcement, the British foreign aid office announced a $60 million "emergency food aid donation" to Ethiopia?[47]

Given the difference in priorities, it is not uncommon for poor governments to ask aid organizations to pay taxes on aid they deliver, especially considering that the foreign aid sector makes up such a large part of the economy. The World Bank, the Inter-American Development Bank, and the Asian Development Bank have agreed to pay nondiscriminatory taxes on projects that they finance.[48] The United States, however, has refused. In 2002, the U.S. Congress learned that the Palestinian Authority had levied millions of dollars of taxes on aid destined for the people of the West Bank and Gaza.[49] This led to the passage of a law that prohibited the payment of such taxes. In 2005, USAID ceased operation in Eritrea after the government proclaimed that aid imports, including food aid, would be taxed and seized United Nations vehicles for nonpayment of taxes.[50]

At the extreme, donors and governments can have opposite preferences concerning public service delivery. Governments that govern through repression or are struggling for control may use denial of food or public services as a weapon against rebellious populations, as did Libyan general Muammar Gaddafi when attempting to subdue rebel-held Misrata. Or they might create and maintain refugees as a means of luring Western foreign aid that could be captured as a revenue source, as did Somali major general Mohammed Siad Barre.

A cautionary example of differing preferences comes from the collapsed effort of the World Bank to assist the government of Chad to develop its oil resources in return for a commitment that the revenues produced would be used for "poverty reducing" spending. Chad is a poor, landlocked, African country that has faced civil war and low-level insurgency for most of the years of independence; at the time of the project it was one of the world's poorest countries. A principal concern of its government has been to quell rebellion and cement territorial control. The World Bank lent the government of Chad the money to help develop its oil.[51] The loan allowed Chad to participate in the construction of an oil pipeline that would carry the oil to a port in neighboring Cameroon, while a consortium of oil companies extracted and sold the oil, paying royalties and dividends to the government. The elaborate deal, based on years of negotiations, was concluded on the condition that Chad pass a law that provided that the majority of the oil revenues would be spent on "priority sectors," including health, education, and infrastructure, and that expenditures would be approved by a council that included civil society representatives.

The Bank rightfully saw the project as risky, acknowledging that Chad's government might seek to allocate the oil revenues otherwise.[52] The passage of the law was seen as one measure to bind Chad's government. Another was to tie future Bank lending to Chad's compliance, on the assumption that Bank financing would be greater than Chad's oil revenue. A final means was to ensure that oil revenues went into an escrow account rather than be paid directly to the government of Chad.

The deal went awry from the very beginning. The government received a $25 million sign-up bonus from the consortium of oil companies. Although it had agreed to treat this revenue as subject to the broader agreement on oil revenue, after several months of prevaricating, it admitted to the Bank that programs and to develop a new poverty reduction strategy that would form the basis for future expenditures.[56] In December 2006, rebel forces reached the capital and were repulsed; World Bank staff were evacuated.[57] In February 2008, rebel forces again attacked the capital, surrounded the presidential palace, and were repulsed.[58] With its new oil revenue, in August 2008, the government paid off the balances on its World Bank loans and the project closed.[59]

The evaluation of the project by the Bank's Independent Evaluation Group found the outcome unsatisfactory, but laid the blame squarely on the lack of government commitment.[60] There is no doubt that the government of Chad did not share the Bank's objectives. The question is whether it could have, given its security challenges and strategies for governance.

A Problem of Knowledge?

We do have a problem with naïveté and lack of understanding of poor governments. We can think of this problem as one of concentric circles of levels of knowledge, the smallest being the people who work on efforts that engage poor governments directly, the next largest being the senior people to whom they report, the next being the politicians that control their funding, and the last being the domestic public that puts pressure on politicians.

The understanding that poor governments govern differently is still not widely shared. In school, we are taught the governance ideal as an empirical description of how our own government works, and it is common to find statements, even in academic literature, that the purpose of government is to provide public goods and services without any acknowledgment that this is a statement of values rather than of fact. We imagine that any government could choose to govern by providing public good and services under the rule of law and with democratic elections. Accordingly, to the extent that people understand that poor governments govern differently, they see it as a consequence of moral failure, not poverty. And indeed, it is hard to make that distinction when the leaders of some poor governments are so self-serving.

Even within the group of those tasked to work with poor governments, many do not understand how they are different. Specialists in areas such as health, education, law, or tax, whose expertise comes from working in the health, education, legal, or tax sectors at home, have no training that would help them understand either the different context of poor governments generally speaking, or the particulars of the specific government with which they are working. They learn on the job or not at all. American lawyers, for example, have engaged in writing constitutions and restructuring justice systems in poor countries as true believers in the rule of law and the governance ideal. And yet, there is nothing in U.S. legal education or the experience of practicing law in the United States that would teach an aspiring development lawyer how governments in poor countries govern, what the role of a justice system is in a poor country, how it operates, or how it fits with respect to the government's other priorities. This is understandable: the goal of a U.S. legal education is to prepare someone to practice law in the United States. European legal education is even more abstract, focused on teaching general principles of law.

To engage poor governments effectively, we need to understand that they govern less and differently. To engage a particular poor government, we need to know how that specific government is governing at a moment in time, in a particular place. We need deeply contextual and ephemeral local information. We need to understand who is in control, with regard to a function or a territory, what rules apply where, what resources are available to the government, what demands are made on them, and what strategies the government uses to hold power.

We need to return to drawing maps of power, as we did before the nature of statehood changed. Where national governments control a function in a territory, they are the right point of engagement to ensure that something happens in the territory in question. Where they do not govern, however, they cannot implement. We will have to think about a more effective way to achieve policy goals in that territory, whether the goal is to contain insurgents or reduce the incidence of child marriage. Real government decision-making authority may be vested in actors who hold no formal position in government. Patronage relationships may result in reporting relationships that are very different than the formal chain of command, as where a seemingly junior functionary in a ministry is a relative or client of a much more powerful politician.

Where rule of law is weak, constitutions and laws are poor guides. We need guides to the actual rules and standards in practice, to the extent that any exist. We also need a better understanding of poor government finances, both revenues and expenditures. This understanding would include off-budget expenditures, the domestic borrowing that happens when governments simply don't pay their bills, and the various informal streams of revenue, such as income from the monetization of government authority and positions, which act in lieu of government salary payments. Finally, we need a better understanding of poor government political constraints. If we want to change the behavior of poor governments, we need to remain in the realm of the possible.

Gathering this information is difficult because it is local and dynamic. Poor governments themselves have not conducted these analyses and may not have this information. Maps of power, diagrams of relationships, and descriptions of informal processes or norms will be subjective, hard to confirm, fluid, and quickly outdated. And poor governments are also likely to resist efforts to gather this information, which raises questions about whether it can be legally collected and reliably sourced. Poor governments are less secure in their seats and fear the political and security implications of sharing sensitive information publicly, especially where it shows the government engaged in activities that violate domestic or international law. Most poor governments do not have a system for classifying information, which puts those who seek or share government information—including information routinely publicly available in rich liberal democracies—at risk of being accused as spies or traitors. Publication of information about the operation of patronage networks can open up demands for renegotiation, as people seek better deals, and may jeopardize the balance of power.

The good news is that over the last twenty years, both foreign aid donors and the military have become more sophisticated in analyzing government power and incentives in poor country governance. Foreign aid donors have crafted analytic frameworks for conducting political economy assessments, generated hundreds, if not thousands, of such assessments, and organized endless workshops on "mainstreaming" political economy analysis to understand how to better structure development projects. This approach "has today been adopted under various names by virtually every Western donor as a means to establish 'political thinking' at the heart of global development policy-making."[61] Intelligence analysts use sophisticated software platforms to analyze social networks. The U.S. Department of Defense's most recent briefing to Congress contains an analysis of the various patronage networks that vie for control in the Afghan National Army.[62] Although this understanding is still limited to enclaves even among those whose work relates to poor governments, there is now more and better quality analysis of these issues than there has ever been before—issues like patronage networks, monetization of offices, the role of the military, and informal practices of governance. A small group of academics and practitioners have argued that we expect too much from poor governments when we attempt to export the governance ideal, sometimes called "the good governance" agenda.[63]

During the same period there has been a more concerted effort to learn from experience. Although the process for evaluating the success of projects is still weak, underfunded, and often biased, evaluations are now routinely conducted for aid interventions and increasingly for military interventions in reconstruction and stabilization. Both aid organizations and the military have made a practice of collecting written accounts of "lessons learned" from their interventions.

The bad news is that, while there is some innovation at the margins, by and large these analyses and lessons learned have not had much impact on how we engage poor governments or conduct foreign policy. In the development community, these analyses are "having little influence on mainstream debates about aid and donors are not questioning their implicit assumptions about how development happens."[64] Within the military, establishing the governance ideal is still seen as the key to ensuring stability in Afghanistan.

Conclusion

Uninformed policies are at best ineffective. At worst, they can have unintended and devastating consequences, singly and collectively. When we press poor governments to take on tasks that outstrip their resources, we undermine their ability to govern. Laws and policies that cannot be implemented become aspirational. The public cannot hold the government accountable because the government has an impossible task and cannot be held responsible for performing it. To the detriment of rule of law and equality before the law, the government's discretion increases as it necessarily picks and chooses which of its policies or laws to implement, or what services to deliver, at what time, and for whose benefit. This discretion in turn allows government officials to sell government implementation (or non-implementation) of laws and policies or access to government services to the highest bidder.

The adoption of policies that cannot be implemented and institutions that cannot be sustained without external funding deepens and continues poor country aid dependence. The dependence of poor country governments on donor funds gives donors strong leverage, which they in turn often use to press for expanded government obligations in a damaging downward spiral. In the extreme case, we can inadvertently attack the very basis of governance, fueling instability, insecurity, and conflict. When we set unrealistic goals, we also pay the price, in money, opportunity cost, and sometimes in lives.

If there has been progress in the last twenty years, it is a growing consensus among academics and practitioners that we should be considering these and similar issues. We should be—but we are not.

A number of explanations have been offered as to why these analyses have had so little impact. One set of explanations points to issues that arise from the way in which engagement with poor governments is conducted. For example, one problem shared by both aid and the military is staff turnover. The constant rotation of personnel means that insights that come from hard experience are soon lost. Yet another analysis points to the perverse incentives of contractors to portray every project as a success and to guard trade secrets in writing up lessons learned.[65] There is no incentive to read the "lessons learned" documents that have been produced, even when these are public information (and many are not). One study considering the lack of uptake of political economy analysis in development blames the fact that political economy analyses are conducted in secret and without involving the government in question, making it "a deeply secretive and exclusionary approach to policymaking." The study suggests that such analyses be conducted together with the government.[66]

I argue that there are several reasons why this work has not had much impact on how we approach poor governments. First, the knowledge about how poor governments govern remains in enclaves of specialists who talk mostly to each other, and it is further fragmented among a number of communities of specialists who only talk to other people in their own communities: political scientists, governance specialists, tax specialists, counterinsurgency experts.

Second, even the best informed specialists do not have a free hand in shaping policy. They are ultimately constrained by domestic public opinion, and the domestic public has strong beliefs about what is right in governance and little reason to know about conditions and constraints in poor countries. Both the demand that poor governments provide more services and the campaign against corruption in poor governments reflect this moralistic base.

But the most important reason why our decision to incorporate insights into the politics of poor governments into our policymaking has not really changed our behavior is that these insights are met with the deep conviction—shared by many of the analyses themselves—that the governance of poor governments is pathological, an evil to be replaced by the governance ideal; that any government, if its leaders only have enough political will, can govern by providing public goods and services under the rule of law, subject to democratic elections; and that therefore, they should be encouraged, or supported, or made to do so.

But what if they can't?

8. A Different Conversation

We see the governance ideal as a moral imperative. The governance of poor governments offends our democratic ideals, our belief in egalitarianism, and our belief in human rights. Our politicians routinely describe a global mission to change the way other countries govern, and this missionary impulse is a constant element in our foreign engagement. The development community has identified good governance as a development objective in itself, as well as the means to the achievement of other valued ends, such as economic growth. The security community has identified good governance as necessary for stability and the suppression of insurgencies and terrorism.

We want to believe that the governance ideal is equally available to every government and all citizens. However, poor governments do not have the resources to provide public goods and services to all their citizens, and especially not the ample basket that has come to be seen as necessary by rich liberal democracies over the last century. Many poor governments are still struggling to control the territories allocated to them during decolonization. As a consequence, they cannot govern exclusively or even primarily by means of the legitimacy that comes from providing universal public goods and services. Instead, they must continue to rely more heavily on strategies of governance we rejected. This includes buying support from elites through the distribution of government largesse (such as jobs, contracts, and monopolies), clientelism, repression, appeals to religious ideology, or cults of personality. Because they cannot provide security, a social safety net, dispute resolution, or contract enforcement services, poor governments have not displaced social mechanisms for meeting these needs, including reliance on extended family, ethnic, and patronage networks.

One attractive answer to this dilemma is to seek to "fix" poor governments so that they can govern according to the governance ideal. If we it had spent the sum unilaterally and had not followed the agreed spending priorities. The government claimed that it was required to respond urgently to repair infrastructure damaged by flooding in the capital and to buy military equipment to respond to an attack by rebels in the north. While the Bank froze work on Chad's request for debt relief for several months, it eventually accepted and reiterated the government's explanation of necessity.

A subsequent audit traced the money to a variety of off-budget expenditures, including an overpayment to a contractor who received a sole source contract, payment of back dues to international organizations of which Chad was a member, and the purchase of thirty-three Peugeot cars for the use of persons in government—although the cars received did not correspond to the cars ordered.[53] The audit noted that foreign currency payments made the same day used different rates of exchange, implicitly raising the question of whether the rate of exchange had been inflated so as to redirect some of the funds. Finally, the audit did point to a number of transfers to the Ministry of Defense, but said that it was impossible to verify that the equipment purchases were made by the ministry and noted that some of the expenditures made on the ministry's account were in reality for the benefit of other government agencies.

While the project had anticipated a maximum price of oil of $19.00 per barrel, the price of oil rose to over $96 per barrel in 2008.[54] The unprecedented rise in the price of oil gave the government of Chad a much larger stream of oil revenue than had been anticipated, making the Bank's loans—and the threat that loans would be withheld—less important. The Bank's leverage collapsed, and the security situation in Chad worsened. Fighting in the north resumed, and the conflict in Darfur on Chad's border brought a wave of refugees. In 2005, the government of Chad unilaterally amended the revenue law. Among other changes, it added security to the list of priority sectors.[55] The president also attached the Ministry of Infrastructure directly to the presidency, allocating contracts sole source rather than bidding them competitively, bypassing all accounting controls. This would have allowed the president to allocate patronage directly in the form of oil revenue-financed contracts for infrastructure, paid for in advance.

After temporarily freezing the Bank's disbursements and Chad's oil escrow account, the Bank negotiated a new, more demanding deal with Chad and resumed lending. The new agreement committed Chad to spend even more of its budget—70 percent of its 2007 budget—on poverty could fix them in short order, we wouldn't need to adapt to or accommodate them, or even know very much about how they govern, except to note that it is unsatisfactory. Much of our effort with respect to poor governments has been directed to this end. The results of these efforts have been disappointing, however.

Alternately, if poor governments can't do it, perhaps rich liberal democracies might consider taking on responsibility for assuring the quality of governance where poor governments fall short. But this is an even more ambitious idea than the idea that we can fix poor governments. We are not willing, and even if willing, would not be able.

Some have suggested that if wealth is a prerequisite of better governance, then we should put the issue of governance aside and focus instead on catalyzing economic growth in poor countries. However, waiting for growth is not a short-term solution either.

Instead we need to admit that the governance ideal is not universally available, that poor governments must govern using a different mix of strategies, and that they will continue to do so for at least the medium term and certainly as long as they are poor. We need to develop effective foreign policies to engage them given how they govern. But this admission and the compromises that it entails are so difficult that we cannot bring ourselves to make them.

Can We Fix Them?

The West has taken a number of different approaches to improving governance in poor countries. If we could fix poor governments, we wouldn't need to adapt to or accommodate their governance in foreign policy. Unfortunately, there are no quick fixes.

Several approaches to improving governance focus on replacing government leaders, reforming government institutions, or incentivizing poor governments to govern according to the governance ideal. All of these approaches assume that poor governments can change the way they hold power if government actors simply change the way they behave.

REPLACEMENT. The corruption, weak rule of law, repression, and informality of poor governments is often attributed to a lack of "political will" for corrective action on the part of government leadership. If the leaders in charge are the problem, replacement with more energetic leaders, whether by means of elections or through force, looks like a quick and simple solution. Foreign aid donors have supported regime change through democratic elections, providing support to civil society organizations that monitor elections and journalists, as well as to opposition political parties. Decapitation of the government by force has proved to be a particularly attractive strategy for the United States given its military might. The United States has used its military power to help replace leaders or governments in countries such as Panama, Grenada, Haiti, Afghanistan, Iraq, and, most recently, Libya.

To be sure, a new leader or government can be better than an old one for any number of reasons. There are better and worse poor governments. A new leader could be more knowledgeable, more intelligent, wiser, have more "political will" to make change, more vision, better values, more respect for human rights, a better work ethic, or better relationships with domestic or foreign constituencies. But replacement in itself could be expected to change the way in which the government holds power only if all the other conditions necessary to achieve the governance ideal are present. If only the problems of poor governments and countries were that simple.

The United States has persistently intervened in Haiti, for example, but no one would say that Haiti epitomizes the governance ideal. Among other interventions, the United States occupied Haiti from 1915 until 1934; forced President Jean-Claude Duvalier to leave in 1986; suspended aid, blocked, and embargoed Haiti; and finally invaded Haiti in 1994 to restore President Aristide after he was deposed by a military regime. The invasion was justified to the American people as a limited operation that was not intended as a nation-building exercise, but rather a response to the human rights abuses of the military regime and an effort to restore democracy. The State Department issued a report that stated that "the de facto government promotes general repression and official terrorism. It sanctions the widespread use of assassination, killing, torture, beating, mutilation, rape, and other violent abuse of innocent civilians, including the most vulnerable, such as orphans."[1] "The criteria would be the removal of the illegal Government, the restoration of civil law and giving the Haitian people an opportunity to have the kind of freely elected Government that they chose in 1990," Secretary of State Warren Christopher told reporters. "That's the fundamental issue."[2]

Even when leaders are replaced, the new leaders of poor governments face the same territorial and political challenges and the same limited domestic resources with which to meet them. As one analysis noted in 2006, regarding the ineffectiveness of Aristide's presidency, "Haiti has been virtually ungovernable. There was no functioning Parliament or judiciary system, no political compromise or consensus, and extreme violence perpetrated by paramilitaries, gangs, and criminal organizations. Corruption and drug trafficking ran rampant. No government enjoyed much legitimacy."[3] Aristide ultimately accepted exile in 2004 in the face of armed revolt.[4]

All of this was of course before the devastating 2010 earthquake that destroyed almost all of Haiti's public buildings, including the Presidential Palace, the parliament building, the tax headquarters, the prison, schools, and hospitals, and killed many of the government workers who were working in them at the time.[5] Although earthquakes can happen anywhere, poor countries are more vulnerable to shocks. One reason for the massive destruction and the high casualty rate was that buildings were not built to withstand earthquakes.

New leaders must build political support for the government among the same small group of elites, leveraging their ability to deliver the support of their constituencies. They face the same set of demands and pressures for redistribution from both political allies and their own family and clients. As a consequence, they must often incorporate the old elites into new patronage positions by folding them into the new government.

It should be no surprise then that the most recent elections in Haiti did not bring a fundamental change in the way in which Haiti is governed. In 2013, Freedom House noted "endemic corruption" under President Martelly, who is himself accused of accepting kickbacks and mismanaging public funds.[6] In addition, "Martelly has appointed a number of individuals to political office who have been credibly accused of human rights abuses, including Jean Morose Villiena, who was appointed mayor of Les Irois despite his facing arson, murder, and attempted murder charges."[7] Freedom House went on to note "the absence of a viable judicial system and widespread insecurity" and violence against and intimidation of the media and human rights activists.

Similarly, in Afghanistan, President Karzai needed to build support among existing Afghan elites. A report by the U.S. Joint Chiefs of Staff explained,

> President Karzai needed to reconcile the local powerbase to GIRoA [the Government of the Islamic Republic of Afghanistan] and did so by placing warlords in key government positions as a way to obtain loyalty. Numerous

political deals allowed Karzai to gain the interim presidency in 2004 and subsequently the presidency in 2009. The 25 GIRoA ministries also served as opportunities to dispense patronage through appointments. . . . Once ensconced within ministries and other government posts, the war-lords-cum-ministers often used their positions to divert GIRoA resources to their constituencies. . . . Due to the extent of CPNS [criminal patronage networks], the removal of one corrupt official typically only resulted in another member of the network taking his place and continuing his corrupt practices. Despite this, president Karzai remained politically dependent on the CPNs; he therefore resisted COMISAF [Commander, International Security Assistance Force] pressure to prosecute corrupt CPN members because, as one senior civilian advisor noted, "[prosecution] meant Karzai would be putting one of his allies in jail."[8]

Instead of replacing government leaders, a more modest people-centered approach has been to seek to identify, support, and engage like-minded partners within poor governments. Foreign aid donors often seek to partner with "champions," individual government actors, ministries, or local governments that share their commitment to the governance ideal. Engaging champions allows donors to meet their immediate institutional need to accomplish projects and missions with the help of partners with whom they are comfortable. It also has the benefit of providing some time-bound protection and benefits for donor-chosen champions. However, this type of engagement is also often presented as a poorly articulated theory of change, involving the construction of "islands" of excellence, integrity, or productivity that will somehow expand or replicate. Implicitly, this approach also assumes that the failure of poor governments to govern according to the governance ideal is a problem of lack of leadership.

This more modest approach to change has not been successful either. Although even in poor governments there are both individuals and government units that embrace the values of the governance ideal, do not monetize their government authority, and work diligently in the public interest, they are outliers operating in and constrained by a broader context. Donors overestimate the power of their champions. Sometimes they are utterly mistaken in their choice of champions. Just as replacing government leaders cannot lead poor governments to govern according to the governance ideal, neither can protecting, financing, or promoting less powerful government actors.

REFORM THE INSTITUTIONS. Another approach focuses on strengthening the capacity of poor governments by providing training, equipment, or infrastructure. Capacity-building is often combined with attempts to change the incentives of government actors by changing laws, procedures, or the organizational structure, or creating or abolishing government organizations, usually to bring them in tighter conformity with those of rich liberal democracies. Rather than replace government leadership, both seek to change the behavior of government actors. On its face, this looks as if reform could be accomplished relatively speedily, even if more slowly than simply replacing offending government officials.

While foreign aid donors promote the governance ideal through capacity building and institutional reform as a development goal in itself, or as a means of supporting economic growth or reducing poverty, the U.S. military sees such reforms as critical to fighting insurgents. The purpose of a counterinsurgency (COIN) campaign, according to the U.S. Counterinsurgency Field Manual, is to "foster development of effective governance by a legitimate government" where "governments described as 'legitimate' rule primarily with the consent of the governed; those described as 'illegitimate' tend to rely mainly or entirely on coercion."[9] To accomplish this, "soldiers and Marines are expected to be nation builders as well as warriors. They must be prepared to help reestablish institutions and local security forces and assist in rebuilding infrastructure and basic services. They must be able to facilitate establishing local governance and the rule of law."[10] Implicit in this statement is the idea that, at one time, institutions were functioning, infrastructure existed, the government delivered basic services, and the rule of law existed. Insurgencies arise as a consequence of dissatisfaction with the government because of its failure to govern according to the governance ideal. The U.S. Government Counterinsurgency Guide states that a condition of a successful COIN operation is that

> the affected government is seen as legitimate, controlling social, political, economic and security institutions that meet the population's needs, including adequate mechanisms to address the grievances that may have fueled support of the insurgency. . . . Almost by definition, a government facing insurgency will require a degree of political "behavior modification" (substantive political reform, anti-corruption and governance improvement) in order to successfully address the grievances that gave rise to insurgency in the first place.[11]

There may be value in institutional reform, and foreign aid donors have often succeeded in persuading poor governments to change their formal institutions and laws. However, there is no evidence that transferring the formal institutions of rich liberal democracies to poor governments will make poor governments govern like rich liberal democracies. Where rule of law is weak, laws and official procedures are not effective instruments for driving behavioral change.

Indeed, the institutional transfer project is likely based on too simple an idea of causality. Formal institutions may indeed constrain and shape behavior, but deeper patterns of social behavior shape and uphold formal institutions. As Vivek Sharma put it in his essay, "Give Corruption a Chance,"

> the outcomes produced by Denmark are not merely the function of possessing good administrative institutions; rather, they are instead a consequence of the emergence of particular configurations of authority that are deeply rooted in the society. The "efficient" and "fair" functioning of Denmark's administrative institutions is a consequence of the fact that these administrative organs are staffed by Danes who take for granted certain patterns of authority in general. Danes did not become prosperous because of the Danish state: they became prosperous because of the way in which they organized their lives in general. The Danish state is a reflection and a consequence of this deeper change in the way in which Danish social organization evolved. Simply taking Danish-style administrative organs and transplanting them to Afghanistan cannot work because the people who would actually staff them would be Afghans, and Afghan institutions are infused with a different category of authority.[12]

Since the beginning of development work in law and governance, scholars and practitioners have cautioned against the "sympathetic magic" practice of exporting Western institutions and laws to poor countries and expecting them to operate the same way or even to operate at all. Allot spoke of "phantom legislation" in Africa in 1968—laws on the books that were simply not enforced or implemented.[13] Economists Acemoglu and Robinson have offered similar cautions about institutional transfer.[14] Harvard public administration specialist Matt Andrews has warned against reforms that "produce new laws, systems, and processes that make governments look better" but go unimplemented.[15] Regarding its efforts at civil service reform, the World Bank's evaluation group noted, in countries where the patronage system is prevalent, reforms that affect pay, recruitment, and promotion are very difficult to achieve. . . . Diagnoses have concluded that the patronage system in developing countries creates a very difficult reform environment. It is important to be realistic that a country's system will not change overnight and that focusing on select entry points and incrementalism will be more successful than any attempt at remodeling an entire system.[16]

INCENTIVIZE THEM TO GOVERN. Another approach is to admit that we don't know how to improve poor governments and instead to incentivize them to deliver the type of governance that we want. This approach also assumes that changing the way poor governments hold power is simply a matter of changing the behavior of government actors.

The Millennium Challenge Corporation (MCC) is a U.S. foreign aid agency that awards grants of hundreds of millions of dollars to governments that perform well on a number of indicators that seek to measure the success of the government in Ruling Justly, Investing in People, and Encouraging Economic Freedom.[17] This selective approach is supposed to ensure that aid money is used well by recipients and to incentivize those that do not qualify for compacts to change the way they govern. Under current legislation, the MCC must also exclude from consideration countries whose governance is considered very bad—although presumably these are exactly the governments that would benefit most from being incentivized to improve. Excluded countries include those in which an elected head of government was deposed by coup (Sudan, Madagascar, Mali, and Guinea-Bissau), those lacking rule of law (Zimbabwe), those lacking fiscal transparency (Cameroon, Central African Republic, The Gambia, Madagascar, Nicaragua, and Swaziland), those supporting international terrorism (Sudan, Syria, North Korea), or those in arrears in debt owed to the United States (Syria, Sudan).[18]

The MCC divides eligible countries into low-income and lower-middle-income categories. Countries are evaluated against other countries in their income group. However, it uses the same criteria to evaluate the governance of all countries regardless of their wealth, implicitly assuming that all governments can and should govern the same way. The indicators include measures of the rule of law, the control of corruption, immunization rates, and public expenditure on health and education—all measures of the ability of the government to govern by providing universal public goods and services under the rule of law.

Reflecting the belief in the universal achievability of the governance ideal, countries that are not precluded from receiving U.S. aid and do not qualify for MCC grants are considered for the Threshold Program, a USAID program that aims to produce quantifiable improvements in governance within two years by providing funding and expert assistance. However, a review of this program concluded that "using a country threshold program to improve performance on MCC's eligibility indicators within a narrow time frame, however, has not been effective in most cases."[19]

Replacement of government leaders, engagement with "champions," reform of government institutions, and incentivizing government actors as ways of achieving the governance ideal are premised on the idea that all governments can govern according to that ideal and that the only constraint is the capacity and bad behavior of government actors. These approaches may be valuable and effective for advancing more limited goals or even worthwhile as prerequisite steps that might set the stage for subsequent change, but there is not a single case in which these approaches have enabled a poor government to abandon reliance on other governance strategies and to govern according to the governance ideal. It does not matter whether we bomb them, invade them, teach them, praise them, reform them, incentivize them, or sanction them. Poor governments cannot govern according to the governance ideal as long as they are poor.

Can We Do It Ourselves?

The creation of the modern state system was accomplished by divorcing the right to govern from the ability to govern. The expectation was that statehood in fact would follow statehood in law; that governments would "grow into" their territories and responsibilities. However, declaring statehood did not assure the governance of the territories of poor countries. The president of Somaliland implicitly tagged the problem with the modern state system when he said, "You can't be donated power."[20]

If poor governments can't govern according to the governance ideal by themselves, one possibility might be for rich liberal democracies to assume responsibility either for governing or for helping poor governments to govern. The responsibilities of poor governments could be reduced to match their capacities by reducing their territorial or functional responsibilities. We would then need to fill the governance vacuum. However, we are not willing to take on these responsibilities, and even if we were willing, we could not fulfill them.

REVISIT THE STATE SYSTEM. Poor governments enjoy the legal rights of governments of states whether or not they are able to carry out the responsibilities of governance. International law usually requires other governments to deal with the recognized government regarding all matters within the state's borders. Although poor governments may not themselves be able to govern their territories, they have the legal authority to prevent others from reaching populations at risk or pursuing criminals or terrorists within their borders, or to set any conditions on access—such as exacting payment for the privilege of delivering aid. This is part of the continuing frustration of the disenfranchised who live in these territories. Although they receive little or no government services, they may not be able to emigrate to richer countries, erect their own governments, or negotiate directly with foreign actors to receive assistance, and other national governments do not have any obligation to them and are not accountable to them.

One possible solution to the puzzle of governance in poor countries is to abandon legal fictions of statehood and realign rights, abilities, and responsibilities. A government's claims to a territory would be recognized only if it could demonstrate that it actually governed according to some minimum standard, such as delivering an adequate level of security and services to the population that lives there. One scholar has suggested that we might think about "decertifying" states.[21] We would once again draw maps that reflect power, rather than international legal claims. This would then allow a conversation about how stateless (not "ungoverned") spaces should be governed, how the needs of the populations who live in them should be met and by whom, and how the problems that arise within them should be resolved. Because recognition of the territorial claims of poor governments would reflect their actual governance to a minimum standard, they would have every incentive to govern to that standard and, by definition, would have adequate resources to do it.

Or instead of all-or-nothing legal rights over territory, we could also imagine increasingly stronger legal rights as a government delivers more to its population, so that stateness becomes a continuum. Poor governments cannot supply even the most minimalist set of public goods and services to all their citizens. Most cannot supply personal security or justice or defend the population against criminals, terrorists, or insurgents. Rather than reducing the territory of poor governments, poor governments could have more limited obligations to supply public goods and services to a subset of the population, rather than attempting to serve so many that their meager resources are diluted to insignificance. When the government's responsibilities are in line with its available resources and capacity, the government could then be held responsible for performance. Perhaps "quasi-states" should have "quasi-sovereignty"—but there is a real question of how a government that delivers very little can win popular support.

This would be a solution to the governance problem only if there were another entity willing and better able to fulfill those responsibilities. The relationship between that entity and the people living in the territory would have to be defined. Without a clearly defined alternative to the present state system, it is hard to say that the disenfranchised would be better off.

In any event, it is not politically feasible. Rich governments (and their citizens) have no incentive to take responsibility for resolving the problems of poor people in other countries except when they threaten to have spillover effects. Poor governments have no incentive to give up any of their territory—even if they cannot govern it—or to give up their functions—even if they cannot perform them.

GIVE THEM MONEY. Yet another alternative would be for rich liberal democracies to subsidize poor governments at a level sufficient to allow them to provide universal public goods and services, the rule of law, and to hold democratic elections. Rich liberal democracies, rather than governing the territory directly or assuming direct responsibility for service delivery, could engage in a form of indirect rule, enabling poor governments to govern as long as their governance conforms to the governance ideal.

Foreign aid donors, NGOs, and even militaries already deliver foreign aid to poor governments and often deliver public goods and services such as health and education services directly. Although foreign aid is critical to the operation of poor governments—on average in 2010, for those from which we have data, foreign aid was half of all government expenditure[22]—the combined efforts of poor governments and foreign actors still fall far short of ensuring that poor country citizens receive basic security, rule of law, and universal public goods and services. It is unclear how much aid would be required to overcome the fiscal constraint to the governance ideal, but it is fair to say that it would be substantially more than donors are currently giving and likely more than they can give. Aid remains volatile, provided by a shifting set of uncoordinated volunteers with their own agendas. They are not accountable to anyone if they fail to deliver on their promises, least of all to aid beneficiaries. Donors tax the limited capacity of poor governments in their demands for reports and interaction, as where by the end of the 1990s, the government of Tanzania was famously made to write more than 2,400 quarterly donor reports and host more than 1,000 donor missions annually.[23] Donors repeatedly promise to coordinate and harmonize their demands so that they are less burdensome to recipients, but their own institutional incentives make it difficult for them to do so.

We are also reluctant to accept responsibility for subsidizing poor governments. Relaxing the expectation that poor governments should be self-financing would mean more than giving them aid seen as charity; it would mean assuming real responsibility for their financing. At present, most donor governments and their citizens do not feel an obligation to deliver aid even when they have pledged it. In economic downturns, donors cut their aid budgets—just when poor governments need the money.[24]

Popular support for foreign aid in the United States is already tenuous. The United States, while not the world's richest country, is one of the world's largest economies and is by far the largest donor of bilateral aid. But many Americans would not eagerly agree to subsidize poor governments indefinitely. They are willing to help the "deserving poor"—those who are impoverished through no fault of their own. However, many believe that hard work and prudence overcome poverty and so tend to find persistent poverty suspect. They worry that someone who is poor for too long is attempting to take advantage of the hard work of others.

Where the aid recipient government is seen to be morally suspect—engaged, for example, in corruption or repression as most poor governments are—there would be very little popular support for subsidizing that government. Foreign aid has been described by conservatives as "pouring money down a rathole." As Douglas Casey quipped, "Foreign aid might be defined as a transfer of money from poor people in rich countries to rich people in poor countries."[25] An editorial in the *Wall Street Journal* titled "To Help Haiti, End Foreign Aid" argued:

Mr. Shikwati and others like Kenya's John Githongo and Zambia's Dambisa Moyo have had the benefit of seeing first hand how the aid industry wrecked their countries. That the industry typically does so in connivance with the same local governments that have led their people to ruin only serves to help keep those elites in power, perpetuating the toxic circle of dependence and misrule that's been the bane of countries like Haiti for generations.[26]

Polls show that Americans do not know how much money is spent in foreign aid, and also think that too much money is dedicated to foreign aid, although the definition of foreign aid that is used by both pollsters and respondents is often unclear. For example, a 2013 poll by the Kaiser Family Foundation found that 61 percent of those surveyed felt that the U.S. spent too much on foreign aid, which for many included military assistance.[27] (The United Kingdom is the second largest bilateral donor, and its citizens are also skeptical of foreign aid. A national poll found that 60 percent believe that foreign aid is wasted.[28])

Finally, even if we were willing to assume responsibility for subsidizing poor governments as needed, this alone would be unlikely to change the way poor governments hold power; the revenue constraint is only one of many. A fundamental shift in the relations of power is not so easily accomplished. To quote Frederick Douglass, "Power concedes nothing without a demand. It never did and it never will."[29] The persistence of patronage and authoritarian governance in wealthier countries demonstrates that while adequate revenue is necessary for good governance, it is not sufficient. Just as there is no automatic adoption of the governance ideal with economic growth, neither is there an automatic adoption as the result of foreign aid. The governance ideal was advanced in the West through conflict and struggle.

A substantial increase in foreign aid might even have the reverse effect. Because poor governments have weak administrations, they cannot rationally spend (much less track or audit) large aid flows, creating waste and new opportunities for capture. Pouring massive amounts of money into poor governments is like trying to fill a teacup with a fire hose—water will go everywhere. In Afghanistan, which not only received military assistance and foreign aid, but also the money that was used by the Coalition for local procurement, the influx of dollars swamped not only the Afghan government but also the Afghan economy.[30] According to one expert, Afghanistan was saturated with inflows within the first year of operations. Not only was the Afghan government unable to track the funds, the U.S. government was also unable to track them.

Increasing aid flows to a poor government may simply result in a class of fabulously wealthy elites, cementing the existing patronage system, or it may allow a strengthening of the security apparatus to be used for repression; in neither case does it advance good governance. We have seen examples of this dynamic in poor governments that received revenue windfalls in the form of oil money to the point that there is a literature about how poor governments can manage the "oil curse."[31] Some scholars believe that the key to good governance is a relationship in which the government is accountable to the people because it depends on them for tax revenue.[32] Financing governments from the outside weakens this link.

Aid skeptics argue that aid is doing more harm than good. Kenyan economist James Shikwati said about development aid for Africa, "For God's sake, please just stop." He went on to explain:

> Huge bureaucracies are financed (with the aid money), corruption and complacency are promoted, Africans are taught to be beggars and not to be independent. In addition, development aid weakens the local markets everywhere and dampens the spirit of entrepreneurship that we so desperately need. As absurd as it may sound: Development aid is one of the reasons for Africa's problems. If the West were to cancel these payments, normal Africans wouldn't even notice. Only the functionaries would be hard hit. Which is why they maintain that the world would stop turning without this development aid.[33]

It is not clear whether delivering larger volumes of aid indefinitely to poor governments would solve their governance problems or just exacerbate them.

Make Them Rich?

Yet another approach to attaining the governance ideal in poor countries might be to wait for or to help catalyze economic growth. Figure 8.1 shows changes in GDP per capita between 1970 and 2008 for 163 countries.[34] A number of countries have been mired in poverty for decades; some were poor dependencies before they became poor countries. If national wealth is a prerequisite of good governance, whether because it increases government revenue or through some other channel, then perhaps we should focus less on making poor governments govern like rich governments and focus more on making them into rich governments.

However, if the answer to achieving the governance ideal is economic growth, we have a few problems. The first is that we do not know how to ensure economic growth. The question of how nations become wealthy was posed by Adam Smith in 1776, and while it has spawned a field of study in economics, there is nothing close to a consensus with respect to the answer. The rapid economic rise of the "East Asian tigers"—Hong Kong, Singapore, South Korea, and Taiwan—was called a "miracle" because such growth stories were historically unprecedented and flouted all of the dominant theories for how national economic growth was accomplished. China is playing that contrarian role today, defying conventional economic thinking, and yet its gross national income per capita has grown at 10 percent per year on average between 1979 and 2011.[35] (By contrast, the rate in high-income countries over the same period was almost 2 percent per year.) Because we do not know what stimulates economic growth—consider the debates about the response to the recent U.S. recession—we are also unable to say with any precision what government policies poor countries should adopt to ensure economic growth, much less how to get poor governments to adopt

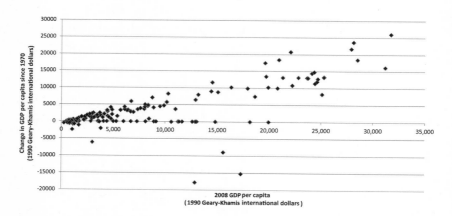

Figure 8.1. GDP Per Capita Between 1970 and 2008 for 163 Countries in 1990 International Geary-Khamis Dollars. (Data from Angus Maddison, *Historical Statistics of the World Economy: 1–2008 AD*, www.ggdc.net/maddison/oriindex.htm)

and implement them. The answers will not be the same for all countries at all times.

In any event, waiting for economic growth in poor countries is likely to be, at best, a medium-term solution to the governance problem. This is because, notwithstanding a handful of outstanding growth stories like those of Singapore and South Korea, most economic growth happens more slowly, and the gap between rich and poor countries is very large. If the gross national income per capita of one of the world's poorest countries, Burundi, were to grow at a respectable 5 percent every year, Burundi would catch up with where Mauritania is today in thirty years and where Botswana is today in about seventy.

Finally, although wealth may be necessary for the governance ideal, it is by no means sufficient. There is a lively debate in both the academic and policy literature about whether better governance causes economic development or the other way around. Both points of view are likely too simple. In rich liberal democracies, increased wealth and gradual changes to governance were mutually reinforcing over centuries. As countries grew richer, their governments had more revenue and more possibilities for implementing policies, and their wealthier and better-educated populations became more demanding. Some countries have grown richer without making a shift to liberal democracy. In some middle-income countries, such as those in the Middle East and North Africa, and oil-rich countries like Gabon and Equatorial Guinea, governments continue to rely heavily on patronage

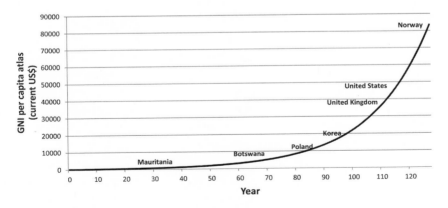

Figure 8.2. How Long Would It Take Burundi to Be as Rich as Norway Is Right Now, if It Grew at 5% GNI Per Capita?

and repression to govern. Recent work in economic theory rejects the idea that countries necessarily progress along a single path toward the governance ideal as they get richer.[36]

There may be many reasons to replace a government leader, reform a government institution, incentivize a poor government, provide foreign aid, or attempt to catalyze economic growth in a poor country. These approaches may even allow some incremental improvement in governance. What they can't do is bring about a rapid shift in how poor governments hold power. They do not allow us to avoid the uncomfortable discussion about how poor governments govern and what this implies for how we must engage them effectively and ethically.

Dealing with Poor Governments

If we cannot "fix" poor governments, and if their strategies of governance are likely to persist for some time, then we must, for the interim, decide how we want to respond to the way they govern. It is tempting to deny, to continue to engage poor governments as if they were simply poorer rich liberal democracies, as if the laws and formal institutional structures of government defined how they operated and as if their interest lay solely in public service delivery, rule of law, and democratic accountability. But as tempting as it is to live in an easier alternate universe, this approach has led us to misunderstand the intentions, actions, and capacities of poor governments, to make investments that are unlikely to bear fruit, to sacrifice lives needlessly, and perhaps even to destabilize poor governments.

GO AROUND. One way to deal with poor governments is to disengage, go around them, and ignore them, at the risk of violating their sovereignty. Foreign aid donors have historically gone around poor governments by "ringfencing" aid projects. Projects are said to be "ringfenced" when donors run aid projects themselves or work with the government to set up stand-alone project implementation units with dedicated government staff. Donors may ringfence projects when they have concerns about the government's capacity or willingness to run an aid project, and in particular, when they are concerned that the government would divert project resources and pose a fiduciary risk (although, for diplomatic reasons, such concerns are rarely voiced publicly).

Ringfencing came under increasing criticism as the number of donors and projects multiplied, creating thousands of uncoordinated, overlapping, and conflicting projects over which the recipient government had little control and often little information. Given that, for poor governments, foreign aid can be the equivalent of the government's own revenues or more, this meant that a substantial percentage of public funds were out of the control of the government. It was argued that the government's ability to make public policy was undermined. In addition, because donor projects offered good salaries, working environments, and professional opportunities, they created a "brain drain" from the recipient government to donor projects and project implementation units, weakening government human resource capacity. Where donors delivered project services directly, some argued that the effect was to marginalize the government in the eyes of the public and undermine the government's legitimacy. Finally, although ringfencing was done in large part to guard against misuse of donor funds, it was not clear that donors were able to monitor their projects adequately to prevent such misuses, even when projects were ringfenced.

For all of these reasons, there have been strong calls to abandon ringfencing and move to direct budget support. Direct budget support is based on the assumption that donors and poor governments have the same kind of governance and priorities, use similar processes and institutions to accomplish similar goals, and that any differences on the ground are attributable to lack of training and capacity. Under direct budget support, instead of financing projects, donors provide financing directly to the government to be managed through the government's own policymaking, budgeting, and public expenditure systems. Direct budget support is accompanied by donor technical assistance designed to help strengthen the capacity of the government to make and implement policy and to manage public funds.

At the end of the day, despite repeated calls to turn to direct budget support, direct budget support comprises less than 3 percent of government development assistance.[37] In part, this reflects donors' need to get individual credit for their projects, whether to gain international reputation and "soft power" or to demonstrate their own institutional effectiveness to a domestic audience. But it is also the case that most donors don't want to relinquish that amount of control, take on that degree of fiduciary risk, and be left to explain to domestic taxpayers how, for example, the aid money that was given to Afghanistan found its way to Kuwait. Donors know, but cannot say out loud, that poor governments do not govern the same way rich liberal democracies do, and they do not have the same priorities. Foreign aid in poor countries continues to "go around" the government.

MEET THEM WHERE THEY ARE. Alternately, we could engage poor governments directly, acknowledging and adapting to their governance strategies. This involves identifying and bargaining with the relevant actors with influence and decision-making authority, regardless of their formal positions. In patronage systems, it may involve acting as a patron and recruiting poor government elites as clients, thereby leveraging their client networks. For example, historian Mark Moyar argued that a COIN approach in Afghanistan that focuses on big development projects that aim to confer broad social and political benefits on the population is unlikely to succeed.[38] This "population-centered" COIN fails both to address the population's principal concerns and to engage the elites that drive public action and opinion. Instead, he argues for targeting spending to elites and allowing them to direct that money to their client networks:

> Channeling aid to elites and demanding their support in return was instrumental to the counterinsurgency triumph in Iraq. During the first few years of the Iraq War, U.S. policymakers forbade this method in the interest of building up a democratic national government and national security forces, a policy that caused large numbers of Iraqi elites to side with the insurgents and did little to bring other elites to the counterinsurgent side. . . .
>
> The insurgency eventually became so bad that the prohibition against cutting deals with local elites was lifted, at which point American commanders quickly co-opted tribal leaders by paying them $35,000 for a $25,000 school and letting them dole out construction contracts to their kinsmen. At American insistence, these Iraqi elites returned the favor by providing intelligence information or recruiting men into local security forces. If the tribal leaders dragged their feet on taking action against the insurgents, the United States could threaten them with a withdrawal of aid, and such threats often achieved the intended effect.[39]

The Central Intelligence Agency has been using a similar strategy in Afghanistan. It began supporting Hamid Karzai as an ally against al Qaeda and continued to drop off bags of cash at his office when he was president.

The payments "totaled tens of millions of dollars since they began a decade ago," according to Afghan officials.[40] With candor and perhaps a bit of puzzlement as to why this had become an issue, Karzai explained that the presidential slush fund "helped pay rent for various officials, treat wounded members of his presidential guard and even pay for scholarships." *The New York Times* explained:

> But it was Mr. Karzai's acknowledgment that some of the money had been given to "political elites" that was most likely to intensify concerns about the cash and how it is used.
>
> In Afghanistan, the political elite includes many men more commonly described as warlords, people with ties to the opium trade and to organized crime, along with lawmakers and other senior officials. Many were the subjects of American-led investigations that yielded reams of intelligence and evidence but almost no significant prosecutions by the Afghan authorities.
>
> "Yes, sometimes Afghanistan's political elites have some needs, they have requested our help and we have helped them," Mr. Karzai said. "But we have not spent it to strengthen a particular political movement. It's not like that. It has been given to individuals."[41]

Afghan, American, and European officials objected that the CIA's cash deliveries "effectively undercut a pillar of the American war strategy: the building of a clean and credible Afghan government to wean popular support from the Taliban."[42]

A third example of this type of engagement is a cautionary tale about the dangers of engaging poor governments on their own terms. The risk is that such engagement could change who we are and challenge some of the victories we have won in our own domestic governance arena.

Formal independence did not end France's relationship with her former African colonies. France continued to exercise strong influence in the selection of government leaders, the military protection of regimes, and in trade agreements, particularly with regard to access to oil. France built and maintained long-term personal social relationships between French and African government elites. The national oil company, Elf Aquitaine, was used as a vehicle for payments to African leaders. The closeness of this relationship is captured in the term to describe it: "FrançAfrique."

These engagements violated French law. When the details became public in 1994, it was a national scandal. The French government was widely criticized for propping up the regimes of African leaders whose governance was marked by human rights violations and corruption. The "Elf Affair" led to criminal prosecutions in what *The Guardian* called "probably the biggest political and corporate sleaze scandal to hit a western democracy since the second world war."[43]

> But the four-month trial, which had France riveted with its tales of political graft and sumptuous living, was also that of a system of state-sanctioned sleaze that flourished in France for years: successive politicians saw the country's state-owned multinationals not just as undercover foreign policy tools, but as a convenient source of ready cash to keep friends happy and enemies quiet.
>
> Le Floch [the former CEO of Elf Aquitaine], whose lawyer said yesterday his client would not be appealing to the court, insisted throughout his trial that he was in "daily contact" with the Elysée palace, and that "all the presidents of France" had known of, and condoned, the company's illicit dealings. . . .
>
> Many of the missing millions were paid out in illegal "royalties" to various African leaders and their families.[44]

But the flow of funds was not unidirectional. "Let's call a spade a spade," said Le Floch in 2002. "The money from Elf goes to Africa and comes back to France."[45] In 2011, French lawyer Robert Bourgi claimed in an interview that between 1997 and 2005 he had transported millions of dollars in campaign contributions to former French president Jacques Chirac and his political ally Dominique de Villepin from Senegal, Burkina Faso, Ivory Coast, Congo-Brazzaville, Gabon, and Equatorial Guinea.[46] The convicted middlemen Tarallo and Sirven also enjoyed substantial benefits. "Much of the money was spent on jewellery, artworks and sumptuous apartments: the magnificent villa that Tarallo bought on Corsica was estimated at €23.1m, while Sirven spent €1m a year for six years on jewels alone."[47]

Meeting poor governments where they are is not an easy alternative either. If a major change to the state system or a commitment to fill the gap in poor countries goes against our key interests, the abandonment of our belief in the universality of our governance ideal goes against our most deeply held values. Patronage systems offend our belief in human equality because they provide unequal access to government positions, authority, resources, and services. Patronage systems are also less effective for policy development and implementation, as the use of government offices, contracts, and powers for patronage may conflict with their use in the public interest. Governance that relies on repression or violates human rights is even more offensive to us. "What happens if we leave Afghanistan?" asked the August 9, 2010 cover of *Time Magazine*. The answer was given by the photograph of eighteen-year-old Aisha, whose nose was cut off by her husband and brother-in-law on the order of a Taliban judge after she fled an abusive marriage. Implicit in the question was the idea that the presence of the United States could help protect human rights. Just that May, Secretary of State Hillary Clinton had promised not to abandon the women of Afghanistan.

Advocates for the governance ideal would likely argue that complacency regarding the injustice, inequality, and repression of poor governments could suppress demand for change where change is in fact possible. If we accept from poor governments what we consider to be unacceptable in richer ones, we will have a dual standard. This is uncomfortably reminiscent of colonialism, when citizens of the metropole and colonial subjects had different legal status and were governed by different institutions, standards, and laws. It is also racially charged because colonial dualism was often justified on a racial basis and because of the racial composition of today's rich and poor countries. Many would see acceptance of the strategies that poor governments use to govern as a statement that the lives and freedoms of people in poor countries are worth less than those of rich liberal democracies—that poor people are somehow less deserving. A dual standard might also undermine standards in rich countries by changing a "bright line" rule ("never do this, it is wrong") to a rule that is contextual ("it's alright under certain circumstances"), threatening governance gains at home.

Coming to Terms

Because we believe that every country can and should be governed by providing public goods and services to all citizens under the rule of law subject to the accountability of democratic elections, we use our power and our position in the world to universalize our governance values. We demand the adoption of the same formal institutions and the passage of laws that criminalize other strategies of governance. Even now, as the development community looks to set new global targets for development post-2015, after the current Millennium Development Goals expire, some are advocating the establishment of global targets for democratic governance, control of corruption, and the rule of law.[48]

But the governance ideal as it is expressed today is historically recent and geographically limited, and the idea that this way of holding power is available to everyone is newer still. Today's rich liberal democracies became states because their governments gradually increased the territory under their control, often through conquest. Today's poor governments were assigned territories and then expected to build a state out to arbitrarily assigned borders. Today's rich liberal democracies relied on cheaper strategies of governance when they were poor, such as appeals to tradition, patronage, religious ideology, and repression. Poor governments are expected to govern their territories without recourse to such strategies. Rich liberal democracies supplied a much more limited basket of public goods and services when they were poor and to a more limited group of people—even a hundred years ago. Poor governments are expected to supply the same basket as today's rich governments do and to everyone. Governments of today's rich liberal democracies were built through centuries of economic growth and gradual government expansion, even as power concentrated among elites was eventually extended to the adult population through political and armed struggle. Poor governments are expected to start with full franchise democracy and deliver the same governance without any intermediate steps and to work this transformation by a graceful consensus in which those who would lose would volunteer to be losers. Finally, poor governments are asked to govern subject to the pressures of the international community, driven by much richer, more powerful, and impatient countries with strong preferences about the way they govern.

There are doubtless many prerequisites for the governance ideal. Scholars and practitioners seeking to explain the way poor governments hold power have pointed to precolonial culture, the impact of colonization on culture, tribalism, ethnic diversity, and greedy, corrupt, exploitative, bloodthirsty, predatory, kleptocratic elites who lack "political will," a mysterious invisible quality that can only be detected by its absence. Some see poor governments as historical throwbacks, because this type of national and governmental poverty is in the Western past. Regional scholars have attempted to understand how poor governments hold power looking only in Sub-Saharan Africa, only in Central Asia, or only in South Asia, and while this narrow focus has enabled them to see idiosyncratic qualities of particular poor governments, it leads them to overlook the common consequences of poverty.

Whether in Africa, Central Asia, or South Asia, poor governments are too poor to satisfy our expectations. Although adequate revenue is not sufficient for the governance ideal, it is absolutely necessary. While we have seen some countries grow wealthier and gradually change the way their governments hold power in tandem, there are a group of governments that are so poor that they cannot govern exclusively or primarily by winning popular support and legitimacy by providing universal public goods and services under the rule of law, subject to democratic accountability. They are too poor to provide minimal services to their entire populations, or even to establish much presence in parts of their territories. They cannot provide basic security or justice, cannot enforce contracts reliably, cannot deal effectively with challengers. They can't even afford to pay for their own national elections. Instead, they provide services to some, buy political support from others, repress political opponents, and ignore parts of their territory and the people who live there. They invoke shared religious beliefs, shared ethnicity, a common enemy, or a common struggle. They look the other way when civil servants pay themselves, because they cannot afford to pay them.

We see these older, cheaper strategies of governance as immoral, corrupt, and evil. When we do acknowledge that poor governments govern differently, we condemn them. We intervene on the theory that stoking popular dissatisfaction and demand for change, tinkering with formal institutions, or replacing government leaders will result in a fundamental change in the way the government holds power without acknowledging that the governance ideal is so expensive that some simply cannot afford it. But the insistence that poor governments hold power and govern the same way that rich liberal democracies do is reminiscent of Rousseau's anecdote about the princess who, when told that the peasants had no bread, said, "Then let them eat pastry!" To pretend that the options of the poor are the same as the options of the rich is false egalitarianism. It is an especially uncomfortable position given the role that the rich West has played in shaping today's poor states.

Because we have labeled their governance as evil, we cannot talk openly about the constraints poor governments face, discuss beneficial incremental changes to the way the government holds power, or discuss adaptive strategies for engagement. When I want to get a laugh from my World Bank colleagues, I ask them when they are going to hold a workshop on "Patronage Best Practices." And then, while they are laughing uncomfortably, I ask them why this is so funny. If we care about improving governance, and if poor governments are compelled to rely on strategies such as patronage to govern, this is exactly what we should be doing. But I already know why they are laughing. Such a frank admission that our governance ideals may not be universally available or any sign of accommodating the disfavored strategies of poor governments would be career suicide both for the unlucky Bank staff and the government officials who participated in the workshop. Our dialogue with poor governments depends on mutual denial.

In part our problem is ignorance, a problem of class and social distance on a global scale, a failure to understand what it means to be poor, a cultural blind spot. But our failure to learn goes much deeper than that. Accepting that not every government can govern the way we would like leads to very hard choices that involve compromising our interests or our values. Our choices are so unappealing and costly; it is easier to avoid them. This—not naïveté—is the real reason why we have been so ineffective in dealing with poor governments. And yet, as the U.S. engagement in Afghanistan should teach us, the failure to make the hard choices is also costly. It causes us to fail to predict the actions of poor governments because we do not know how they govern, or what incentives or constraints they face. When we stigmatize the governance strategies of poor governments, we make it difficult to have real conversations about how poor governments work or how they can work better. When we base our development and security strategies on unattainable changes in the way in which poor governments hold power, they fail, at the cost of money and lives. When we set ethical and performance standards for poor governments that are unachievable no matter what they do, ironically we free poor governments from being accountable for ethical behavior and performance. If poor governments can't afford the kind of governance we want, then campaigning to universalize our governance values as the only legitimate basis of governance risks destabilizing poor governments without offering any viable alternative. At the same time, the failure to develop an explicit foreign policy to engage poor governments effectively delegates that responsibility to the clandestine services and field-level personnel. This means that the approach will be piecemeal and focused on solving immediate problems without consideration of the full scope of the national interest. It also leaves these on-the-ground problem solvers without useful guidance and vulnerable to later reproach or punishment.

Most people want to turn the discussion back immediately to the question of how poor countries can become rich in the hope that this will obviate the need to develop an adaptive foreign policy for the long interim. But this is not a book about how to fix poor governments, and it does not offer a technical solution. It does not suggest how poor governments should govern or how poor countries should become rich. This is because the problem with which this book is concerned is a political problem, not a technical one, and it is a problem with us, not poor governments. If poor governments cannot change the way they govern in the medium or perhaps even the long term, then we must change the way we respond to them. This book is an appeal to allow a different kind of conversation about the governance of poor governments.

DESTIGMATIZE. By painting poor country governance as an exclusively moral issue, we drive the issue underground; but it cannot be the case that to be moral one must be rich. Destigmatizing the governance of the poor would allow a more honest exchange with poor governments and their citizens about the way they are governing and why and what types of reforms and improvements might be possible. Accepting the governance strategies of the poor would mean abandoning denunciations and ultimatums because we would not want to undermine the government's ability to govern, and we do not have workable suggestions for alternative ways for the government to hold power. We would drop the use of the word "corruption" to describe governments that govern through patronage. "Corruption" is not accurate to describe patronage systems, insofar as it refers to deviant, not routine, behavior; nor is it helpful, since it is also a term of moral condemnation.

DECRIMINALIZE. We would also have to decriminalize these governance practices and allow them to be legalized in international and poor country domestic law. For example, if the government cannot pay civil servants regular and adequate salaries, then civil servants must legally be allowed to monetize their offices or to hold outside employment, just as government officials were allowed to do when Western countries were too poor to pay them salaries. If legalized and thereby made more transparent, such practices might more easily be publicly discussed and bounded by norms, like public-private partnerships or outsourcing. Poor governments would not be pressured into signing treaties that criminalize their strategies of governance, such as the United Nations Convention Against Corruption. The human rights community would need to, at a minimum, take a much more limited view of the role of poor governments in guaranteeing human rights and, at a maximum, be willing to tolerate some degree of political repression. By bringing the domestic law back in line with the possibilities, actualities, and norms of poor government governance, the legal system could be made meaningful and rule of law might become more possible.

DEVELOP REALISTIC EXPECTATIONS. We would lower our expectations of poor governments substantially, and in particular we would not encourage them to overpromise, by, for example, pressing them to pass laws, sign treaties, or hew to benchmarks that commit them to provide services or guarantee rights that they cannot afford to provide or guarantee. We would limit our demands on poor governments for information, interaction, reform and implementation, the protection of human rights, transparency and democracy, and the delivery of more and better quality public goods and services to a wider set of users. Poor government accountability would be strengthened if the responsibilities of poor governments were reduced and brought back into alignment with their capacities, resources, and governance strategies.

DEVELOP NEW STANDARDS. All poor governments are not the same. We would develop more nuanced standards appropriate to poor governments to judge the quality of their governance. Instead of measuring poor governments against a single unattainable governance ideal (an ideal that even rich liberal democracies do not attain), we would judge them against governance possibilities that are within their grasp, keeping in mind the way in which they do and must hold power and comparing them to other similarly situated governments. We would distinguish between strategies we liked better (perhaps patronage) from strategies we did not like as much (perhaps repression). We could even distinguish between better and worse patronage systems and between better and worse repressive governments. Just as citizens in poor countries do today, we would distinguish between those who take and those who take "too much"; those who share with others and those who "eat alone"; and those who take but get things done and those who take but do not deliver. We may distinguish between patronage systems based on their inclusion, stability, legitimacy, or involvement with international crime. Likewise, we could distinguish between repressive governments that use repression modestly and in predictable ways and those that have such disproportionate and unpredictable responses to challengers or conduct themselves with such impunity that even apolitical citizens live in fear of their government. There is a qualitative difference, for example, between North Korea and Rwanda.

We would encourage deeper thinking about how better outcomes are achieved in the world of second-best governance, which can only be done by acknowledging how poor governments do and must govern. The question is not whether such regimes are desirable, but whether they are the best available under existing constraints, and at the center of this analysis must be the question of how a government is to govern because a government that cannot govern cannot do any other thing. The governance of poor governments should be compared with a counterfactual, not an ideal, vision.

Some scholars are drawing such distinctions already, although our foreign policy has not. Fukuyama, for example, has argued that a distinction should be drawn between clientelism—in which democratic politicians and political parties deliver benefits to their electoral supporters—and corruption—in which politicians simply take for themselves.[49] Other studies have drawn distinctions between the impact of bribe demands when the amounts to be paid and the persons to whom they should be paid are well known and the services paid for are reliably delivered, and decentralized corruption, where there is uncertainty about whom to pay, how much services cost, and whether they will be delivered once payment is made.[50] Similarly, Johnston has argued that political machines are superior to decentralized corruption because they do deliver some level of services and that the existence of cartels of elites can be consistent with economic growth and gradually improving governance.[51] A large body of scholarly work has debated the benefits of development-minded authoritarian regimes, such as those of Singapore, China, predemocracy South Korea, and Rwanda, as long as they deliver the goods in terms of economic growth, human development, and the gradual expansion of the quality, breadth, and depth of public goods and services.

PRESS FOR IMPROVEMENTS THAT ACKNOWLEDGE HOW THE GOVERN-
MENT HOLDS POWER. Within the community of Western governance
experts, the problem of strengthening governance in poor countries has
often been seen as a problem of sequencing: figuring out the optimal order
of steps and focusing on building "the basics" first. This approach embod-
ies an optimistic view of our understanding of how complex social systems
operate and the possibilities of social engineering, as if governments were
designed and built by clever technocrats instead of emerging as the product
of political processes. (It is worth remembering James Madison's caution
that the U.S. Constitution is a political outcome, rather than the product of
an ingenious theorist working in his closet.[52]) But even if it were allowed
that Western governance experts have the ability to design and create other
peoples' governments, the problem is not simply one of sequencing if we
don't know what the end product is. The sequence of steps in building a
skateboard is not the same as the sequence of steps in building a sports car;
nor should the two be judged by the same criteria.

Understanding that poor governments hold power differently would
mean abandoning the insistence on transferring "best practices" in governance, laws, institutions, or ethics codes to poor governments that cannot
use them, given how they govern, and cannot afford to implement them.
The transfer of Western formal institutions is unlikely to change the way
poor governments hold power, and therefore, if transferred, such institutions are not likely to work the same way for poor governments as they do
for rich ones. Scholars and practitioners have raised this point, repeatedly,
since the beginning of this institutional transfer project.

We can and should still press for better governance, but it would be better governance within the framework of the strategies available to the government for holding power. Instead of starting as a point of departure with
what governments that are thousands of times richer do, much less what
an unattainable governance ideal looks like, we would ask, "What does a
good $200 or $300 or $600 per person per year government look like? How
would it garner political support? How would it hold power? How would
it deal with challengers? What functions can it carry out? How much of its
territory could it really govern? Who, if anyone, can govern the territory it
cannot?" There can be no single right answer to these questions.

Because governance according to the governance ideal is not an option,
taking the constraints of poor governments seriously might mean supporting a shift in governance strategies from one suboptimal strategy to

another. It might involve working to support the establishment of a political machine as a better alternative to a decentralized and disorganized corrupt state that delivers no services, helping to build more effective, equitable, transparent, or stable patronage systems, or working to replace an unpredictable and violent system of political repression with a more restrained and predictable one.

Finally, acceptance of the governance implications of poverty calls into question the transferability of the expertise of Western technocrats in the governance domain. There is no reason to assume, for example, that the domestic experience of Western procurement specialists or lawyers equips them with an understanding of the role and possibilities of procurement and legal systems in poor governments that hold power differently. We may know how to be a good rich government (although some would question that given our own struggles with good governance at home). However, it is much less clear that we know how to be a good poor government. The West's experience of governing while poor is too long behind it for Western experts to have much advice on how to run a better patronage system or repressive regime, even if they were inclined to do so. There is also the question of having moral standing to advise on the difficult trade-offs that poor governments and their citizens must make. While the West lacks expertise in this domain, it could foster South-South cooperation on governance issues between countries that have similar constraints, but only if it allows people to speak freely about how they govern without fear of condemnation or reprisal.

CHANGE THE RULES OF ENGAGEMENT. Acceptance of the ways in which poor governments govern would then allow us to discuss how to engage these governments effectively, ethically, and productively. This means identifying and engaging the decision makers regardless of their formal roles and engaging poor government processes even if they are not those written in the law. It would mean developing an understanding of how poor governments hold power and both their political constraints and the limits of their capacities. It may even mean cultivating government elites as clients in order to leverage their patronage networks. In practice, we already do these things episodically, but because the way that poor governments govern is not considered legitimate, these practices of engagement are also considered illegitimate and usually hidden from the public eye. Destigmatizing the governance of poor governments would also allow us to destigmatize these engagements with poor governments and allow the formulation of a more transparent and thoughtful foreign policy on engagement.

This pragmatic approach is not a relativist one; it is not a repudiation of our governance values. People everywhere should continue to seek government that is more effective, just, accountable, predictable, inclusive, responsive, and peaceful. However, the governance of very poor governments will never look like the governance of rich liberal democracies. It will necessarily follow a different logic and fall far short of our desires. The path to better government will be imperfect, incremental, and contextual, and more possibilities open with increasing wealth. However, the refusal to acknowledge the limitations that poverty imposes on governance not just in terms of capacity but also in terms of how governments must hold power is too expensive.

Notes

1. Blind Spot

1. "Poverty 'Fuelling Terrorism,'" *BBC News*, March 22, 2002, http://news.bbc.co.uk/2/hi/1886617.stm.

2. "President Bush's Speech at the United Nations Financing for Development Conference in Monterrey, Mexico," *PBS*, March 22, 2002, www.pbs.org/newshour/updates/march02/bush_3-22.html.

3. Total of official aid received from 2001 to 2010 from the World Development Indicators, World Bank, in constant 2010 dollars. http://data.worldbank.org/data-catalog/world-development-indicators.

4. Office of the Special Inspector General for Afghanistan Reconstruction, "Commander's Emergency Response Program in Laghman Province Provided Some Benefits, but Oversight Weaknesses and Sustainment Concerns Led to Questionable Outcomes and Potential Waste," January 27, 2011, www.sigar.mil/pdf/audits/2011-01-27audit-11-07.pdf.

5. U.S. Library of Congress, Congressional Research Service, *The Cost of Iraq, Afghanistan, and Other Global War on Terror Operations Since 9/11*, by Amy Belasco, CRS RL 33110 (Washington, D.C.: Office of Congressional Information and Publishing, March 29, 2011), 1.

6. U.S. Library of Congress, Congressional Research Service, *Afghanistan Casualties: Military Forces and Civilians*, by Susan Chesser, CRS R41084 (Washington, D.C.: Office of Congressional Information and Publishing, December 6, 2012).

7. Steve Schooner and Colin Swan, "Dead Contractors: The Un-Examined Effect of Surrogates on the Public's Casualty Sensitivity," *Journal of National Security Law and Policy* 6 (2012): 11, http://jnslp.com/2012/04/16/dead-contractors-the-un-examined-effect-of-surrogates-on-the-publics-casualty-sensitivity/.

8. U.S. Library of Congress, Congressional Research Service, "Afghanistan Casualties," 3.

9. Thomas Barfield, *Afghanistan: A Cultural and Political History* (Princeton: Princeton University Press, 2010), 318–31.

10. Freedom House, "Freedom in the World 2012: Afghanistan," 2013, www.freedomhouse.org/report/freedom-world/2013/afghanistan-0.

11. U.S. Department of State, "Country Reports on Human Rights Practices for 2012: Afghanistan," 2012, www.state.gov/j/drl/rls/hrrpt/humanrightsreport/#wrapper.

12. Transparency International, "Corruption Perceptions Index 2012," www .transparency.org/cpi2012/results.

13. United Nations, United Nations Office on Drugs and Crime, "The Global Afghan Opium Trade: A Threat Assessment," July 2011, 1, www.unodc.org/documents/data -and-analysis/Studies/Global_Afghan_Opium_Trade_2011-web.pdf.

14. Matthew Rosenberg, "An Afghan Mystery: Why Are Large Shipments of Gold Leaving the Country?" *The New York Times*, December 15, 2012.

15. Office of the Special Inspector General for Afghanistan Reconstruction, "Anticorruption Measures: Persistent Problems Exist in Monitoring Bulk Cash Flows at Kabul International Airport," SIGAR SP-13–1, December 11, 2012.

16. John Allen, "A Transformation: Afghanistan Beyond 2014," Testimony Before the Senate Foreign Relations Committee, April 30, 2014, www.foreign.senate.gov/imo /media/doc/Allen_Testimony.pdf.

17. U.S. Library of Congress, Congressional Research Service, "The Cost," 12 (Table 1), 17 (Table 3).

18. Anthony Cordesman, *Afghanistan: The Failed Metrics of Ten Years of War* (Washington, D.C.: Center for Strategic and International Studies, February 9, 2012).

19. Steven Metz, "Strategic Horizons: U.S. Must Learn the Real 'Lessons' of Afghanistan," *World Politics Review*, January 16, 2013, 3, www.worldpoliticsreview.com /articles/print/12627.

20. Majority Staff of Senate Committee on Foreign Relations, *Evaluating U.S. Foreign Assistance to Afghanistan*, 112th Congr., 1st Sess. (Washington, D.C.: U.S. Government Printing Office, June 8, 2011), 8–9.

21. This book illustrates the poverty of poor governments using comparative revenue per capita figures. The figures are derived from revenue data in the U.S. Central Intelligence Agency *World Factbook*, which are in current exchange rates. U.S. Central Intelligence Agency, *World Factbook*, 2014, www.cia.gov/library/publications /the-world-factbook/geos/af.html.

22. U.S. Government Accountability Office, "Afghanistan's Donor Dependence," GAO-11–948R (Washington, D.C., September 20, 2011), 3.

23. U.S. GAO, "Afghanistan's Donor Dependence," 1.

24. Kevin Sieff, "Afghan Economy Faces Serious Revenue Shortfall Amid Tenuous Political Transition," *The Washington Post*, April 15, 2014, www.washingtonpost .com/world/asia_pacific/afghan-economy-facing-serious-revenue-shortage/2014/04/15 /6ddce38a-5be9–46ad-8f3b-1eb2ef4ed9bd_story.html.

25. Barfield, *Afghanistan*, 311.

26. Barfield, *Afghanistan*, 68.

27. Max Weber, *The Vocation Lectures*, eds. David Owen and Tracy B. Strong, trans. Rodney Livingstone (Indianapolis: Hackett, 2004), 32.

28. Max Weber, *The Theory of Social and Economic Organization* (New York: Free Press, 1964).

29. Weber, *The Vocation Lectures*, 33.

30. Frances Romero, "Kim Jong-Il," *Time Magazine*, September 22, 2008, www.time .com/time/world/article/0,8599,1843207,00.html.

31. See Douglass C. North, John Joseph Wallis, and Barry R. Weingast, *Violence and Social Orders: A Conceptual Framework for Interpreting Recorded Human History* (Cambridge: Cambridge University Press, 2009).

32. Jan Banning, "Bureaucratics," www.janbanning.com/gallery/bureaucratics/.

33. See, for example, Patrick Chabal and Jean-Pascal Daloz, *Africa Works: Disorder as Political Instrument*, African Issues (Bloomington: Indiana University Press, 1999); North, Wallis, and Weingast, *Violence and Social Orders*; Daron Acemoglu and James Robinson, *Why Nations Fail: The Origins of Power, Prosperity, and Poverty* (New York: Crown, 2012).

34. M. A. Thomas, "Rich Donors, Poor Countries," *Policy Review* no. 175 (2012), www.hoover.org/publications/policy-review/article/129006; Merilee S. Grindle, "Good Enough Governance: Poverty Reduction and Reform in Developing Countries," *Governance* 17, no. 4 (2004): 525–48; Lant Pritchett and Frauke de Weijer, *Fragile States: Stuck in a Capability Trap?* (Washington, D.C.: World Bank, 2010).

35. Stanislav Andreski, *The African Predicament* (London: Joseph, 1968), 92–109; Stanislav Andreski, "Kleptocracy as a System of Government in Africa," in *Political Corruption: Readings in Comparative Analysis*, ed. Arnold Heidenheimer (New York: Holt, Rinehart and Winston, 1970), 346–57.

2. The Governance Ideal

1. Millennium Declaration, G.A. Res. 55/2, U.N. Doc. A/RES/55/2 (September 8, 2000).

2. U.S. Agency for International Development, "Democracy, Human Rights, and Governance," last updated February 6, 2014, www.usaid.gov/what-we-do/democracy -human-rights-and-governance.

3. U.S. Library of Congress, Congressional Research Service, *Foreign Aid: An Introduction to U.S. Programs and Policy*, by Curt Tarnoff and Maria Lawson, CRS R40213 (Washington, D.C.: Office of Congressional Information and Publishing, February 10, 2011), 5.

4. World Bank, *Governance: The World Bank's Experience* (Washington, D.C.: World Bank, 1994), vii; World Bank, *Governance and Development* (Washington, D.C.: World Bank, 1992).

5. World Bank, *Annual Report of the World Bank* (Washington, D.C.: World Bank, 2013), 15, http://go.worldbank.org/ZJCK7BDUY0.

6. Millennium Declaration, G.A. Res. 55/2, U.N. Doc. A/RES/55/2 (September 8, 2000).

7. United Nations Convention against Corruption, G.A. Res., U.N. Doc A/58/422 (October 7, 2003).

8. U.S. Interagency Counterinsurgency Initiative, "U.S. Counterinsurgency Guide," January 2009, 4, 12, www.state.gov/documents/organization/119629.pdf.

9. U.S. Joint Chiefs of Staff, "Report on Progress toward Security and Stability in Afghanistan," 2008, www.dod.mil/pubs/foi/joint_staff/jointStaff_jointOperations/10F _0018Report_on_Progress_toward_Security_and_Stability_in_Afghanistan.pdf.

10. Joint Chiefs, "Report on Progress."

11. Margaret C. Jacob, *The Enlightenment: A Brief History with Documents* (Boston: Bedford/St. Martins, 2001); James Van Horn Melton, *The Rise of the Public in Enlightenment Europe* (Cambridge: University Press, 2009).

12. Pauline Gregg, *King Charles I* (Berkeley: University of California Press, 1984), 432, http://ark.cdlib.org/ark:/13030/ft9v19p2p6/.

13. Lucy Aikin, *Memoirs of the Court of King Charles the First: In Two Volumes*, vol. 2 (Philadelphia: Carey, Lea and Blanchard, 1833), 365–66.

14. Ibid., 363.

15. *Declaration of the Rights of Man and the Citizen*, August 26, 1789.

16. Robert Neild, *Public Corruption: The Dark Side of Social Evolution* (London: Anthem Press, 2002).

17. William Doyle, *Venality: The Sale of Offices in Eighteenth Century France* (Oxford: Oxford University Press, 1996).

18. W. D. Rubinstein, "The End of Old Corruption in Britain 1780–1860," *Past and Present* 101 (1983): 55–86, 65.

19. Ibid., 73, quoting "A Peep at the Peers," Black Dwarf.

20. Neild, *Public Corruption*.

21. Ibid., 21–32.

22. Rubinstein, "The End of Old Corruption," 75.

23. Ari Hoogenboom, "The Pendleton Act and the Civil Service," *The American Historical Review* 64, no. 2 (1959): 301–18, 301, quoting H.R. Rep. No. 47 (1868), 40.

24. Neild, *Public Corruption*, 51.

25. Gustavus Myers, *The History of Tammany Hall*, 2nd ed. (New York: Boney and Liveright, 1917); Roy V. Peel, "The Political Machine of New York City," *American Political Science Review* 27, no. 4 (1933): 611–18.

26. William. L. Riordan, *Plunkitt of Tammany Hall: A Series of Very Plain Talks on Very Practical Politics* (New York: Signet Classic, 1995), xxiv.

27. Merriam-Webster, "Corruption," www.merriam-webster.com/dictionary/corruption.

28. "Blagojevich Impeached; Governor Blagojevich, Resign; Get the Latest on the Blagojevich Case," *Chicago Tribune*, December 10, 2008, Chicagotribune.com; "Details from Rod Blagojevich's 74-Page Affidavit," *CNN*, December 9, 2008, http://edition.cnn .com/2008/POLITICS/12/09/blagojevich.affidavit/.

29. Choire Sicha, "Glengarry Rod Blagojevich," *Salon*, December 10, 2008, www .salon.com/opinion/feature/2008/12/10/mamet/index.html.

30. See Laughlin McDonald, *American Indians and the Fight for Equal Voting Rights* (Oklahoma: University of Oklahoma Press, 2011).

31. William Collins and Melissa Thomasson, "Exploring the Racial Gap in Infant Mortality Rates, 1920–1970," Department of Economics, Vanderbilt University, Working Paper No. 02-W01, 2002, 9.

32. "Late Night: Jon Stewart Calls Fox's Megyn Kelly a Hypocrite," *Los Angeles Times*, August 12, 2011, http://latimesblogs.latimes.com/showtracker/2011/08/late-night-jon -stewart-calls-foxs-megyn-kelly-a-hypocrite-.html.

33. Universal Declaration of Human Rights, G.A. Res. 217A (III), UN Doc A/810 (December 10, 1948), 71.

34. Ibid.

35. Johannes Morsink, *The Universal Declaration of Human Rights: Origins, Drafting, and Intent* (Philadelphia: University of Pennsylvania Press, 1999), 229–30.

36. David Banisar, *Freedom of Information Around the World 2006* (Privacy International: 2006), www.privacyinternational.org/foi/foisurvey2006.pdf.

37. Jesse Jackson, Jr., "Do We Have a Right to Health Care?" *ABC News*, October 13, 2006, http://abcnews.go.com/WNT/PrescriptionForChange/Story?id=2563706&page=1.

38. Scott Wilson, "Obama Defends Health-Care Law, Calling Health Insurance 'a Right,'" *The Washington Post*, September 26, 2013, www.washingtonpost.com/politics/obama-defends-health-care-law-calling-health-insurance-a-right/2013/09/26/9e1d946e-26b8-11e3-b75d-5b7f66349852_print.html.

39. Chester Hartman, "The Case for a Right to Housing," *Housing Policy Debate* 9, no. 2 (1998): 223–46.

40. Pew, "The American-Western European Values Gap: American Exceptionalism Subsides," Pew Research Center Global Attitudes Project, 2011, www.pewglobal.org/files/2011/11/Pew-Global-Attitudes-Values-Report-FINAL-November-17–2011–10AM-EST1.pdf.

41. See Mark Benjamin, "Obama's Speech is Similar to Bush's Second Inaugural Address," *Time U.S., Battleland: Military Intelligence for the Rest of Us*, May 20, 2011, http://battleland.blogs.time.com/2011/05/20/obama-speech-contains-echoes-of-bush-inaugural-address/.

42. Federal News Service, "There Is No Justice Without Freedom," *The Washington Post*, January 21, 2005, www.washingtonpost.com/wp-dyn/articles/A23747–2005Jan20.html.

43. Ben Feller, "Obama Middle East Speech Covers Arab Spring, Need For Reform In Region," *Huffington Post*, May 19, 2011, www.huffingtonpost.com/2011/05/19/obama-middle-east-speech-_n_864153.html.

44. U.S. Const. art. II § 1.

45. The White House, "Text of Obama's Speech on Afghanistan," *The Seattle Times*, June 22, 2011, www.archives.gov/press/press-kits/charters.html#pressrelease1; Milton Gustafson, "Travels of the Charters of Freedom," *Prologue* 34, no. 4 (2002), www.archives.gov/publications/prologue/2002/winter/travels-charters.html.

46. President Truman, "The National Archives Experience," 1952, www.archives.gov/national-archives-experience/visit/truman_transcript.html.

47. Transcript, "Saving the National Treasures," *PBS*, February 15, 2005, www.pbs.org/wgbh/nova/transcripts/3206_charters.html.

48. National Institute of Standards and Technology, "Origins of the Charters of Freedom Project," www.nist.gov/centennial/encasements.cfm.

49. Michael Beschloss, "Remarks by Michael Beschloss at the Ceremony to Unveil Page Two of the U.S. Constitution in Its New Encasement," Speech, Rotunda of the National Archives Building, Washington, D.C., September 15, 2000, www.archives.gov/about/speeches/09–15–00-b.html.

50. G. K. Chesterton, "What Is America?" in *What I Saw in America / The Resurrection of Rome / Side Lights*, vol. 21 of *The Collected Works of G. K. Chesterton*, ed. George Marlin (San Francisco: Ignatius Press, 1990), 37–50.

51. Douglass C. North, John Joseph Wallis, and Barry R. Weingast, *Violence and Social Orders: A Conceptual Framework for Interpreting Recorded Human History* (Cambridge: Cambridge University Press, 2009); Daron Acemoglu and James Robinson, *Why Nations Fail: The Origins of Power, Prosperity, and Poverty* (New York: Crown Publishers, 2012).

52. Francis Fukuyama, *The Origins of Political Order: From Prehuman Times to the French Revolution* (New York: Farrar, Straus and Giroux, 2011).

53. Mick Moore, "Revenues, State Formation, and the Quality of Governance in Developing Countries," *International Political Science Review* 25, no. 3 (2004): 297–319.

54. See Mark Dincecco, "Fiscal Centralization, Limited Government, and Public Revenues in Europe, 1650–1913," *The Journal of Economic History* 69, no. 1 (2009): 48–103.

55. Acemoglu and Robinson, *Why Nations Fail*; Mark Dincecco and Gabriel Katz, "State Capacity and Long-Run Performance," October 29, 2012, SSRN, http://ssrn.com/abstract=2044578.

56. See Dincecco, "Fiscal Centralization."

57. The figure for 1902 U.S. government spending is from U.S. Census Bureau, *Historical Statistics of the United States: Millennial Edition Online*, "Table Ea10–23, Total government revenue and expenditure, by level: 1902–1995," www.census.gov/population/www/censusdata/hiscendata.html. The figure for the U.S. population of 76,212,168 is from U.S. Census Bureau, "Selected Historical Decennial Census Population and Housing Counts," *1900 US Census Bureau, Historical Statistics*, "Table 2: Population, Housing Units, Area Measurements, and Density: 1790 to 1990," www.census.gov/population/www/censusdata/files/table-2.pdf. The constant dollar figure was calculated using the GDP deflator and calculator provided by Louis Johnston and Samuel H. Williamson at www.measuringworth.com. The figure for 2012 U.S. government spending is from the Office of Management and Budget, "Historical Tables, Budget of the U.S. Government, Table 15.1—TOTAL GOVERNMENT RECEIPTS IN ABSOLUTE AMOUNTS AND AS PERCENTAGES OF GDP: 1948–2013," www.whitehouse.gov/omb/budget/historicals. The U.S. population data is from U.S. Census Bureau, "Annual Estimates of the Resident Population for the United States, Regions, States, and Puerto Rico: April 1, 2010 to July 1, 2013 (NST-EST2013–01)," 2014, Table 1, Annual Estimates of the Population for the United States, Regions, States, and Puerto Rico: April 1, 2010 to July 1, 2013, www.census.gov/popest/data/national/totals/2013/index.html.

3. Paper Empires, Paper Countries

1. Ola Olsson, "Unbundling Ex-Colonies: A Comment on Acemoglu, Johnson and Robinson 2001," Department of Economics, University of Gothenburg, Working Paper No. 146, 2004.

2. D. K. Fieldhouse, *The Colonial Empires: A Comparative Survey from the Eighteenth Century* (New York: Delacorte Press, 1966), 372.

3. Margery Perham, *The Colonial Reckoning: The End of Imperial Rule in Africa in Light of the British Experience* (New York: Alfred A. Knopf, 1962), 157–58, 126.

4. A. Adu Boahen, *African Perspectives on Colonialism* (Baltimore: Johns Hopkins University Press, 1987), 78–93, 32.

5. Thomas Pakenham, *The Scramble for Africa: The White Man's Conquest of the Dark Continent from 1876 to 1912* (New York: Random House, 1991), 22.

6. I. M. Cumpston, "The Discussion of Imperial Problems in the British Parliament, 1880–1885," *Transactions of the Royal Historical Society*, Fifth Series 13 (1963): 29–47; House of Lords, Hansard, "Debate 09 May 1884," vol. 287, cc 1827–36, 1834, http://hansard.millbanksystems.com/lords/1884/may/09/resolution.

7. Pakenham, *The Scramble for Africa*, 22; Jeffery Herbst, "The Creation and Maintenance of National Boundaries in Africa," *International Organizations* 43, no. 4 (1989): 678.

8. Herbst, "National Boundaries."

9. Ibid.

10. Antony Anghie, "Finding the Peripheries: Sovereignty and Colonialism in Nineteenth Century International Law," *Harvard International Law Journal* 40, no. 1 (1999): 1–80.

11. Frank Moore Colby, Harry Thurston Peck, and Edward Lathrop Engle, *The International Year Book* (New York: Dodd, Mead and Company, 1903), 8.

12. Frederick Quinn, *The French Overseas Empire* (Westport, CT: Praeger, 2000), 268. See also Boahen, *African Perspectives*, 29.

13. Fieldhouse, *The Colonial Empires*, 373.

14. See Michael Havinden and David Meredith, *Colonialism and Development: Britain and Its Tropical Colonies, 1850–1960* (New York: Routledge, 1993), 307.

15. Robert. H. Jackson, *Quasi-States: Sovereignty, International Relations, and the Third World* (Cambridge: Cambridge University Press, 1990), 67–71.

16. Anghie, "Finding the Peripheries."

17. Henry Wheaton, *Elements of International Law: With a Sketch of the History of the Science* (London: B. Fellowes, 1836), 15.

18. Anghie, "Finding the Peripheries."

19. "Convention Revising the General Act of Berlin, February 26, 1885, and the General Act and Declaration of Brussels, July 2, 1890," *The American Journal of International Law* 15, no. 4 (1921): 314–21.

20. Anghie, "Finding the Peripheries."

21. David Killingray, "The Maintenance of Law and Order in British Colonial Africa," *African Affairs* 84, no. 340 (1986): 436.

22. See, for example, Peter Karibe Mendy, "Portugal's Civilizing Mission in Colonial Guinea-Bissau: Rhetoric and Reality," *The International Journal of African Historical Studies* 36, no. 1 (2003): 38, 41.

23. Havinden and Meredith, *Colonialism and Development*, 154, 183.

24. Robert Aldrich, *Greater France: A History of French Overseas Expansion* (London: MacMillan, 1996), 167; Patrick Manning, *Francophone Sub-Saharan Africa, 1880–1985* (Cambridge: Cambridge University Press, 1988; 2nd edition, revised and expanded, 1999), 54.

25. Havinden and Meredith, *Colonialism and Development*, 247.

26. Lord Hailey, *An African Survey: A Study of Problems Arising in Africa South of the Sahara* (London: Oxford University Press, 1938), 546, 620–26.

27. Vali Jamal, "Taxation and Inequality in Uganda, 1900–1964," *The Journal of Economic History* 38, no. 2 (1978): 421, quoting Government of Uganda, *Report of the Treasurer on Revenue and Taxation, 1936* (Entebbe, 1937), 4.

28. Andrew Hardy, "The Economics of French Rule in Indochina: A Biography of Paul Bernard (1892–1960)," *Modern Asian Studies* 32, no. 4 (1988): 807–48.

29. Michael Crowder, *West Africa Under Colonial Rule* (Ann Arbor: University of Michigan, 1968), 276.

30. Mario Azvedo, "The Human Price of Development: The Brazzaville Railroad and the Sara of Chad," *African Studies Review* 24, no. 1 (1981): 1–19; Lord Hailey, *An African Survey: Revised 1956* (London: Oxford University Press, 1957), 1537–39.

31. Lord Hailey, *An African Survey: Revised 1956*, 1537–39.

32. "Logistics in Africa," *The Economist*, October 16, 2008, www.economist.com /business/displayStory.cfm?story_id=12432456.

33. Calculation from Geobytes, City Distance Tool, www.geobytes.com/CityDistanceTool .htm?loadpage.

34. Catherine Coquery-Vidrovitch, "Colonisation ou Impérialisme: La Politique Africaine de la France entre les Deux Guerres," *Le Mouvement Social*, no. 107 (April–June 1979): 51–76.

35. Charles Robequain, Isabel A. Ward, James Russell Andrus, and Katrine R. C. Greene, *The Economic Development of French Indo-China*, trans. Isabel A. Ward (London; New York: Oxford University Press, 1944), 89.

36. Havinden and Meredith, *Colonialism and Development*, 151.

37. CAB 23/80, Cabinet Conclusions, October 3, 1934, Cabinet 33 (34) 5, www .nationalarchives.gov.uk/cabinetpapers/cabinet-gov/cab23-interwar-conclusions .htm#Cabinet%20Conclusions%201935%20to%201937.

38. Manning, *Francophone Sub-Saharan Africa*, 54.

39. Ibid., 47.

40. Havinden and Meredith, *Colonialism and Development*, 141, 169.

41. Hardy, "The Economics of French Rule."

42. Ibid.

43. Havinden and Meredith, *Colonialism and Development*, 255.

44. Aaron Benavot and Phyllis Riddle, "The Expansion of Primary Education, 1870–1940: Trends and Issues," *Sociology of Education* 61, no. 3 (1988): 191–210, 201.

45. E. Eastman Irvine, ed., *The World Almanac and Book of Facts for 1946* (New York: New York World-Telegram, 1946), 313.

46. Calculations based on data from Irvine, *The World Almanac 1946*, 345.

47. Ibid., 366.

48. Ibid., 361.

49. C. M. Andre and A. S. Kanya-Forstner, "The French 'Colonial Party': Its Composition, Aims and Influence, 1885–1914," *The Historical Journal* 14, no. 1 (1971): 99, 101.

50. A. Wauters, "Belgian Policy in the Congo," *Journal of the Royal Institute of International Affairs* 9, no. 1 (1930): 51; Pierre Wigny, "Methods of Government in the Belgian Congo," *African Affairs* 50, no. 201 (1951): 313.

51. Klaus Epstein, "Erzberger and the German Colonial Scandals, 1905–1910," *The English Historical Review* 74, no. 293 (1959): 637–63, 638.

52. James Duffy, *Portugal in Africa* (Baltimore: Penguin Books, 1962), 152.

53. Hardy, "French Rule"; Paul S. Reinsch, *Colonial Administration* (New York: MacMillan, 1912), 83; Mendy, "Portugal's Civilizing Mission," 49; Epstein, "Erzberger," 638.

54. A. H. M. Kirk-Greene, "The Thin White Line: The Size of the British Colonial Service in Africa," *African Affairs* 79, no. 314 (1980): 25–44, 26.

55. Ibid.

56. Perham, *The Colonial Reckoning*, 157–58.

57. Martin Stuart-Fox, "The French in Laos: 1887–1945," *Modern Asian Studies* 29, no. 1 (1995): 111, 122, 132.

58. Patrick Kakwenzire, "Resistance, Revenue and Development in Northern Somalia, 1905–1939," *The International Journal of African Historical Studies* 19, no. 4 (1986): 659–77.

59. Ibid., 664.

60. Ibid., 663.

61. Aldrich, *Greater France*, 56–57.

62. Raymond Gervais, "La Plus Riche des Colonies Pauvres: La Politique Monétaire et Fiscal de la France au Tchad 1900–1920," *Canadian Journal of African Studies/Revue Canadienne des Études Africaines* 16, no. 1 (1982): 93–112.

63. Reinsch, *Colonial Administration*, 85.

64. Ibid., 87.

65. Jedrzej George Frynas, Geoffrey Wood, and Ricardo M. S. Soares de Oliveira, "Business and Politics in São Tomé e Príncipe: From Cocoa Monoculture to Petro-State," *African Affairs* 102, no. 406 (2003): 51–80.

66. Lord Hailey, *An African Survey*, 1465.

67. Edward Schieffelin and Robert Crittenden, *Like People You See in a Dream: First Contact in Six Papuan Societies*, 1st ed. (Stanford: Stanford University Press, 1991), 43.

68. See *First Contact*, directed by Bob Connolly and Robin Anderson (Filmmakers Library, 1983).

69. Frederick Lugard, *The Rise of Our East African Empire: Early Efforts in Nyasaland and Uganda* (Edinburgh: W. Blackwood and Sons, 1983), 659.

70. M. Crowder, "Indirect Rule, French and British Style," *Africa: Journal of the International African Institute* 34, no. 3 (1964): 198.

71. August Ibrum Kituai, *My Gun, My Brother: The World of the Papua New Guinea Colonial Police, 1920–1960*, Pacific Islands Monograph Series 15 (Honolulu: University of Hawai'i Press, 1998), 5.

72. Crowder, "Indirect Rule," 198.

73. See R. Delavignette, "Lord Lugard et la Politique Africaine," *Africa: Journal of the International African Institute* 21, no. 3 (1951): 177–87; Crowder, "Indirect Rule"; Peter Geschiere, "Chiefs and Colonial Rule in Cameroon: Inventing Chieftaincy, French and British Style," *Africa: Journal of the International African Institute* 63, no. 2 (1993): 151–75; Veronique Dimier, *Le Gouvernement des Colonies: Regard Croisés Franco-Britanniques* (Brussels: Université de Bruxelles, 2004); David Killingray, "The Maintenance of Law and Order in British Colonial Africa," *African Affairs* 84, no. 340 (1986): 428.

74. Hubert Deschamps, "Et Maintenant, Lord Lugard?" *Africa: Journal of the International African Institute* 33, no. 4 (1963): 296.

75. Killingray, "Law and Order," 419.

76. Ibid., 417; Emily Lynn Osborn, "'Circle of Iron': African Colonial Employees and the Interpretation of Colonial Rule in French West Africa," *Journal of African History* 44, no. 1 (2003): 29–50.

77. Osborn, "'Circle of Iron,'" 29.

78. Kirk-Greene, "The Thin White Line," 26.

79. Epstein, "Erzberger," 641.

80. Kituai, *My Gun, My Brother*, 11; Roger Keesing and Peter Corris, *Lightning Meets the West Wind: The Malaita Massacre* (Melbourne: Melbourne University Press, 1980).

81. C. W. Monckton, *Some Experiences of a New Guinea Resident Magistrate* (London: John Lane, 1921), 208.

82. Mendy, "Portugal's Civilizing Mission," 41, quoting L. Loff de Vasconcellos, *A Defeza das Victimas da Guerra de Bissau: O Eterminio da Guiné* (Lisbon: Impr. L. da Silva 1916), 36.

83. Adam Hochschild, *King Leopold's Ghost* (Boston: Houghton Mifflin, 1998), 164–65.

84. Boahen, *African Perspectives*, 79; Mendy, "Portugal's Civilizing Mission," 42; Frederick Quinn, *The French Overseas Empire* (Westport, CT: Praeger, 2000), 189, 196.

85. Epstein, "Erzberger," 648.

86. Fieldhouse, *The Colonial Empires*, 373.

87. Killingray, "Law and Order," 432.

88. Gavin White, "Firearms in Africa: An Introduction," *The Journal of African History* 12, no. 2 (1971): 173–84.

89. Risto Marjoma, "The Martial Spirit: Yao Soldiers in British Service in Nyasaland (Malawi), 1895–1939," *The Journal of African History* 44, no. 3 (2003): 418; Killingray, "Law and Order," 430; Osborn, "'Circle of Iron.'"

90. Marjoma, "The Martial Spirit," 418; Quinn, *The French Overseas Empire*, 139.

91. Mendy, "Portugal's Civilizing Mission," 42.

92. Killingray, "Law and Order," 431.

93. Ibid., 423.

94. Mendy, "Portugal's Civilizing Mission," 39; Boahen, *African Perspectives*, 54–55.

95. Killingray, "Law and Order," 431.

96. D. A. Low, *Lion Rampant: Essays in the Study of Imperialism* (London: Frank Cass, 1973), 23.

97. Kenneth Robinson, "World Opinions and Colonial Status," *International Organization* 8, no. 4 (1951): 468–83.

98. Martin Deming Lewis, "One Hundred Million Frenchmen: The 'Assimilation' Theory in French Colonial Policy," *Society for Comparative Studies in Society and History* 4, no. 2 (1962): 129; see also Quinn, *The French Overseas Empire*, 176–80.

99. Woodruff D. Smith, "The Ideology of German Colonialism, 1840–1906," *The Journal of Modern History* 46, no. 4 (1974): 641–62.

100. Benjamin Madley, "From Africa to Auschwitz: How German Southwest Africa Incubated Ideas and Methods Adopted and Developed by the Nazis in Eastern Europe," *European History Quarterly* 35 (2005): 431.

101. Epstein, "Erzberger," 647.

102. Madley, "From Africa to Auschwitz," 431.

103. Rudolf Von Albertini, *Decolonization: The Administration and Future of the Colonies 1919–1960* (Garden City, NY: Doubleday, 1971), 4–5.

104. League of Nations, Covenant of the League of Nations, April 28, 1919, available at: www.refworld.org/docid/3dd8b9854.html (accessed March 18, 2014), art. 22.

105. Robinson, "World Opinions and Colonial Status," 471.

106. The Avalon Project, "The Atlantic Conference: Joint Statement by President Roosevelt and Prime Minister Churchill, August 14, 1941," http://avalon.law.yale.edu /wwii/at10.asp, citing U.S. Department of State, *Executive Agreement Series* No. 236.

107. William Roger Louis, "American Anti-Colonialism and the Dissolution of the British Empire," *International Affairs* 61, no. 3 (1985): 400.

108. William Roger Louis, *Imperialism at Bay*: The United States and the Decolonization of the British Empire, 1941–1945 (New York: Oxford University Press, 1978).

109. Ernst B. Haas, "The Attempt to Terminate Colonialism: Acceptance of the United Nations Trusteeship System," *International Organization* 7, no. 1 (1953): 1–21, 8.

110. Louis, *Imperialism at Bay*, 198.

111. Boahen, *African Perspectives*, 78–93.

112. Perham, *The Colonial Reckoning*, 72–75, 79–80; Boahen, *African Perspectives*, 91.

113. Louis, *Imperialism at Bay:* 533–43.

114. Ibid., *Imperialism at Bay*, 24.

115. "The United Nations and Decolonization," www.un.org/en/decolonization /index.shtml.

116. "The Government of the Pitcairn Islands," www.government.pn/.

117. Louis, *Imperialism at Bay*, 546–47.

118. Ibid., 540, citing Minutes of the American Delegation, 18 May 1945, at 797.

119. Aristotle, *The Politics*, trans. T.A. Sinclair, rev. Trevor Saunders (London: Penguin Books, 1992), Book I, Part 2.

120. "Empire or Commonwealth?" *Time*, January 25, 1943, www.time.com/time /magazine/article/0,9171,850240,00.html.

121. See, for example, William Henderson, "United States Policy and Colonialism," *Proceedings of the Academy of Political Science* 26, no. 3 (1957): 58.

122. Robinson, "World Opinions and Colonial Status," 479.

123. Margery Perham, "African Facts and American Criticisms," *Foreign Affairs* 22, no. 3 (1944): 444–47, 453.

124. See League of Nations Covenant, art. 22; James H. Mittelman, "Collective Decolonisation and the UN Committee of 24," *The Journal of Modern African Studies* 14, no. 1 (1973): 41–64, 53.

125. Eirene White, "Last Steps Towards Independence: The Three African Protectorates," *African Affairs*, 64, no. 257 (1965): 261–70.

126. 2006 data from World Bank, "World Development Indicators," http://data .worldbank.org/data-catalog/world-development-indicators.

127. Francis B. Sayre, "The Problem of Underdeveloped Areas in Asia and Africa," *Proceedings of the American Academy of Arts and Sciences* 81, no. 6 (1952): 284–98.

128. See J. K. Thompson, "Abolition of Colonialism," *The Journal of Negro History* 37, no. 1 (1952): 81–89, 88; Margery Perham, "The British Problem in Africa," *Foreign Affairs* 29, no. 4 (1951): 637–50.

129. Sayre, "Underdeveloped Areas"; White, "Last Steps Towards Independence."

130. Melville Herskovits, "Native Self-Government," *Foreign Affairs* 22, no. 3 (1944): 413–23.

131. Ernst Wilhelm Meyer, "National Self-Determination: Forgotten and Remembered," *American Journal of Economics and Sociology* 5, no. 4 (1946): 449–67, 466. See also Daniel Philpott, "In Defense of Self-Determination," *Ethics* 105, no. 2 (1995): 352–85.

132. Declaration on the Granting of Independence to Colonial Countries and Peoples, G.A. Res. 1514 (XV), U.N. Doc. A/RES/1514/15 (December 14, 1960).

133. Perham, *The Colonial Reckoning*, 86–87.

134. Declaration on the Granting of Independence to Colonial Countries and Peoples, G.A. Res. 1514 (XV), U.N. Doc. A/RES/1514/15 (December 14, 1960).

135. United Nations, "United Nations Member States," United Nations Press Release ORG/1469, www.un.org/News/Press/docs/2006/org1469.doc.htm.

136. MSN Encarta Encyclopedia, http://encarta.msn.com/encyclopedia_761564397/french_west_africa.html.

137. Round Table, "Shipping and World Trade: Overview," www.marisec.org/shippingfacts/worldtrade/index.php?SID=3411af4dcfabcod85e2ed96495e34f7d.

138. United Nations Office of the High Representative for the Least Developed Countries, "Landlocked Developing Countries and Small Island Developing States: List of Landlocked Developing Countries," www.un.org/special-rep/ohrlls/lldc/list.htm.

139. John Luke, Jeffrey D. Sachs, and Andrew D. Mellinger, "Geography and Economic Development," *International Regional Science Review* 22, no. 2 (1999): 179–232, 181.

140. See, for example, Herbst, "National Boundaries," 687.

141. See, for example, ibid., and cites therein.

142. See, for example, ibid.; Pierre Englebert, Stacy Tarango, and Matthew Carter, "Dismemberment and Suffocation: A Contribution to the Debate on African Boundaries," *Comparative Political Studies* 35, no. 10 (2002): 1093–118.

143. Herbst, "National Boundaries."

144. Francine Hirsch, "The Soviet Union as a Work-in-Progress: Ethnographers and the Category Nationality in the 1926, 1937, and 1939 Censuses," *Slavic Review* 56, no. 2 (1997): 251–78; Francine Hirsch, "Toward an Empire of Nations: Border-Making and the Formation of Soviet National Identities," *Russian Review* 59, no. 2 (2000): 201–26.

145. Shahram Akbarazadeh, "Keeping Central Asia Stable," *Third World Quarterly* 25, no. 4 (2004): 689–705; Shahram Akbarazadeh, "Why Did Nationalism Fail in Tajikistan?" *Europe-Asia Studies* 48, no. 7 (1996): 1105–29.

146. Charles Tilly, ed., *The Formation of National States in Western Europe* (Princeton: Princeton University Press, 1975); Jeffrey Herbst, "War and the State in Africa," *International Security* 14, no. 4 (1990): 117–39.

147. Herbst, "War and the State."

148. Ibid.

149. Data on civil conflict from Meredith Reid Sarkees, "The Correlates of War Data on War: An Update to 1997," *Conflict Management and Peace Science* 18, no. 1 (2000): 123–44, www.correlatesofwar.org.

150. Nils Petter Gleditsch, Peter Wallensteen, Mikael Eriksson, Margareta Sollenberg, and Hårvard Strand, "Armed Conflict 1946–2001: A New Dataset," *Journal of Peace Research* 39, no. 5 (2002): 615–37, 623; Indra De Soysa and Nils Petter Gleditsch, "The Liberal Globalist Case," in *Global Governance in the 21st Century: Alternative Perspectives on World Order*, ed. Björn Hettne and Bertil Odén (Stockholm: Almkvist and Wiksell, 2002), 26–73, 50.

151. See U.S. Department of State, *Cameroon: Country Reports on Human Rights Practices 2007*, 2008, www.state.gov/g/drl/rls/hrrpt/2007/100470.htm.

152. Ian S. Spears, "Reflections on Somaliland and Africa's Territorial Order," *Review of African Political Economy* 30, no. 95 (2003): 89–98.

153. Michael O'Neill, Larissa Fast, Elizabeth Rowley, and Faith Freeman, "Collaborative Learning Approach to NGO Security Management," USAID and Save the Children (2011), 5, www.eisf.eu/resources/library/acceptance-white-paper.pdf.

154. Ed Vuilliamy, "How a Tiny West African Country Became the World's First Narco State," *The Observer*, March 9, 2008, www.guardian.co.uk/world/2008/mar/09/drugstrade.

155. See, for example, Bonnie Campbell, "Neocolonialism, Economic Dependence and Political Change: A Case Study of Cotton and Textile Production in the Ivory Coast 1960 to 1970," *Review of African Political Economy* 2 (1975): 36–53.

156. Stephen Weissman, "An Extraordinary Rendition," *Intelligence and National Security* 25, no. 2 (2010): 198–222.

157. Norwegian People's Aid, "Striving to Secure Rights for 89,000 Land Users," www.npaid.org/en/news/?module=Articles&action=Article.publicShow&ID=19266.

158. World Bank, "World Development Indicators," http://data.worldbank.org/data-catalog/world-development-indicators.

159. Robert H. Jackson, *Quasi-States: Sovereignty, International Relations, and the Third World* (Cambridge: Cambridge University Press, 1990).

160. Gerard Kriejen, *State Failure, Sovereignty and Effectiveness* (Leiden: Martinus Nijhoff, 2004), 93.

161. "After Oil and Gas, Sahara Sunshine?" *Associated Press*, August 11, 2007, www.boston.com/news/science/articles/2007/08/11/after_oil_and_gas_sahara_sunshine/.

162. See Thomas D. Grant, "Defining Statehood: The Montevideo Convention and Its Discontents," *Columbia Journal of Transnational Law* 37 (1999): 403–57.

163. D. J. Devine, "The Requirements of Statehood Re-examined," *The Modern Law Review* 34, no. 4 (1971): 410–17, 417.

4. Poor Countries, Poor Governments

1. Lael Brainard and Derek Chollet, eds., *Too Poor for Peace? Global Poverty, Conflict, and Security in the 21st Century* (Washington, D.C.: Brookings Institution, 2007).

2. Central Intelligence Agency, *World Factbook 2014*, www.cia.gov/library/publications/the-world-factbook/.

3. In 2006, it was correlated with GDP per capita at about 0.8, but it is orders of magnitude smaller, reflecting both the fact that the public sector by design does not usually consume all economic output, as well as the difficulties that poor country governments have capturing economic output through taxation.

4. See note 57 in chapter 2 for information on sources.

5. Population data and budget data from the Central Intelligence Agency, *World Factbook 2012*, www.cia.gov/library/publications/download/download-2012/index.html; data on aid from the Organisation for Economic Co-operation and Development, "International Development Statistics," www.oecd.org/dac/stats/idsonline. Revenue data are in current U.S. dollars, not in purchasing power parity exchange rates.

6. "LIBERIA: Civil servants begin three-day strike to demand pay arrears," *IRIN*, July 6, 2005, www.irinnews.org/Report/55314/LIBERIA-Civil-servants-begin-three-day-strike -to-demand-pay-arrears.

7. Nazmul Chaudhury, Jeffrey Hammer, Michael Kremer, Karthik Muralidharan, and F. Halsey Rogers, "Missing in Action: Teacher and Health Worker Absence in Developing Countries," *Journal of Economic Perspectives* 20, no. 1 (2006): 91–116, 96.

8. International Crisis Group, "Bangladesh: Getting Police Reform on Track," *Asia Report*, no. 182, December 11, 2009, www.crisisgroup.org/~/media/Files/asia/south -asia/bangladesh/182%20Bangladesh%20Getting%20Police%20Reform%20on%20 Track.pdf, 10.

9. Celia W. Dugger, "Cambodia Tries Nonprofit Path to Health Care," *The New York Times*, January 8, 2006, www.nytimes.com/2006/01/08/international/asia/08cambodia .html?pagewanted=all.

10. Ibid.

11. World Bank, "World Development Indicators," http://data.worldbank.org/data -catalog/world-development-indicators.

12. According to the 2009 World Development Indicators, of the forty-one low-income economies, only North Korea, Liberia, The Gambia, and Ghana had urban populations over 50 percent. World Bank, "World Development Indicators."

13. United Nations, "Millennium Development Goals Indicators: Slum Population as Percentage of Urban, Percentage, 2007," http://mdgs.un.org/unsd/mdg/Search .aspx?q=slum%20population.

14. United Nations, "We Can End Poverty: 2015 Millennium Development Goals," www.un.org/millenniumgoals/education.shtml.

15. Eirene White, "Last Steps Towards Independence: The Three African Protectorates," *African Affairs* 64, no. 257 (1965): 261–70.

16. Barbara Bruns, Alain Mingat, and Ramahatra Rakotomalala, *Achieving Universal Primary Education by 2015: A Chance for Every Child* (Washington, D.C.: World Bank, 2003), 10.

17. Government of Uganda, Ministry of Education and Sports, "Status of Education for Rural People in Uganda: A Presentation by Hon. Geraldine Namirembe Bitamazire (MP), Minister of Education and Sports, Uganda at the Ministerial Seminar on Education for Rural People in Africa, to Be Held Between 7th–9th September 2005 in Addis Ababa, Ethiopia," August 2005, http://edu.txtshr.com/docs/index-10184 .html; Klaus Deininger, "Does Cost of Schooling Affect Enrollment by the Poor?

Universal Primary Education in Uganda," *Economics of Education Review* 22, no. 3 (2003): 291–305.

18. Anne Look, "Overcrowding, Stalled Reform Keep Guinea's Children Out of School," *Voice of America*, May 13, 2011, www.voanews.com/english/news/africa /Overcrowding-Stalled-Reform-Keep-Guineas-Children-Out-of-School-93694144.html.

19. Fidelis Haambote and Jon Oxenham, "Regaining Momentum Towards UPE in Zambia," in *Maintaining Universal Primary Education*, ed. Lalage Bown (London: Commonwealth Secretariat, 2009), 55.

20. Alba De Souza and Gituro Wainaina, "Kenya's Three Initiatives in UPE," in *Maintaining Universal Primary Education*, ed. Lalage Bown, 47.

21. David Stasavage, "The Role of Democracy in Uganda's Move to Universal Primary Education," *Journal of Modern African Studies* 43, no. 1 (2005): 53–73.

22. Ishmael Kasooha, "Country Top in Teacher Absenteeism," *New Vision*, August 31, 2008, http://allafrica.com/stories/200809011156.html.

23. Another study also based on 2001 data concluded that while the probability of a child entering school before the age of eight rose about 9 percent, the probability that the child could complete a simple reading test fell by 10 percent. Louise Grogan, "Who Benefits from Universal Primary Education in Uganda?" Unpublished report, Department of Economics, University of Guelph, 2006. A more recent study finds that in a sample of school-aged children, more than half had repeated the same grade once, and about a quarter had repeated it twice. M. Nishimura, T. Yamano, and Y. Sasaoka, "Impacts of the Universal Primary Education Policy on Education Attainment and Private Costs in Rural Uganda," *International Journal of Educational Development* 28 (2008): 161–75.

24. Terra Lorenz, Executive Director of Ekyaro Kyaife—Our Village Uganda, personal correspondence, March 30, 2013.

25. Tim Cocks, "Uganda Free Secondary Education Starts," *Reuters Alertnet*, February 19, 2007, www.alertnet.org/thenews/newsdesk/L19223537.htm.

26. Lalage Bown, "Lessons for the Future," in *Maintaining Universal Primary Education*, ed. Lalage Bown, 126 (emphasis in the original).

27. UNESCO, *Financing Education in Sub-Saharan Africa: Meeting the Challenges of Expansion, Equity and Quality* (UNESCO Institute for Statistics, 2011).

28. Global Health Observatory Data Repository, Aggregated Data, Density per 1,000, http://apps.who.int/ghodata/#.

29. Abdoulaye Massalatchi, "Niger to Double Current Number of Doctors," *Reuters*, May 5, 2011, www.reuters.com/article/2011/05/05/us-niger-double-doctors -idUSTRE7447KK20110505.

30. Adam Nossiter, "In Sierra Leone, New Hope for Children and Pregnant Women," *The New York Times*, July 17, 2011, www.nytimes.com/2011/07/18/world/africa/18sierra .html?pagewanted=all.

31. World Bank, "World Development Indicators."

32. U.S. Agency for International Development, *Findings from the Health Facility Survey 2005, Al Jawf Governorate, Yemen* (Partners for Health Reformplus, 2006), 22, www.mophp-ye.org/docs/Survey_Health_Facility/HFS_AlJawf_Report_EN%20.pdf.

33. A. Hauri, Y. Hutin, and G. Armstrong, "Contaminated Injections in Health Care Settings," in Majid Ezzati, Alan D. Lopez, Anthony Rodgers, and Christopher

J. L. Murray, eds., *Comparative Quantification of Health Risks*, vol. 2 (Geneva: World Health Organization, 2004), 1803–50; Savanna Reid, "Injection Drug Use, Unsafe Medical Injections, and HIV in Africa: A Systematic Review," *Harm Reduction Journal* 6 (2009): 24.

34. USAID, "Health Facility Survey 2005," 27.

35. Celia W. Dugger, "Maternal Deaths Focus Harsh Light on Uganda," *The New York Times*, July 29, 2011, www.nytimes.com/2011/07/30/world/africa/30uganda.html.

36. Michael Wines, "The Forgotten of Africa, Wasting Away in Jails Without Trial," *The New York Times*, November 6, 2005, www.nytimes.com/2005/11/06/international/africa/06prisons.html.

37. "ZIMBABWE: Even a Short Prison Sentence Could Mean Death," *IRIN*, October 31, 2008, www.irinnews.org/report.aspx?ReportID=81228.

38. Rose Skelton, "Drug Hub Guinea-Bissau Awaits First Prisons," *BBC News Africa*, July 15, 2010, www.bbc.co.uk/news/world-africa-10611635.

39. ACE Electoral Knowledge Network, "How Much Do Elections Cost?" http://aceproject.org/ace-en/focus/core/crb/crb03.

40. Marina Ottway and Theresa Chung, "Toward a New Paradigm," *Journal of Democracy* 10, no. 4 (1999): 99–113.

41. Center for Transitional and Post-Conflict Governance, International Foundation for Electoral Systems, and Bureau for Development Policy, United Nations Development Programme, *Getting to the CORE: A Global Survey on the Cost of Registration and Elections*, 2005, http://content.undp.org/go/cms-service/stream/asset/?asset_id=472992.

42. Anne Gearan, "Kerry Pledges $30 Million in Aid for Congo Elections," *The Washington Post*, May 4, 2014, www.washingtonpost.com/world/kerry-sets-aid-conditions-for-congo/2014/05/04/3240c75e-d377-11e3-8f7d-7786660fff7c_story.html.

43. Data from NASA Socioeconomic Data and Applications Center, "Gridded Population of the World (GPW), v3," http://sedac.ciesin.columbia.edu/gpw/maps/mlidens.pdf.

44. "Mali," *The New York Times*, July 7, 2012, http://topics.nytimes.com/top/news/international/countriesandterritories/mali/index.html.

45. Richard Goode, *Government Finance in Developing Countries* (Washington, D.C.: The Brookings Institution, 1984), 102.

46. Roger Gordon and Wei Li, "Tax Structures in Developing Countries: Many Puzzles and a Possible Explanation," 2006, www1.gsm.pku.edu.cn/userfiles/0708–13.pdf.

47. Ibid., Table 1, 33.

48. S. Akbar Zaidi, "Pakistan's Roller-Coaster Economy: Tax Evasion Stifles Growth," Carnegie Endowment Policy Brief No. 88, 2010, 5, http://carnegieendowment.org/files/pakistan_tax.pdf.

49. Martin Stuart-Fox, "The Political Culture of Corruption in the Lao PDR," *Asian Studies Review* 30, no. 1 (2006): 59–75, 74.

50. Gordon and Li, "Tax Structures."

51. Sanjeev Gupta and Shamsuddin Tareq, *Mobilizing Revenue: Strengthening Domestic Revenue Bases Is Key to Creating Fiscal Space for Africa's Developmental Needs* (Washington, D.C.: International Monetary Fund, 2008); see also Michael Keen and

4. POOR COUNTRIES, POOR GOVERNMENTS

Ben Lockwood, "The Value-Added Tax: Its Causes and Consequences," International Monetary Fund Working Paper WP/07/183, 2007, 4, 5.

52. Richard Krever, ed., *VAT in Africa* (Pretoria: Pretoria University Law Press, 2008), 10–11.

53. Ibid., 10–11, 12.

54. World Bank, "World Development Indicators."

55. See, for example, Global Witness, *Cambodia's Family Trees: Illegal Logging and the Stripping of Public Assets by Cambodia's Elites* (London: Global Witness, 2007).

56. Lord Hailey, *An African Survey: A Study of Problems Arising in Africa South of the Sahara* (London: Oxford University Press, 1938), 1312.

57. Data from International Trade Centre, "Trade Competitiveness Map, Trade Performance HS," http://legacy.intracen.org/marketanalysis/TradeCompetitivenessMap.aspx.

58. Roumeen Islam and Gianni Zanini, *World Trade Indicators: Benchmarking Policy and Performance* (Washington, D.C.: World Bank, 2008), 52.

59. Alĕs Bulir and A. Javier Hamann, "Volatility of Development Aid: An Update," *IMF Staff Papers* 54, no. 4 (2007): 727–34.

60. Roger England, "Are We Spending Too Much on HIV?" *BMJ* (2007): 334–44.

61. See, for example, Joong Shik Kang, Alessandro Prati, and Alessandro Rebucci, *Aid, Exports, and Growth: A Time-Series Perspective on the Dutch Disease Hypothesis* (Washington, D.C.: Inter-American Development Bank, 2010).

62. See, for example, David Roodman, "Aid Project Proliferation and Absorptive Capacity," Center for Global Development Working Paper No. 75, 2006.

63. See Mick Moore, "Revenues, State Formation, and the Quality of Governance in Developing Countries," *International Political Science Review* 25, no. 3 (2004): 297–319.

64. Audrey Sacks, "Can Donors and Non-State Actors Undermine Citizens' Legitimating Beliefs?" World Bank Policy Research Working Series 6158, 2012.

65. See, for example, World Bank, "Guinea-Bissau Public Expenditure Review (PER) Update: Enhancing Growth and Adjustment through Civil Service Reform," 2007, x, http://ddp-ext.worldbank.org/EdStats/GNBper07.pdf.

66. International Development Association and International Monetary Fund, *Heavily Indebted Poor Countries (HIPC) Initiative and Multilateral Debt Relief Initiative (MDRI)—Status of Implementation* (Washington, D.C.: International Development Association and International Monetary Fund, 2008), 37, Figure 5.

67. International Development Association and International Monetary Fund, *Review of Low-Income Country Debt Sustainability Framework and Implications of the MDR* (Washington, D.C.: International Development Association and International Monetary Fund, 2006), 2.

68. Alan Beattie and Eoin Callan, "China Loans Create 'New Wave of African Debt,'" *Financial Times*, December 7, 2006, www.ft.com/cms/s/0/640a5986–863a-11db-86d5-0000779e2340.html.

69. "China Announces $3 Billion Loan Plan for Africa," *The New York Times*, January 30, 2007, www.nytimes.com/2007/01/30/world/africa/30fbrief-chinaandafrica.html?ex=1327813200&en=4ae0ce0c2a049a87&ei=5088&partner=rssnyt&emc=rss.

70. Larry Elliot, "Vultures in Pursuit of £1bn Threaten Debt-Relief Deal," *The Guardian*, October 22, 2007, www.guardian.co.uk/business/2007/oct/22/debt.imf.

71. Gordon and Li, "Tax Structures," Table 1, 33.

72. Angus Shaw, "Zimbabwe's Leader Says He'll Print More Cash," *The Washington Post*, July 29, 2007, www.washingtonpost.com/wp-dyn/content/article/2007/07/28/AR2007072801288.html.

73. "Zimbabwe: Hyperinflation," *Africa Research Bulletin 17299*, February 16–March 15, 2007.

74. Nelson Banya, "Zimbabwe's Currency Crashes, Prices Rocket," *Reuters*, June 5, 2008, www.reuters.com/article/2008/06/05/idUSL04243842.

75. Blessing Zulu, "Zimbabwe Government Unveils Aid Programs Ahead of Presidential Run-Off," *Voice of America News*, May 28, 2008, http://voanews.com/english/Africa/Zimbabwe/2008-05-28-voa53.cfm.

76. Banya, "Zimbabwe's Currency Crashes."

77. "More Than a Year Before Dollar Returns," *The Zimbabwean*, May 15, 2009, www.thezimbabwean.co.uk/index.php?option=com_content&task=view&id=21199&Itemid=104.

78. Omar Bongo, *Blanc Comme Negre* (Paris: Bernard Grasset, 2001), 289.

79. Benjamin A. Olken and Monica Singhal, "Informal Taxation," *American Economic Journal: Applied Economics* 3, no. 4 (2011): 1–28.

80. Deo Namujimbo, "Global Integrity Report: Reporter's Notebook: D.R. Congo" (Washington, D.C.: Global Integrity, 2008).

81. Stuart-Fox, "Corruption in the Lao PDR," 61.

82. Ibid., 62.

83. U.S. Library of Congress, Congressional Research Service, *Drug Trafficking and North Korea: Issues for U.S. Policy*, by Raphael Perl, Order Code RL 32167 (Washington, D.C.: Office of Congressional Information and Publishing, Updated January 25, 2007), 5; U.S. Department of State, "International Narcotics Control Strategy Report [INCSR]," March 1998, 623.

84. U.S. Library of Congress, Congressional Research Service, *North Korean Counterfeiting of U.S. Currency*, by Dick K. Nanto, Order Code RL 33324 (Washington, D.C.: Office of Congressional Information and Publishing, June 12, 2009). See also U.S. Library of Congress, Congressional Research Service, *North Korea Crime-for-Profit Activities*, by Liana Sun Wyler and Dick K. Nanto, Order Code RL33885 (Washington D.C.: Congressional Research Service, August 25, 2008).

85. U.S. Library of Congress, *North Korean Counterfeiting*.

86. U.S. Library of Congress, *Drug Trafficking*.

87. U.S. Department of State, "*International Narcotics Control Strategy Report [INCSR]*," March 2003, VII-43, www.state.gov/documents/organization/18168.pdf.

88. Andrei Lankov and Seok-hyang Kim, "A New Face of North Korean Drug Use: Upsurge in Methamphetamine Abuse across the Northern Areas of North Korea," *North Korean Review* 9, no. 1 (2013): 45–60.

89. U.S. Library of Congress, *North Korea Crime-for-Profit Activities*.

90. Sebastian Strangio, "Inside Pyongyang, the North Korean Chain with Restaurants across Asia," *Slate*, March 27, 2010, www.slate.com/id/2247402/.

91. United Nations Security Council, *Final Report of the Panel of Experts on the Illegal Exploitation of Natural Resources and Other Forms of Wealth of the Democratic Republic of Congo*, October 16, 2002 (S/2002/1146), www.un.org/news/dh/latest/drcongo.htm.

92. Human Rights Watch, "The Curse of Gold," 2005, www.hrw.org/reports/2005/drc0505/index.htm.

93. Alfred Wasike, "Keep Out of Trouble, Museveni Warns Saleh," *New Vision*, June 9, 2006, www.newvision.co.ug/D/8/12/503025.

94. United Nations Security Council, *Final Report of the Panel of Experts*, 15.

5. Governing Cheaply

1. Mark N. Hopkins, "Congo Film w/English Subtitles," Vimeo.com/28190004.

2. Afrobarometer, "Afrobarometer Round 5 (2010–2013): Essential Characteristics of Democracy," www.afrobarometer-online-analysis.com/aj/AJBrowserAB.jsp.

3. In political science, patronage, clientelism, patrimonialism, neopatrimonialism, and corruption have in common the idea of personal rule in which a political leader or party provides private rewards to supporters, which may include cash, jobs, government appointments, government contracts, or government authority that may be used to generate a private income stream. The political science literature is extensive and in the context of the development literature, for historical reasons, strongly focused on Africa. Interested readers may wish to consult the following works to start: Christopher Clapham, ed., *Private Patronage and Public Power: Political Clientelism in the Modern State* (New York: St. Martin's Press, 1982); Daniel Bach and Mamoudou Gazibo, *Neopatrimonialism in Africa and Beyond* (New York: Routledge, 2012); D. Beekers and B. van Gool, *From Patronage to Neopatrimonialism: Postcolonial Governance in Sub-Sahara Africa and Beyond* (Leiden: African Studies Centre, 2012); Jean-François Bayart, *The State in Africa: The Politics of the Belly* (London: Longman, 1996); Michael Bratton and Nicolas Van de Walle, "Neopatrimonial Regimes and Political Transitions in Africa," *World Politics* 46, no. 4 (1994): 453–89; Peter Ekeh, "Colonialism and the Two Publics in Africa: A Theoretical Statement," *Comparative Studies in Society and History* 17, no. 1 (1975): 91–112; S. N. Eisenstadt, *Traditional Patrimonialism and Modern Neopatrimonialism* (Beverly Hills: Sage, 1973); S. N. Eisenstadt and René Lemarchand, eds., *Political Clientelism, Patronage and Development*, Contemporary Political Sociology vol. 3 (Beverly Hills: Sage, 1981); S. N. Eisenstadt and Luis Roniger, *Patrons, Clients, and Friends: Interpersonal Relations and the Structure of Trust in Society* (Cambridge: Cambridge University Press, 1984); Arnold J. Heidenheimer, Michael Johnston, and Victor T. Le Vine, *Political Corruption: A Handbook* (New Brunswick: Transaction, 1989); Allen Hicken, "Clientelism," *Annual Review of Political Science* 14 (2011): 289–310; Victor T. Le Vine, "African Patrimonial Regimes in Comparative Perspective," *The Journal of Modern African Studies* 18, no. 4 (1980): 657–73; Joel S. Migdal, *Strong Societies and Weak States: State-Society Relations and State Capabilities in the Third World* (Princeton: Princeton University Press, 1988); William Reno, *Warlord Politics and African States* (Boulder: Lynne Reinner, 1998); Guenther Roth, "Personal Rulership, Patrimonialism, and Empire-Building in the New

States," *World Politics* 20, no. 2 (1968): 194–206; Donald Rothchild and Naomi Chazan, eds., *The Precarious Balance: State and Society in Africa* (London: Westview Press, 1988); Steffan W. Schmidt, James C. Scott, Carl Landé, and Laura Guasti, *Friends, Followers, and Factions: A Reader in Political Clientelism* (Berkeley: University of California Press, 1977); James C. Scott, "Patron-Client Politics and Political Change in Southeast Asia," *The American Political Science Review* 66, no. 1 (1972): 91–113; Max Weber, *The Theory of Social and Economic Organization* (New York: Free Press, 1964).

4. S. E. Finer, *The History of Government: I. Ancient Monarchies and Empires* (Oxford: Oxford University Press, 2003), 1311.

5. Ibid., 1330–31.

6. April Longley Alley, "The Rules of the Game: Unpacking Patronage Politics in Yemen," *The Middle East Journal* 64, no. 3 (2010): 395–409, 395.

7. S. Akiner, "IV. Political Processes in Post-Soviet Central Asia," *Perspectives on Global Development and Technology* 3, no. 4 (2003): 435.

8. Martin Stuart-Fox, "The Political Culture of Corruption in the Lao PDR," *Asian Studies Review* 30, no. 1 (2006): 67.

9. Ibid.

10. Ibid.

11. *The Phnom Penh Post*, "It's a Family Affair" (February 23–March 8, 2007), 8–9, www .cambodia.org/blogs/editorials/uploaded_images/Inter-marriages_in_Cambodian _political_spheres-788546.jpg.

12. Omar Bongo, *Blanc Comme Negre* (Paris: Bernard Grasset, 2001), 289–90.

13. Finer, *The History of Government: I*, 1309.

14. Ibid., 1310, 1321.

15. Barbara Nunberg and Robert Taliercio, "Sabotaging Civil Service Reform in Aid-Dependent Countries: Are Donors to Blame?" *World Development* 40, no. 10 (2012): 1970–81.

16. International Monetary Fund, "Zimbabwe 2011 Article IV Consultation," IMF Country Report No. 11/135, 2011, www.imf.org/external/pubs/ft/scr/2011/cr11135.pdf.

17. Leonardo Arriola, "Patronage Circulation and Party System Fragmentation in Africa," Draft, University of California, Berkeley, 2011, www.polisci.ucla.edu/department -workshops/cp-workshop-pdfs/Leonardo%20Arriola%20Paper%2002–23–11.pdf.

18. A. M. Mwenda, "Personalizing Power in Uganda," *Journal of Democracy* 18 (2007): 23–37.

19. Elliott Green, "Patronage, District Creation, and Reform in Uganda," *Studies in Comparative International Development* 45 (2010): 83–103, 93.

20. Hermann Levy, *Monopoly and Competition: A Study in English Industrial Organization* (London: MacMillan, 1911), 17. Quoting F. W. Hirst, *Monopolies, Trusts and Kartells* (London: Metheun, 1905), 17.

21. Alley, "The Rules of the Game," 388.

22. Ibid., 389.

23. Fakhri Al-Arashi, "The Shadow Cabinet of Sheikhs," *National Yemen*, April 22, 2012, http://nationalyemen.com/2012/04/22/the-shadow-cabinet-of-sheikhs/.

24. "Analysis: Patronage Stalls Yemen's Transition," *IRIN*, August 8, 2012, www .irinnews.org/Report/96052/Analysis-Patronage-stalls-Yemen-s-transition.

25. Max Weber, *The Vocation Lectures*, eds. David Owen and Tracy B. Strong, trans. Rodney Livingstone (Indianapolis: Hackett, 2004), 35 (emphasis in the original).

26. Benjamin Reilly and Robert Phillpot, "'Making Democracy Work' in Papua New Guinea: Social Capital and Provincial Development in an Ethnically Fragmented Society," *Asian Survey* 42, no. 6 (2002): 906–27, 923.

27. Coalition for Accountable Political Financing, *Campaign Finance and Corruption: A Monitoring Report on Campaign Finance in the 2007 General Election* (Nairobi, 2008), 24, www.capf.or.ke/document/CAPF%202007%20Election%20Campaign%20Finance%20Report.pdf.

28. Afrobarometer, "Online Data Analysis," www.afrobarometer-online-analysis.com/aj/AJBrowserAB.jsp.

29. Talato Sîîd Saya, "Editorial: Le Nomadisme Politique Est un Jeu Dangereux," *L'Indépendant*, June 8, 2010, www.independant.bf/article.php3?id_article=771?&sq=arti.

30. Abdoulaye Diakité, "MALI: Réformes Constitutionnelles: Le Nomadisme Politique désormais Sanctionné," *Kassataya*, April 22, 2010, www.kassataya.com/index.php?option=com_content&view=article&id=396:mali—reformes-constitutionnelles—le-nomadisme-politique-desormais-sanctionne-&catid=4:afrique&Itemid=4.

31. Maïdawa Tchiwaké, "Nomadisme Politique: Désertions dans les Rangs du RDP-JAMA'A," *Nigerdiaspora*, May 13, 2009, www.nigerdiaspora.info/actualites-du-pays/politique/4695-nomadisme-politique-desertions-dans-les-rangs-du-rdp-jamaa.

32. Constitution of the Republic of Senegal, art. 60, www.gouv.sn/-Constitution-du-Senegal-.html; Henry Okole, "The 'Fluid' Party System of Papua New Guinea," *Commonwealth and Comparative Politics* 43, no. 3 (2005): 362–81; Constitution of Bangladesh, art. 70, www.pmo.gov.bd/pmolib/constitution/part1.htm; Diakité, "MALI." See also Kenneth Janda, "Laws Against Party Switching, Defecting, or Floor-Crossing in National Parliaments," The Legal Regulation of Political Parties Working Paper 2, 2009, www.partylaw.leidenuniv.nl/uploads/wp0209.pdf.

33. Hari Bahadur Thapa, "Nepal: Fox in the Henhouse," in *The Corruption Notebooks 2008*, eds. Jonathan Werve and Global Integrity (Washington, D.C.: Global Integrity, 2009), 219–26, 221.

34. Thomas Bierschenk, "The Local Appropriation of Democracy: An Analysis of the Municipal Elections in Parakou, Republic of Benin," *The Journal of Modern African Studies* 44 (2006): 543–71, 548, quoting *Le Cordon*, July 19, 2001.

35. Coalition for Accountable Political Financing, *Campaign Finance and Corruption.*

36. Alphonce Shiundu, "We'll Not Pay a Penny, Swear MPs in Tax Row," *Daily Nation*, June 23, 2011, www.nation.co.ke/News/We+ll+not+pay+a+penny++swear+MPs+in+tax+row+/-/1056/1188148/-/3jljmu/-/.

37. James Macharia, "Kenyan MPs Take First Pay Cut, But Allowances Mount," *Reuters*, June 12, 2103, www.reuters.com/article/2013/06/12/us-kenya-parliament-pay-idUSBRE95B0Y220130612.

38. D. J. Gould, "Patrons and Clients: The Role of the Military in Zaire Politics," in Isaac Mowoe, ed., *The Performance of Soldiers as Governors: African Politics and the African Military* (Washington, D.C.: University Press of America), 473–92, 485.

39. Jean-François Bayart, *The State in Africa* (London: Longman, 1993), 235. See also Frank Polzenhagen and Hans-Georg Wolf, "Culture-Specific Conceptualization of

Corruption in African English," in *Applied Cultural Linguistics*, eds. Farzad Sharifian and Gary P. Palmer (Philadelphia: John Benjamins, 2007), 125.

40. The term "big man" to describe an influential man or man of status, for example, was used before 1830 as part of Nigerian pidgin English (see Hugh Crow, *Memoirs of the Late Captain Hugh Crow, of Liverpool* [London: Longman, Rees, Orme, Brown and Green, 1830], 140); and in 1854 as part of pidgin English spoken by American Indians in the United States (see Rufus B. Sage, *Scenes in the Rocky Mountains, and in Oregon, California and New Mexico*, 2nd ed. rev. [Philadelphia: Carey and Hart, 1847], 26). It was then applied and popularized in the literature on Melanesia, which up until the 1950s used the term "chief" rather than "big man." The switch was motivated by the desire of researchers to find a new term to characterize Melanesian leadership, which did not fit the European expectations that accompanied the word "chief." Lamont Lindstrom, "Big Man: A Short Terminological History," *American Anthropologist, New Series* 83, no. 4 (1981): 900–905, 900. ("The first time we match word to concept we use language; the second time, repeated, language begins to use us.") See also Marshall D. Sahlins, "Poor Man, Rich Man, Big-Man, Chief: Political Types in Melanesia and Polynesia," *Comparative Studies in Society and History* 5, no. 3 (1963): 295–303. Similarly, the common use of the word "sabby" (to know) in pidgin English in a number of different countries has been argued to be "the result of vocabulary borrowing among the European colonizers and slave traders . . . a part of conquistador/slavetrader jargon." Hans Heinrich Hock, *Principles of Historical Linguistics* (Berlin: Walter de Gruyer, 1991), 518. The possibilities of borrowing, projection, and importation suggest caution when attempting to impute something unique about cultural mindset from language usage.

41. Nina Tuhaika, "Reporter's Notebook: Solomon Island," Global Integrity Report 2008, http://report.globalintegrity.org/Solomon%20Islands/2008/notebook.

42. "Probe for Kenya's Biggest Scandal," *BBC News*, February 24, 2003, http://news .bbc.co.uk/2/hi/africa/2794385.stm; "Moi 'Ordered' Goldenberg Payment," *BBC News*, February 17, 2004, http://news.bbc.co.uk/2/hi/africa/3495689.stm.

43. John O. Kollie, "Liberia: Corruption's Legacy," in *The Corruption Notebooks 2009*, eds. Hazel Feigenblatt and Global Integrity (Washington, D.C.: Global Integrity, 2010), 231–37, 235.

44. Jan Van Dijk, John van Kesteren, and Paul Smit, *Criminal Victimization in International Perspective: Key Findings from the 2004–2005 ICVS and EU ICS* (The Hague: Boom Legal, 2007), 90.

45. Stuart-Fox, "Corruption in the Lao PDR," 63.

46. Nguyen Qui Duc, "Vietnam: A Life of Envelopes" in *The Corruption Notebooks 2009*, eds. Hazel Feigenblatt and Global Integrity (Washington, D.C.: Global Integrity, 2010), 95–103, 98–99.

47. Syful Islam, "Bangladesh: Tomorrow's Corrupt Leaders," in *The Corruption Notebooks 2008*, eds. Jonathan Werve and Global Integrity (Washington, D.C.: Global Integrity, 2009), 17–24, 21.

48. Islam, "Bangladesh: Tomorrow's Corrupt Leaders," 21.

49. Charlie J. Hughes, "Sierra Leone: New Broom, Same Old Dirt," in *The Corruption Notebooks 2009*, eds. Hazel Feigenblatt and Global Integrity (Washington, D.C.: Global Integrity, 2010), 141–47, 145–46.

50. "Burma: Light and Hope Amid Brutality," *National Catholic Reporter*, July 24, 2010, http://ncronline.org/news/global/burma-light-and-hope-amid-brutality.

51. "The UK Bribery Act: What Does It Mean for NGOs?" *European Interagency Security Forum*, July 18, 2011, www.eisf.eu/alerts/item.asp?n=13140.

52. Abdurrahman Warsameh, "Somalia: Paying to Stay Alive," in *The Corruption Notebooks 2008*, eds. Jonathan Werve and Global Integrity (Washington, D.C.: Global Integrity, 2009), 289–95, 291–92.

53. Yulia Savchenko, "Kyrgyz Republic: The Second Salary," in *The Corruption Notebooks 2008*, eds. Jonathan Werve and Global Integrity (Washington, D.C.: Global Integrity, 2009), 183–89.

54. Stuart-Fox, "Corruption in the Lao PDR," 63–64.

55. Duc, "A Life of Envelopes."

56. World Bank, "World Bank Statement on Padma Bridge," June 29, 2012, www.worldbank.org/en/news/2012/06/29/world-bank-statement-padma-bridge.

57. Graeme Smith, "Two Former SNC-Lavalin Executives Charged with Corruption," *The Globe and Mail*, June 22, 2012, www.theglobeandmail.com/globe-investor/two-former-snc-lavalin-executives-charged-with-corruption/article4364648/.

58. Tuhaika, "Reporter's Notebook: Solomon Islands."

59. Jérôme Y. Bachelard, "The Anglo-Leasing Corruption Scandal in Kenya: The Politics of International and Domestic Pressures and Counter-Pressures," *Review of African Political Economy* 37, no. 124 (2010): 187–200.

60. Jody Clarke, "$47m of Donor Money Stolen in Kenya," *Irish Times*, June 16, 2011, www.irishtimes.com/newspaper/world/2011/0616/1224298999695.html.

61. Njabulo Ncube, "Zimbabwe: Rotting from the Head Down," in *The Corruption Notebooks 2009*, eds. Hazel Feigenblatt and Global Integrity (Washington, D.C.: Global Integrity, 2010), 279–87, 285.

62. Bongo, *Blanc Comme Negre*, 290.

63. Xan Rice, "Papa Bongo's 40 Years in Power: Record-Breaking Rule Thanks to Oil Cash but Cronyism and Corruption Taint Future," *The Guardian*, May 5, 2008. www.guardian.co.uk/world/2008/may/05/1?gusrc=rss&feed=worldnews.

64. David Pallister, "Scandals Cast Shadow Over Kenya's Government: Senior Officials Suspended After Alleged Corruption over Multimillion-Pound Contracts Involving British-Based Firm," *The Guardian*, July 6, 2004, www.guardian.co.uk/world/2004/jul/06/kenya.davidpallister.

65. Siri Schubert, "Haiti: The Long Road to Recovery: Public Money Stolen by a Corrupt President Finally to Be Returned," *Frontline: World Stories from a Small Planet*, May 22, 2009, www.pbs.org/frontlineworld/stories/bribe/2009/05/haiti-the-long-road-to-recovery.html.

66. Nicolas van de Walle, "The Democratization of Political Clientelism in Sub-Saharan Africa," Typescript, 3rd European Conference on African Studies, Leipzig, Germany, June 4–7, 2009.

67. Alley, "The Rules of the Game," 392.

68. Steven Pierce, "Looking Like a State: Colonialism and the Discourse of Corruption in Northern Nigeria," *Comparative Studies in Society and History* 48, no. 4 (2006): 887–914, 893.

69. Afrobarometer, "Online Data Analysis," 2005–2006, www.afrobarometer-online -analysis.com/aj/AJBrowserAB.jsp ("Q58A.- For each of the following please indicate whether you think the act is not wrong at all, wrong but understandable, or wrong and punishable. A government official gives a job to someone from his family who does not have adequate qualifications.")

70. Afrobarometer, "Online Data Analysis," 2005–2006, www.afrobarometer-online -analysis.com/aj/AJBrowserAB.jsp.. ("Q58B.- For each of the following please indicate whether you think the act is not wrong at all, wrong but understandable, or wrong and punishable. A government official demands a favour or an additional payment for some service that is part of his job.")

71. See, for example, Gerhard Anders, *Civil Servants in Malawi: Cultural Dualism, Moonlighting and Corruption in the Shadow of Good Governance* (Rotterdam: Erasmus University, 2005).

72. Ibid.

73. G. Blundo and J-P Olivier De Sardaan, *Everyday Corruption and the State in Africa* (New York: Zed Books, 2006), 133.

74. Robert Klitgaard, *Controlling Corruption* (Berkeley: University of California Press, 1988), 106–7, quoting Second Report of the Commission of Enquiry Under Sir Alastair Blair-Kerr (Hong Kong, 1973), paragraphs 92, 93, 96–100.

75. J. L. M. De Gain-Montagnac, ed., *Memoires de Louis XIV, Part 1–2* (Paris: Garnery, 1806), 19. (Translation by author.)

76. Njabulo Ncube, "Reporter's Notebook: Zimbabwe," Global Integrity Report 2008, Global Integrity, http://report.globalintegrity.org/Zimbabwe/2008/notebook.

77. van de Walle, "The Democratization of Political Clientelism."

78. Ari Hoogenboom, "The Pendleton Act and the Civil Service," *The American Historical Review* 64, no. 2 (1959): 40.

79. Freedom House, "Freedom in the World 2014," www.freedomhouse.org/report /freedom-world/freedom-world-2014#.U2uDxiiPO4o.

80. Simon J. Powelson, "Enduring Engagement Yes, Episodic Engagement No: Lessons for SOF from Mali," Naval Postgraduate School, 2012, http://hdl.handle.net /10945/38996, 26, 31.

81. American Embassy Bamako, "Closing Ceremony of JCET training of Malian Army ETIA 4 in Gao," Ref. Bamako 813, December 17, 2009, www.wikileaks.org/plusd /cables/09BAMAKO815_a.html.

82. U.S. State Department, "Burundi. Country Reports on Human Rights Practices for 2012," www.state.gov/j/drl/rls/hrrpt/humanrightsreport/index.htm?year=2012&dlid =204095.

83. Peter Shadbolt and Thair Shaikh, "Report: Torture, Starvation Rife in North Korea Political Prisons," *CNN World*, May 4, 2011, www.cnn.com/2011/WORLD/asiapcf /05/04/north.korea.amnesty/.

84. Freedom House, "Eritrea: Freedom in the World 2013," 2013, http://freedomhouse .org/report/freedom-world/2013/eritrea-0#.U2qF2yiPO4o.

85. Celia W. Dugger, "General Says Mugabe Rival Is a Threat to Zimbabwe," *The New York Times*, June 23, 2011, www.nytimes.com/2011/06/24/world/africa/24zimbabwe .html?_r=1&pagewanted=print.

86. Ibid.

87. Robert F. Worth, "Yemen on the Brink of Hell," *The New York Times*, July 20, 2011, www.nytimes.com/2011/07/24/magazine/yemen-on-the-brink-of-hell.html.

88. Freedom House, "Rwanda: Freedom in the World 2013," 2013, www.freedomhouse .org/report/freedom-world/2013/rwanda.

89. Edmund Blair and Jenny Clover, "Rwanda's Foreign Adventures Test West's Patience," *Reuters*, April 5, 2014, www.reuters.com/article/2014/04/05/us-rwanda-politics -idUSBREA3406L20140405.

90. John B. Londregan and Keith T. Poole, "Poverty, the Coup Trap, and the Seizure of Executive Power," *World Politics* 42, no. 2 (1990): 151–83, 151.

91. Monty G. Marshall and Donna Ramsey Marshall, "Coup d'Etat Events, 1946–2010," Center for Systemic Peace, 2011, www.systemicpeace.org/inscr/CSPCoupsList2010.xls.

92. Michael Beckel and Chris Zubak-Skees, "Wanna Be Ambassador to Argentina?" *Slate*, February 7, 2014, www.slate.com/articles/news_and_politics/politics/2014/02/map _of_ambassador_posts_given_to_obama_s_top_fundraisers_noah_bryson_mamet .html.

93. Jonathan Allen and Amie Parnes, *HRC: State Secrets and the Rebirth of Hillary Clinton* (New York: Crown, 2014), 10.

6. The Rule of Law

1. The Associated Press, "Text of Obama's Speech on Afghanistan," *The Seattle Times*, June 22, 2011, http://seattletimes.nwsource.com/html/nationworld/2015398345 _apususafghanistantext.html.

2. William L. Riordan, *Plunkitt of Tammany Hall: A Series of Very Plain Talks on Very Practical Politics* (New York: Signet Classic, 1995), 13.

3. Roscoe Pound, "Law in Books and Law in Action," *American Law Review* 44 (1910): 12–36.

4. April Longley Alley, "The Rules of the Game: Unpacking Patronage Politics in Yemen," *The Middle East Journal* 64, no. 3 (2010): 395–409.

5. ARD, Inc., "Democracy and Governance Assessment of Yemen: Final Report," February 2004 (Work Conducted under Core TO [Task Order No. 1] under USAID Contract No. AEP-I-00–99–00041–00 General Democracy and Governance Analytical Support and Implementation Services Indefinite Quantity Contract).

6. Zerick Smith, Elizabeth Hart, Jaque Koussé, Ryan McCannell, and Bernic Noude-gbessi, "Benin Democracy and Governance Assessment Report," November 2004, 15–16 (Under USAID Contract No. IQC # AEP-I-00–00–00040–00 TO #21).

7. Sue Nelson, Bishnu Adhikari, Harry Blair, Judy Dunbar, and Veeraya Somvongsiri, "Nepal: Democracy and Governance Assessment," September 2005, v (emphasis in the original).

8. Charles Y. Mansfield, "Tax Administration in Developing Countries: An Economic Perspective," Staff Papers, *International Monetary Fund* 35, no. 1 (1998): 181–97, 182.

9. Syed Giasuddin Ahmed and Mohammad Mohabbat Khan, "Bangladesh," in *Public Administration in the Third World: An International Handbook*, ed. V. Subramanian (New York: Greenwood Press, 1990), 17–41, 38.

10. David Cingranelli and David L. Richards, "Dataset Version: 2010.05.30," *The Cingranelli-Richards (CIRI) Human Rights Dataset*, www.humanrightsdata.org.

11. U.S. Department of State, *2009 Human Rights Report: Central African Republic*, www.state.gov/g/drl/rls/hrrpt/2009/af/135944.htm.

12. Ibid.

13. Ibid.

14. Joseph Attila, "How Do African Populations Perceive Corruption: Microeconomic Evidence from Afrobarometer Data in Twelve Countries," CERDI-CNRS, Etudes et Documents E.2008.11, 2008, 9.

15. Duncan Brack, "Controlling Illegal Logging: Consumer-Country Measures," *Energy, Environment and Development Programme EED/LOG BP 07/01* (London: Chatham House, 2007), 2, www.illegal-logging.info/uploads/1_Illegal_logging_bp_07_01 .pdf. See, for example, Ron Corben, "Environmental Group Links Vietnam's Military to Laos Timber Smuggling," *Voice of America*, July 29, 2011, www.voanews.com/english/news /asia/southeast/Environmental-Group-Links-Vietnams-Military-to-Laos-Timber -Smuggling-126395423.html; Charles Victor Barber and Kirk Talbott, "The Chainsaw and the Gun," *Journal of Sustainable Forestry* 16, no. 3/4 (2003): 131–60; Global Witness, "Cambodia's Family Trees," *Global Witness*, 2007, www.globalwitness.org/library /cambodias-family-trees.

16. See, for example, Jim Lobe, "Rule of Law Strongest in Rich Nations, Weakest in Poor," *Interpress Services*, June 14, 2011, http://ipsnews.net/news.asp?idnews=56066.

17. See Abram Chayes and Antonia Handler Chayes, "On Compliance," *International Organization* 47, no. 2 (1993): 194.

18. Varun Gauri, "The Cost of Complying with Human Rights Treaties: The Convention on the Rights of the Child and Basic Immunization," *Review of International Organizations* 6, no. 1 (2011): 33–56, 54.

19. Pamela S. Chasek, "Confronting Environmental Treaty Implementation Challenges in the Pacific Islands," *Pacific Islands Policy 6: East-West Center*, 2010, www .eastwestcenter.org/fileadmin/stored/pdfs/pip006.pdf.

20. Ernesto Londoño, "Survey of Afghans Points to Rampant Corruption in Government," *The Washington Post*, July 8, 2010, A08.

21. Manzoor Hasan, "'Corruption in Bangladesh' Surveys: An Overview," Transparency International-Bangladesh Chapter, http://unpan1.un.org/intradoc/groups/public /documents/APCITY/UNPAN004880.pdf.

22. Julian Go, "Modeling the State: Postcolonial Constitutions in Asia and Africa," *Southeast Asian Studies* 39, no. 4 (2002): 558–83; Julian Go, "A Globalizing Constitutionalism? Views from the Postcolony, 1945–2000," *International Sociology* 18, no. 1 (2003): 71–95.

23. In his study of compliance with the law in the United States, "Why People Obey the Law," Tom Tyler argues that a principal reason for legal compliance is that the laws themselves accord with what people think is fair and morally correct behavior.

Alternately, people may obey the law because they think the process by which the law was made and the application of the law is fair and legitimate. Tom Tyler, *Why People Obey the Law* (Princeton: Princeton University Press, 2006).

24. Organisation for Economic Co-operation and Development, Development Centre, "Social Institutions and Gender Index," http://my.genderindex.org/.

25. United Nations Treaty Collection, "Status, Convention on the Elimination of All Forms of Discrimination against Women," *United Nations*, Treaty Series, vol. 1249, 13, http://treaties.un.org/Pages/ViewDetails.aspx?src=TREATY&mtdsg_no=IV-8&chapter =4&lang=en.

26. Cynthia Gorney, "Too Young to Wed: The Secret World of Child Brides," *National Geographic*, June 2011, http://ngm.nationalgeographic.com/2011/06/child-brides /gorney-text.

27. United Nations Population Fund, "Child Marriage Fact Sheet, 2005," guard www .unfpa.org/swp/2005/presskit/factsheets/facts_child_marriage.htm.

28. Immigration and Refugee Board of Canada, "Chad: Forced Marriage; Application of the Law of 2002; The Existence of Organizations That Defend the Rights of Women Who Are Forced to Marry; The Family Code Project (November 2004–January 2007)," January, 23, 2007, www.unhcr.org/refworld/docid/469cd6c81e.html.

29. Global Integrity, "Cambodia: Thieves Can't Catch Thieves," in Jonathan Werve and Global Integrity, eds., *The Corruption Notebooks 2008* (Washington, D.C.: Global Integrity, 2009), 39–45, 42.

30. Anas Aremeyaw Anas, "Ghana: Smuggling to Live," in Jonathan Werve and Global Integrity, eds., *The Corruption Notebooks 2008* (Washington, D.C.: Global Integrity, 2009), 117–24, 117.

31. Kepher Otieno, "Kenya: Who Will Follow the Law If the Leaders Don't?" in Hazel Feigenblatt and Global Integrity, eds., *The Reporter's Notebook 2009* (Washington, D.C.: Global Integrity, 2010), 115–24, 118.

32. David Leigh, "Wikileaks Cables: Tanzania Official Investigating BAE 'Fears for His Life,'" *The Guardian*, December 19, 2010, www.guardian.co.uk/world/2010/dec/19 /wikileaks-cables-tanzania-bae-fears.

33. David Leigh, "Fraud Office Inquiry into BAE Tanzania Deal," *The Guardian*, November 12, 2006, www.guardian.co.uk/politics/2006/nov/13/armstrade.foreignpolicy.

34. American Embassy Dar Es Salaam, "Big Fish Still Risky Catch in Tanzania: The Prevention of Corruption Bureau of Tanzania Is Before Its First Big Case," 07DARESSA-LAAM1037, July 23, 2012, http://cablegategame.com/cable/07DARESSALAAM1037. See also Leigh, "Wikileaks Cables."

35. U.K. Department for International Development, "Safety, Security, and Accessible Justice: Putting Policy into Practice," 2002, 58, www.gsdrc.org/docs/open/SSAJ23.pdf.

36. John Dempsey and Noah Coburn, "Traditional Dispute Resolution and Stability in Afghanistan," Peacebrief 10, *United States Institute for Peace*, 2010, www.usip.org/files /resources/PB%2010%20Traditional%20Dispute%20Resolution%20and%20Stability %20in%20Afghanistan.pdf.

37. Fergus Kerrigan, Anne Louise McKay, Annali Kristiansen, Helene Kyed, Lise Dahl, Paul Dalton, Mie Roesdahl, and NuriaVehils, "Informal Justice Systems: Charting

a Course for Human-Rights Based Engagement," *United Nations Women, UNICEF, and United Nations Development Programme*, September 26, 2012, 74, www.undp.org/content /undp/en/home/librarypage/democratic-governance/access_to_justiceandruleoflaw /informal-justice-systems/.

38. Anatole France, *Le Lys Rouge* (Paris: Calmann-Levy, 1906), https://archive.org /details/lelysrouge00franuoft.

39. J-P. Olivier de Sardaan and A. Elhadji Dagobi, "La Gestion Communautaire Sert-elle l'Intérêt Public? Le Cas de l'Hydraulique Villegoise au Niger," *Politique Africaine* 4, no. 80 (2000): 153–68.

40. Marcel Fafchamps and Bert Minten, "Property Rights in a Flea Market Economy," *Economic Development and Cultural Change* 49, no. 2 (2001): 229–67.

41. Martin Stuart-Fox, "The Political Culture of Corruption in the Lao PDR," *Asian Studies Review* 30, no. 1 (2006): 70.

42. Ibid., 62.

43. Nguyen Qui Duc, "A Life of Envelopes," in Hazel Feigenblatt and Global Integrity, eds., *The Corruption Notebooks 2009* (Washington, D.C.: Global Integrity, 2010), 95–103, 100–01.

44. Deo Namujimbo, "Global Integrity Report: Reporter's Notebook: D.R. Congo" (Washington, D.C.: Global Integrity, 2008).

45. Anas, "Ghana: Smuggling to Live," 117.

46. Katherine Xin and Jone Pearce, "Guanxi: Connections as Substitutes for Formal Institutional Support," *The Academy of Management Journal* 39, no. 6 (1996): 1641–58.

47. Ibid., 1653.

48. Ibid., 1646.

49. Daniel Jordan Smith, *A Culture of Corruption: Everyday Deception and Popular Discontent in Nigeria* (Princeton: Princeton University Press, 2007), 57.

50. Ibid., 57–60.

51. Ibid., 60.

52. Ministry of Justice, Government of Madagascar, *Justice Selon Les Justiciables: Une Enquête aupres les Usagers du Systéme Judiciaire* (Antananarivo, Madagascar: Government of Madagascar, 1999).

53. Stuart-Fox, "Corruption in the Lao PDR," 72.

54. John O. Kollie, "Liberia: Corruption's Legacy," in Hazel Feigenblatt and Global Integrity, eds., *The Corruption Notebooks 2009* (Washington, D.C.: Global Integrity, 2010), 231–37.

55. United Nations Office on Drugs and Crime, "Corruption in Afghanistan: Bribery as Reported by the Victims," January 2010, 21, www.unodc.org/documents/data-and -analysis/Afghanistan/Afghanistan-corruption-survey2010-Eng.pdf

56. Robert H. Mnookin, R. Cooter, and S. Marks, "Bargaining in the Shadow of the Law: A Testable Model of Strategic Behavior," *Journal of Legal Studies* 11 (1982): 225–51.

57. F. A. Hayek, *The Road to Serfdom* (Chicago: University of Chicago Press, 1994), 82–83. See also Jeremy Waldron, "The Rule of Law in Contemporary Liberal Theory," *Ratio Juris* 2, no. 1 (2007): 84–85.

58. David Trubek, "Max Weber on Law and the Rise of Capitalism," *Wisconsin Law Review* 3 (1972): 720–53, 735; see also Max Weber, *Economy and Society*, vol. 1, eds. Guenther Roth and Claus Wittich (Berkeley: University of California Press, 1978), 1847.

59. See, for example, Hayek, *The Road to Serfdom*. Some legal scholars have argued that the law has no predictive value and has nothing to do with the way judges decide cases. Instead, it is used only to disguise and legitimate the judge's personal decisions.

60. Oliver Wendell Holmes, Jr., "The Path of the Law," *Harvard Law Review* 10, no. 457 (1897).

61. Stuart-Fox, "Corruption in the Lao PDR," 68.

62. Smith, *A Culture of Corruption*, 56.

63. Goren Hyden, *African Politics in Comparative Perspective* (1980; reprint, Cambridge: Cambridge University Press, 2006), 72.

64. Gerhard Anders, *In the Shadow of Good Governance* (Leiden, Boston: Brill, 2010).

65. Alley, "The Rules of the Game."

66. Antony Allot, "The Unification of Laws in Africa," *American Journal of Comparative Law* 16, no. 51 (1968): 51–87, 52; see also Paul O. Proehl and Henry J. Richardson III, "Crossroads for Law in Africa," *UCLA Law Review* 18 (1970–1971): 219–51, 224.

67. Stuart-Fox, "Corruption in the Lao PDR," 72.

7. Governance as It Is

1. World Health Organization, *Health Systems Financing: The Path to Universal Coverage* (Geneva: World Health Organization, 2010), 5, www.who.int/whr/2010/10_summary_en.pdf.

2. Edmund Sanders, "In Kenya, Patients Held Hostage to Medical Bills," *Los Angeles Times*, June 28, 2009, http://articles.latimes.com/2009/jun/28/world/fg-kenya-healthcare28.

3. Human Rights Watch, "Burundi: A High Price to Pay: Detention of Poor Patients in Hospitals," September 2006, www.hrw.org/reports/2006/09/07/high-price-pay.

4. Human Rights Watch, "Health and Human Rights," www.hrw.org/sites/default/files/related_material/Health_Human_Rights.pdf.

5. Manasseé Nimpargaritse and Maria Paola Bertone, "The Sudden Removal of User Fees: The Perspective of a Frontline Manger in Burundi," *Health Policy and Planning* 26 (2011): ii63–ii71, ii66.

6. Letter from David A. Smith, Director, Department of Public Policy, AFL-CIO, to Timothy Geithner, Under Secretary for International Affairs, U.S. Treasury Department, October 11, 2000. Quoted by Robert Naiman, "Is the U.S. Treasury above the Law?" Center for Economic and Policy Research, June 7, 2001, www.policyarchive.org/handle/10207/bitstreams/20847.pdf.

7. *An Act Making Appropriations for Foreign Operations, Export Financing, and Related Programs for the Fiscal Year Ending September 30, 2001, and for Other Purposes*, 106th Congr., Public Law 106–429, Section 596, U.S. Statutes at Large 114 (2000): 1900.

8. Bruno Meessen, David Hercot, Mathieu Noirhomme, Valéry Ridde, Abdelmajid Tibouti, Abel Bicaba, Christine Kirunga Tashobya, and Lucy Gilson, *Removing User Fees in the Health Sector in Low-Income Countries: A Multi-Country Review* (New York: UNICEF, 2009), 20.

9. David Hercot, Bruno Meessen, Valéry Ridde, and Lucy Gilson, "Removing User Fees for Health Services in Low-Income Countries: a Multi-Country Review Framework for Assessing the Process of Policy Change," *Health Policy and Planning* 26 (2011): ii5–ii15.

10. Meessen et al., *Removing User Fees*, ii1.

11. Nimpargaritse and Bertone, "The Sudden Removal of User Fees," ii64.

12. Ibid.

13. Ibid., ii63–ii71.

14. Ibid.

15. Transparency International, "The East African Bribery Index," 2011, 58, www.transparency.org/files/content/pressrelease/20111020_Tanzania_EABI2011_EN.pdf.

16. Valéry Ridde, Emilie Robert, and Bruno Meessen, "Les Pressions Exercées par l'Abolition du Paiement des Soins sur les Systèmes de Santé," World Health Organization, World Health Report Background Paper No. 18, 2010, www.who.int/healthsystems/topics/financing/healthreport/UserFeesNo18FINAL.pdf.

17. Meessen et al., *Removing User Fees*, 20.

18. Maureen Lewis, "Informal Payments and the Financing of Health Care in Developing and Transition Countries," *Health Affairs* 26, no. 4 (2007): 984–97.

19. Meessen et al., *Removing User Fees*, 25, 28.

20. Organisation for Economic Co-operation and Development, "OECD Anti-Bribery Convention: Entry into Force of the Convention," www.oecd.org/daf/anti-bribery/anti-briberyconvention/oecdanti-briberyconventionentryintoforceoftheconvention.htm.

21. UN General Assembly, *United Nations Convention Against Corruption*, October 31, 2003, A/58/422, art. 5(1), www.unodc.org/documents/treaties/UNCAC/Publications/Convention/08-50026_E.pdf.

22. United Nations, "United Nations Convention Against Corruption: UNCAC Signature and Ratification as of 27 September 2013," www.unodc.org/unodc/en/treaties/CAC/signatories.html.

23. United Nations News Centre, "Time to Fight Back Against 'Cancer' of Corruption—UN Chief," December 8, 2011, www.un.org/apps/news/story.asp?NewsID=40661&Cr=corruption&Cr1.

24. U.K. Department for International Development, "UK's Fight Against Corruption Boosts World's Poorest People: Millions of Pounds Stolen by a Corrupt Nigerian Politician Will Be Returned to the Country's Poorest People, International Development Secretary Andrew Mitchell Said Today," February 27, 2012, www.dfid.gov.uk/News/Latest-news/2012/UKs-fight-against-corruption-boosts-worlds-poorest-people/.

25. UN General Assembly, *United Nations Convention Against Corruption*, October 31, 2003, A/58/422, Foreword, www.unodc.org/documents/treaties/UNCAC/Publications/Convention/08-50026_E.pdf.

26. Sebastian Mallaby, "Blinkered By His Big Ideas," *The Washington Post*, April 23, 2006, www.washingtonpost.com/wp-dyn/content/article/2006/04/21/AR2006042101756.html.

27. Business Anti-Corruption Portal, "Snapshot of the Uganda Country Profile," www.business-anti-corruption.com/country-profiles/sub-saharan-africa/uganda/.

28. International Crisis Group, "Burundi: A Deepening Corruption Crisis," *Africa Report* no. 185, March 21, 2012, www.crisisgroup.org/en/regions/africa/central-africa /burundi/185-burundi-la-crise-de-corruption.aspx.

29. President of the United States, "To Suspend Entry as Immigrants or Nonimmigrants of Persons Engaged in or Benefiting from Corruption; Proclamation 7750," 69 *Federal Register* 9 (January 14, 2004): 2287–88.

30. Millennium Challenge Corporation, "Millennium Challenge Corporation Report on the Criteria and Methodology for Determining the Eligibility of Candidate Countries for Millennium Challenge Account Assistance for Fiscal Year 2011," September 2010, 2, www.mcc.gov/documents/reports/report-2010001039502 -selection-criteria-and-methodology.pdf.

31. International Crisis Group, "The Insurgency in Afghanistan's Heartland," *Asia Report* no. 207–27, June 2011, www.crisisgroup.org/~/media/Files/asia/south-asia /afghanistan/207%20The%20Insurgency%20in%20Afghanistans%20Heartland.pdf.

32. Anushka Asthana, Mark Townsend, and Peter Beaumont, "Hamid Karzai Given Timetable by G8 to Tackle Corruption in Afghanistan," *The Guardian*, June 27, 2010, www .guardian.co.uk/world/2010/jun/27/g8-tells-karzai-tackle-corruption; Andrew Taylor, "House Panel Denies Aid to Afghanistan," *Washington Post*, June 30, 2010, www .washingtonpost.com/wp-dyn/content/article/2010/06/30/AR2010063004741.html.

33. International Crisis Group, "Burundi: A Deepening Corruption Crisis."

34. U.S. Department of Defense, "Progress Toward Security and Stability in Afghanistan," July 2013, 146, www.defense.gov/pubs/Section_1230_Report_July_2013.pdf.

35. World Bank, "Brief Assessment of Global Experiences with Civil Service Reform: The IEG Experience," http://go.worldbank.org/M4UHQoWM00. The Bank assesses the sustainability of outcomes separately from the quality of the outcome—a peculiar distinction in this case.

36. Anne Evans, "Civil Service and Administrative Reform: Thematic Paper Background Paper to Public Sector Reform: What Works and Why? An IEG Evaluation of World Bank Support," IEG Working Paper 2008/8, 14, http://siteresources.worldbank .org/EXTPUBSECREF/Resources/civil_service_thematic_paper.pdf.

37. United States Agency for International Development, "USAID's Anticorruption Strategy: A Mandatory Reference for ADS Chapter 200," January 2005, 22.

38. Institute for Health Metrics and Evaluation, *Financing Global Health 2013: Transition in an Age of Austerity* (Seattle: IHME 2014).

39. Bernard Gauthier, "PETS-QDS in Sub-Saharan Africa; A Stocktaking Study," 2006, 30, http://siteresources.worldbank.org/INTPUBSERV/Resources/477250–1165937779670 /Gauthier.PETS.QSDS.Africa.STOCKTAKING.7Sept06.pdf.

40. Ibid., 31.

41. Office of the Inspector General, The Global Fund to Fight AIDS, Tuberculosis and Malaria, "Audit of Global Fund Grants to the Federal Democratic Republic of Ethiopia," April 20, 2012, Report No: GF-OIG-10–014, revised, May 14, 2012, www.theglobalfund .org/documents/oig/OIG_GFOIG10014AuditEthiopia_ExecutiveSummary_en/.

42. Marwa Farag, A. K. Nandakumar, Stanley S. Wallack, Gary Gaumer, and Dominic Hodgkin, "Does Funding From Donors Displace Government Spending for Health in Developing Countries?" *Health Affairs* 28, no. 4 (2009): 1045–55.

43. Institute for Health Metrics and Evaluation, "Financing Global Health 2010," 50.

44. Ibid., 52.

45. Celia W. Dugger, "Maternal Deaths Focus Harsh Light on Uganda," *The New York Times*, July 29, 2011, www.nytimes.com/2011/07/30/world/africa/30uganda.html. The report referenced is Institute for Health Metrics and Evaluation, "Financing Global Health."

46. Xan Rice, "MPs Back Ugandan President's Plea for £24m Jet Upgrade," *The Guardian*, December 20, 2007, www.guardian.co.uk/world/2007/dec/20/uganda.international.

47. Thomas Mountain, "Ethiopia Buys Arms as Millions Starve," *Foreign Policy Journal*, July 8, 2011, www.foreignpolicyjournal.com/2011/07/08/ethiopia-buys-arms-as-millions-starve/.

48. International Tax Dialogue, "Tax Treatment of Donor-Financed Projects," October 3, 2006, www.itdweb.org/documents/taxtreatmentofdonorfinancedprojectsOct06.pdf.

49. U.S. General Accounting Office, "Subject: Foreign Assistance: USAID and the Department of State Are Beginning to Implement Prohibition on Taxation of Aid," GAO-04–314, February 20, 2004, www.gao.gov/assets/100/92457.pdf.

50. "Eritrea Suspends US Aid Efforts," *BBC News*, August 26, 2005, news.bbc.co.uk/2/hi/africa/4186728.stm.

51. World Bank, "Petroleum Development and Pipeline Project: Abstract," www.worldbank.org/projects/P044305/petroleum-development-pipeline-project?lang=en.

52. Chad and Cameroon Petroleum Pipeline and Development Project (IBRD Loans 4558 and 7020); see World Bank. 2000. Chad and Cameroon - Petroleum Development and Pipeline Project. Washington, DC: World Bank. http://documents.worldbank.org/curated/en/2000/04/693181/chad-cameroon-petroleum-development-pipeline-project, Appendix 11, 98.

53. Government of Chad, "Le Rapport Provisoire d'Audit du Bonus Pétrolier," www.coursupreme.td/cs_ccrapbonus.htm.

54. See U.S. Energy Information Administration, "Petroleum and Other Liquids," www.eia.gov/dnav/pet/pet_pri_spt_s1_a.htm.

55. "CHAD: Parliament Defies World Bank, Scraps 'Future Generations' Oil Fund," *IRIN*, December 30, 2005, www.irinnews.org/Report/57696/CHAD-Parliament-defies-World-Bank-scraps-future-generations-oil-fund.

56. World Bank, "World Bank, Govt of Chad Sign Memorandum of Understanding on Poverty Reduction," Press Release 2007/19/EXC, July 14, 2006, http://go.worldbank.org/HPVWZXVTB0.

57. "UN Condemns Rebel Attack in Chad," *BBC News*, April 14, 2006, http://news.bbc.co.uk/2/hi/africa/4908836.stm.

58. Moumine Ngarmbassa, "Rebels Surround President's Palace in Chad Capital," *Reuters*, February 2, 2008, www.reuters.com/article/2008/02/03/idUSL02234686.

59. World Bank Group, Independent Evaluation Group, "The World Bank Group Program of Support for the Chad-Cameroon Petroleum Development and Pipeline Construction Program Performance Assessment Report: CHAD (WB LOAN 4558-CD; IDA CREDITS 3373-CD and 3316-CD; IFC LOAN 4338); CAMEROON (WB LOAN 7020-CM; IDA CREDIT 3372-CM; IFC LOAN 4338); CHAD IFC ADVISORY

SERVICES (537745, 534603, 33974)," Report No. 51315, November 20, 2009, http://siteresources.worldbank.org/INTOED/Resources/ChadCamReport.pdf.

60. World Bank, "Chad and Cameroon—Petroleum Development and Pipeline Project; Cameroon—Petroleum Capacity Enhancement Project; Chad—Petroleum Sector Management Capacity-Building Project; and Chad—Petroleum Economy Management Project," September 16, 2009, http://documents.worldbank.org /curated/en/2009/09/11137766/chad-cameroon-petroleum-development-pipeline -project-cameroon-petroleum-capacity-enhancement-project-chad-petroleum-sector -management-capacity-building-project-chad-petroleum-economy-management -project.

61. Jonathan Fisher and Heather Marquette, "Donors Doing Political Economy Analysis™: From Process to Product (and Back Again?)," *Typescript*, 2013, 1, http://papers.ssrn.com/sol3/papers.cfm?abstract_id=2206474.

62. U.S. Department of Defense, "Progress Toward Security and Stability in Afghanistan," 146.

63. See, for example, M. A. Thomas, "Rich Donors, Poor Countries," *Policy Review* no. 175 (2012), www.hoover.org/publications/policy-review/article/129006; M. Grindle, "Good Enough Governance Revisited," *Development Policy Review* 25 (2007): 533–74; Lant Pritchett, "Fragile States: Stuck in a Capability Trap?" World Bank Development Report 2011 Background Paper, 2010, http://siteresources.worldbank.org/EXTWDR2011 /Resources/6406082–1283882418764/WDR_Background_Paper_Pritchett.pdf.

64. Sue Unsworth, "What's Politics Got to Do with It? Why Donors Find It So Hard to Come to Terms with Politics, and Why This Matters," *Journal of International Development* 21 (2009): 883–94, 883.

65. Wade Channell, "Lessons Not Learned: Problems with Western Aid for Law Reform in Post Communist Countries," Carnegie Endowment No. 57, 2005, http://carnegieendowment.org/files/CP57.Channell.FINAL.pdf.

66. Fisher and Marquette, "Donors Doing Political Economy Analysis™," 1.

8. A Different Conversation

1. Elaine Sciolino, "Invasion of Haiti Would Be Limited, Clinton Aides Say," *The New York Times*, September 13, 1994.

2. Sciolino, "Invasion of Haiti Would Be Limited."

3. Terry F. Buss and Adam Gardner, "Why Foreign Aid to Haiti Failed (and How to Do It Better Next Time)," National Academy of Public Administration, Academy International Affairs Working Paper Series, 2006, 4.

4. Freedom House, "Haiti: Freedom in the World 2013," www.freedomhouse.org /report/freedom-world/2013/haiti#.U24RgiiPO4o.

5. Aislinn Laing, "Haiti Earthquake: Public Buildings Demolished," *Telegraph*, January 14, 2010, www.telegraph.co.uk/news/worldnews/centralamericaandthecaribbean/haiti /6990875/Haiti-earthquake-public-buildings-demolished.html.

6. Freedom House, "Haiti: Freedom in the World 2013."

7. Ibid.

8. U.S. Joint Chiefs of Staff, Joint and Coalition Operational Analysis, "Operational-izing Counter/Anticorruption Study," February 28, 2014, 9–10.

9. Headquarters Department of the Army, "Counterinsurgency: Field Manual No. 3–24," Marine Corps Warfighting Publication No. 3–33.5, 2006, 1–21, www.fas.org/irp/doddir/army/fm3–24.pdf.

10. Headquarters Department of the Army, "Counterinsurgency," Preface.

11. United States Counterinsurgency Initative, "U.S. Counterinsurgency Guide," January 2009, 16, 24, www.state.gov/documents/organization/119629.pdf.

12. Vivek Sharma, "Give Corruption a Chance: Two Cheers for Corruption—Though the West Hates It, in Some Societies It Produces Good Outcomes," *The National Interest*, November–December 2013, http://nationalinterest.org/article/give-corruption-chance-9276.

13. Antony Allot, "The Unification of Laws in Africa," *American Journal of Comparative Law* 16, no. 51 (1968): 51–87, 52; see also Paul O. Proehl and Henry J. Richardson III, "Crossroads for Law in Africa," *UCLA Law Review* 18 (1970–1971): 219–251, 224.

14. Daron Acemoglu and James Robinson, *Why Nations Fail: The Origins of Power, Prosperity, and Poverty* (New York: Crown, 2012).

15. Matt Andrews, *The Limits of Institutional Reform in Development: Changing Rules for Realistic Solutions*, (Cambridge: Cambridge University Press), 215.

16. World Bank, "Brief Assessment of Global Experience with Civil Service Reform," http://go.worldbank.org/M4UHQ0WM00.

17. Millennium Challenge Corporation, "Guide to the MCC Indicators and the Selection Process: Fiscal Year 2011," 2011, 3, www.mcc.gov/documents/reports/reference-2010001040503-fy11guidetotheindicators.pdf.

18. U.S. Library of Congress, Congressional Research Service, *Millennium Challenge Corporation*, by Curt Tarnoff, CRS RL 32427 (Washington, D.C.: Office of Congressional Information and Publishing, April 8, 2014), 4.

19. Millennium Challenge Corporation, "MCC Threshold Program Lessons Learned," 2010, www.mcc.gov/documents/press/factsheet-2010002048002-threshold-program-lessons-learned.pdf.

20. "SOMALIA: Hundreds of Drought-Displaced Seek Shelter in Somaliland," *IRIN*, July 29, 2011, www.irinnews.org/report.aspx?reportid=93375.

21. Jeffrey Herbst, *States and Power in Africa* (Princeton: Princeton University Press, 2000).

22. World Bank, "World Development Indicators: Net ODA Received (% of Central Government Expense)."

23. Nancy Birdsall and Brian Deese, "Hard Currency: Unilateralism Doesn't Work for Foreign Aid Either," *Washington Monthly*, March 2004, www.washingtonmonthly.com/features/2004/0403.birdsall.html.

24. Organisation for Economic Co-operation and Development, Development Assistance Committee, "Development: Aid to Developing Countries Falls Because of Global Recession," 2012, www.oecd.org/dac/developmentaidtodevelopingcountriesfalls-becauseofglobalrecession.htm.

25. Douglas Casey, "Opportunity in Mozambique," *Escape From America Magazine*, www.escapeartist.com/Offshore/Doing_Business_Overseas/Mozambique/.

26. Bret Stephens, "To Help Haiti, End Foreign Aid," *Wall Street Journal*, January 19, 2010, http://online.wsj.com/article/SB10001424052748704541004575010860014031260.html.

27. The Henry J. Kaiser Family Foundation, "2013 Survey of Americans on the U.S. Role in Global Health," November 7, 2013, http://kff.org/global-health-policy/poll-finding/2013-survey-of-americans-on-the-u-s-role-in-global-health/.

28. Jason Groves, "Just One in Four Support David Cameron Over Decision to Spend Billions on Foreign Aid," December 28, 2012, *MailOnline*, www.dailymail.co.uk/news/article-2254304/Just-support-David-Cameron-decision-spend-billions-foriegn-aid.html?ito=feeds-newsxml.

29. Frederick Douglass, *Two Speeches By Frederick Douglass, One on West India Emancipation, Delivered at Canandaigua, Aug 4th, and the Other on the Dred Scott Decision, Delivered in New York, on the Occasion of the Anniversary of the American Abolition Society, May 1857* (Rochester, NY: C. P. Dewey, Printer, American Office, 1857).

30. U.S. Joint Chiefs of Staff, "Operationalizing Counter/Anticorruption Study," 12.

31. See, for example, Michael Ross, *The Oil Curse: How Petroleum Wealth Shapes the Development of Nations* (Princeton: Princeton University Press, 2012).

32. See, for example, Mick Moore, "Revenues, State Formation, and the Quality of Governance in Developing Countries," *International Political Science Review* 25, no. 3 (2004): 297–319.

33. "For God's Sake, Please Stop the Aid!" *Der Spiegel*, August 27, 2005, www.spiegel.de/international/spiegel/spiegel-interview-with-african-economics-expert-for-god-s-sake-please-stop-the-aid-a-363663.html.

34. Data from Angus Maddison, "Historical Statistics," www.ggdc.net/MADDISON/Historical_Statistics/horizontal-file_02–2010.xls. Data in 1990 International Geary-Khamis dollars.

35. World Bank, "World Development Indicators," http://data.worldbank.org/data-catalog/world-development-indicators.

36. Douglass C. North, John Joseph Wallis, and Barry R. Weingast, *Violence and Social Orders: A Conceptual Framework for Interpreting Recorded Human History* (Cambridge: Cambridge University Press, 2009); Acemoglu and Robinson, *Why Nations Fail*.

37. Marcus Manuel, "Budget Support—Good or Bad for Development?" Presentation at Overseas Development Institute, July 13, 2011, www.odi.org.uk/events/presentations/919.pdf.

38. Mark Moyar, "Development in Afghanistan's Counterinsurgency: A New Guide," *Orbis Operations*, March 2011, http://smallwarsjournal.com/blog/development-in-afghanistans-counterinsurgency.

39. Ibid., 7.

40. Matthew Rosenberg, "Karzai Says He Was Assured C.I.A. Would Continue Delivering Bags of Cash," *The New York Times*, May 4, 2013.

41. Ibid.

42. Ibid.

43. Jon Henley, "Gigantic Sleaze Scandal Winds Up as Former Elf Oil Chiefs Are Jailed: Trial for Huge Kickbacks by Publicly Owned Firm Reveals Years of Corruption at Top of French State," *The Guardian*, November 12, 2003, www.guardian.co.uk /business/2003/nov/13/france.oilandpetrol.

44. Ibid.

45. Christophe Boisbouvier, "50 Years Later, Françafrique Is Alive and Well," *RFI*, February 16, 2010, www.english.rfi.fr/africa/20100216–50-years-later-francafrique-alive -and-well.

46. Hugh Schofield, "Chirac-Villepin Allegations Revive Sleazy Memories," *BBC News Europe*, September 12, 2011, www.bbc.co.uk/news/world-europe-14886113.

47. Henley, "Gigantic Sleaze Scandal."

48. United Nations Development Programme, "Governance and the Post-2015 Development Framework," February 1, 2013, www.undp.org/content/undp/en/home /librarypage/democratic-governance/dg-publications/governance-and-the-post -2015-development-framework/.

49. Francis Fukuyama, *Political Order and Political Decay: From the French Revolution to the Present* (New York: Farrar, Straus and Giroux, 2014), Chapter 5.

50. Andrei Shleifer and Robert Vishny, "Corruption," *Quarterly Journal of Economics* 108, no. 3 (1993): 599–617.

51. Michael Johnston, *Syndromes of Corruption: Wealth, Power, and Democracy* (Cambridge: Cambridge University Press, 2005); Michael Johnston, *Corruption, Contention, and Reform: The Power of Deep Democratization* (Cambridge: Cambridge University Press, 2014).

52. Federalist No. 37 (James Madison).

Index

academic disciplines, disjointed political theories in, 15

Afghanistan: attempt to restructure government, 21; budget shortfall consequences, 7; civilian death toll, 3; COIN strategy, 25; contractors death toll, 2; control of corruption, 165; destructive influence of foreign aid on, 190–191; fixers in, 151; government restructuring attempts, 21; inability to afford governance ideal, 14; myth of democratic elections, 100; parliamentary elections, 2; police bribes, 139; as poor government, 12; presidential elections, 2; provisional government, 1; quality of life gains, 3; reasons for failure, 4–13; revenue per capita, 78; support building among elites, 181; as top opium producer, 4; U.S. and coalition death toll, 2; U.S. embroilment in, 1; U.S. spending, 2

Africa: colonial border problems, 70; devastation by slave trade, 45; donor focus on HIV/AIDS, 91–92; economy of affection, 154; failures in universal primary education, 85; low-income economies, 46; scramble for, 47

Aiddata 3.0, 2

American religiosity, 35, 38; in governance ideal, 22

Amnesty International, 23

antibribery laws, 115

anticorruption campaigns, 141, 163–164; attacking political opponents by, 142; foreign aid donors, 165; low success rates, 165; *versus* patronage politics, 141; unsustainability, 166; zero tolerance policies, 164–165

authoritarianism, 13; benefits of development-minded, 205; persistence of, 190

authority, differing cultural concepts, 184

Axis of Evil, 35

Bangladesh: aid project cancellation, 117; bribes to education officials, 113; corruption in, 139; disconnect between laws and practice, 135; supply problems, 80–81

behavioral change, law as instrument of, 155–156

Benin: impunity in, 134; party hopping in, 110; weak rule of law, 134

Berlin Congo Conference, 48

best practices, insistence on transferring, 206

big fish, escape of, 141–142

big man, 230

Blagojevich, Ron, 30; Al Capone cartoon, 31

blind spot, 16; cultural, 202

Bonn Agreement, 2

boom-bust cycles, 52; due to narrow export base, 90

border policing, 90

bribes, 136; antibribery laws, 115; to avoid dirty needles, 115; in customs services, 146–147; Democratic Republic of Congo, 146–147; to education officials, 113; in import/export dealings, 115; for information, 151; from lower- to higher-level government employees, 117; for medical services, 162–163; nurses' demands for, 86; for permission to deliver foreign aid, 114; police, 95; *versus* private payments, 95; to render government services, 113; as revenue source, 95; in Somalia, 115; in taxation system, 89; during train travel, 116

Burkina Faso, party hopping in, 109

Burundi: anticorruption movement, 165; encouraging economic growth in, 193; governance challenges, 77; human rights abuses, 125–126; revenue per capita, 78; user fees abolishment, 160–161

Bush, President George W., 35; anticorruption proclamation, 165; on rule of law, 132

Cambodia: bureaucratic embezzlement, 81; patronage networks, 103–104

capacity building, failures, 183–185

capitalism, association with rule of law, 153

Caribbean, low-income economies, 46

Carter Center, 23

cash basis economy, 89